Cocktails with
George and Martha

What Becomes a Legend Most: The Biography of Richard Avedon

Wagstaff: Before and After Mapplethorpe

Photography After Frank

Cocktails with George and Martha

Movies, Marriage, and the Making of
Who's Afraid of Virginia Woolf?

Philip Gefter

BLOOMSBURY PUBLISHING

NEW YORK · LONDON · OXFORD · NEW DELHI · SYDNEY

BLOOMSBURY PUBLISHING
Bloomsbury Publishing Inc.
1385 Broadway, New York, NY 10018, USA

BLOOMSBURY, BLOOMSBURY PUBLISHING, and the Diana logo are
trademarks of Bloomsbury Publishing Plc

First published in the United States 2024

Bloomsbury Publishing Plc does not have any control over, or responsibility for, any
third-party websites referred to or in this book. All internet addresses given in this
book were correct at the time of going to press. The author and publisher regret any
inconvenience caused if addresses have changed or sites have ceased to exist, but can
accept no responsibility for any such changes.

ISBN: HB: 978-1-63557-962-8; EBOOK: 978-1-63557-963-5

LIBRARY OF CONGRESS CATALOGING-IN-PUBLICATION DATA IS AVAILABLE

2 4 6 8 10 9 7 5 3 1

Typeset by Westchester Publishing Services
Printed and bound in the U.S.A.

To find out more about our authors and books visit www.bloomsbury.com and
sign up for our newsletters.

Bloomsbury books may be purchased for business or promotional use.
For information on bulk purchases please contact Macmillan Corporate and
Premium Sales Department at specialmarkets@macmillan.com.

For Peter and Leah

Tevye
Do you love me?

Golde
Do I *what?*

—FROM "DO YOU LOVE ME,"
FIDDLER ON THE ROOF, 1964

TABLE OF CONTENTS

PROLOGUE

W hat a dump."

Edward Albee's *Who's Afraid of Virginia Woolf?* begins with these three words. They are a proclamation and a provocation. Albee might as well be Beethoven taking the podium to commence a performance of his own Fifth Symphony. A flick of the baton. A breath:

Da da da DUM.

What a dump.

The first four indelible notes of Beethoven's "Symphony of Fate" (as the Fifth is sometimes known) form the essential DNA of that piece. The assertive theme unfurls in a trail of echoes and iterations, galloping through various instruments and multiple harmonies, building to crescendos, returning again and again to that unquenchable motif. So, too, we may see "What a dump" as a strand of DNA that will replicate and mutate and evolve throughout a nocturnal odyssey of taunts and dares, with its own thunderous crescendos and touching adagios.

The 1966 film *Who's Afraid of Virginia Woolf?*, directed by Mike Nichols, opens with George and Martha, a married couple, arriving home after a late-night party. Martha, played by Elizabeth Taylor, turns on a light, surveys their living room, takes a long drag on her cigarette, and levels a sorry appraisal. "What a dump," she utters with casual disdain. Then, suddenly, a glimmer of amusement animating her face, she swings around to George, played by Richard Burton. "Hey, what's that from?" she blurts out, repeating the phrase—"Wha*T* a Dum*P*"—with exacting elocution. She looks at him expectantly. "How would I know?" George says, turning away with an air of impatience and leaving the room.

Martha thinks she's imitating Bette Davis's performance in "some *goddamn* Warner Brothers epic." She's mistaken. *Beyond the Forest*, directed by King Vidor, is the 1949 film in which Davis says "What a dump," but it's a throwaway line, uttered in passing, without the Hollywood diva's usual precise diction. In the original 1962 stage version of *Who's Afraid of Virginia Woolf?*, the actress Uta Hagen, starring as Martha, hyperarticulated the line, out-Bette-Davis-ing Davis herself. Taylor's performance, in turn, is an homage to Hagen's, which Taylor heard on the cast recording of the Broadway production as she prepared for the role.

At least Martha gets the name of the studio right: It was, indeed, Warner Brothers that was left holding the bag for *Beyond the Forest*, a film noir flop, universally panned. "If Bette Davis had deliberately set out to wreck her career, she could not have picked a more appropriate vehicle," the columnist Hedda Hopper wrote at the time. In her later years, Davis, appearing on television talk shows, was asked repeatedly about the line "What a dump." She endured the question with forced levity. By then, *Who's Afraid of Virginia Woolf?* was an artistic monument, and an infinitely greater number of people knew the line in Taylor's exaggerated form than had ever heard Davis's original. "Wha*T* a Dum*P*" had taken hold, traded back and forth between dinner party guests and hosts. Whether grudgingly or genuinely, Davis would say she gave all credit to Taylor.

This was one small testament to the impact of *Who's Afraid of Virginia Woolf?* It could transform even this deliberately misremembered snippet, plucked from the waste bin of American cultural oblivion, into a shibboleth of sophisticated taste. How deliciously ironic. How camp.

In the 1980s, Davis starred in a one-woman show on Broadway. As the performance opened, she would walk onstage, survey the theater, and let fly: "Wha*T* a Dum*P*." Laughter. Applause.

~

Who's Afraid of Virginia Woolf? is a film (and before that, a play) about a marriage. It is, equally, about *marriage*. That contention underlies the story I am telling, in which a simple, free-floating idea about a married couple hovers in the mind of Edward Albee—a young, bohemian writer in Greenwich Village in the early 1950s—and inspires his first three-act play, completed in 1961. Through a sequence of events that appears virtually preordained, the play gets produced on Broadway, becomes a succès de scandale, and generates enough highbrow controversy to get Hollywood's attention. At the time, the movie industry's preferred image of coupledom tended toward sweet—if insipid—romantic comedies such as *Pillow Talk; Kiss Me, Stupid; The Parent Trap*; and *Under the Yum Yum Tree*. Even as he sold the film rights to his play, Albee joked with great trepidation that he wouldn't be surprised if Rock Hudson and Doris Day were cast as George and Martha. Fortunately, *Who's Afraid of Virginia Woolf?* would have an entirely different destiny. It would earn piles of money and a raft of prizes, and even herald the death of the Production Code, Hollywood's mid-century censorship regime.

While marriage is the essential subject of *Virginia Woolf*, the tale I am telling is also about artmaking—the reach for something true and an attempt to experiment with form—in this case, both theater and film. A number of larger-than-life figures propel this narrative: Edward Albee, one of the original Theatre of the Absurd playwrights, despite his discomfort with the term; Mike Nichols, the first-time film director who would become a legendary auteur; Richard Burton and Elizabeth Taylor, the movie stars whose illicit romance and subsequent glamorous marriage made them, in that period, the most famous couple in the world; and Ernest Lehman, the producer-screenwriter, who facilitated the imperious demands of a novice director and navigated the wildly indulgent whims of his stars with an unwavering eye on the finish line—and his own legacy.

In fact, the travails of *Virginia Woolf*'s production should have militated against its success at every turn, yet when the film was released in

1966, it both anticipated and precipitated the currents of its time, eventually securing its place as an American touchstone. At Warner Brothers, the assemblage of unlikely characters, the practical constraints of budget, and the perfectionist standards required of greatness left their mark on the process of making the film, often in laughable ways. The production was divided between one side compelled to neuter Albee's play to appeal to mainstream, big-screen audiences, and the other determined to coax out an exacting fidelity to Albee's sometimes incendiary words. It is an entertaining alchemy of talent, vision, tension, drama, ego, and rigor that brought *Virginia Woolf* to the big screen. During filming, the balance of power careened back and forth between director Nichols and producer Lehman, in a battle of wills and canny mind games. Meanwhile, the real-life marriage of Burton and Taylor, the dazzling superstars, lent prismatic verisimilitude to George and Martha, and created outsized drama—and not a little chaos—on and off the set.

Who's Afraid of Virginia Woolf? is my standard against which all movies about marriage are measured, but obviously not because George and Martha's marriage is ideal. On the contrary, though their love is genuine, their marriage is imperfect and, in that sense, typical of all marriages. We are catching them on a particularly bad night when their demons have been let loose on each other and on their guests. Those demons prove to be more familiar to us than we would like to admit, and that's really the point. No matter how tempered, decorous, or respectful the daily comportment of any couple, their underlying feelings of attachment dwell in a private, unpredictable universe subject to its own solar flares of displeasure, shooting meteors of pain, and exploding stars of rage. In *Virginia Woolf*, we are witness to a profound shift in George and Martha's marital orbit. Their bawdy, vicious, painful, yet witty display of unharnessed human emotion reminds us of what lurks beneath the surface in our own lives. Their drama offers, perhaps, a hard lesson about how to manage our own messy and, at times, uncontrollable feelings in the realm of love and deep attachment.

George and Martha go at each other with blatant vulgarity and vicious accusation. Their hatred tangles with love, their rage follows on the heels of affection—a protracted, if extreme, version of all marital discord, for better or for worse.

~

My interest in writing this book stemmed in part from my front-row seat to my parents' marriage. In my young eyes, marriage was large, an institution equal in magnitude to government or religion—at least in the mid-twentieth-century American suburbia in which I grew up. All things considered, my parents were respectable; they set a civilized standard for my siblings and me. My father would come home from work at six P.M. He and my mother would sit down together with a cocktail—he a scotch on the rocks, she a scotch and soda—and talk quietly about the events of the day. Then we would all gather for dinner, my sister, my brother, and I, describing our activities at school.

My parents bickered, too, of course. And sometimes, bitter arguments would erupt between them, with *Who's Afraid of Virginia Woolf?* intensity. I distinctly remember one evening when my sister corralled my brother and me, huddling us to safety behind her closed bedroom door. In the living room, we could hear my mother shriek and my father bellow, arguing about issues both philosophical and psychological that, ultimately, unearthed deep fault lines in their marriage. Their words meant nothing to me at the age of nine, but the conflict felt like a powerful, rumbling earthquake. In my terror, I imagined the house collapsing all around us. I lived with the persistent fear of their divorce, but it never happened. They stuck it out until the very end. Why they did and what it said about them is the riddle that drew my interest in marriage itself. Later, the riddle would deepen through the ongoing process of understanding my own marriage. I remain fascinated by the nature of bonding, coupling, that is so near the core of what it means to be human.

I was fifteen when I first heard about *Who's Afraid of Virginia Woolf?* the movie. The name alone got my attention. I encountered it in *Playboy*, a magazine my father subscribed to and that I actually read, as it was my tutorial on the secrets of the adult world beyond my awareness. Mike Nichols gave *Playboy* an interview about the movie, and I consumed his every word with vociferous interest. I asked my parents if I could see the movie, and while they didn't object, they cautioned that I wouldn't understand it.

They were right. I couldn't really make sense of it, but I recognized my parents in it, as well as the parents of my friends. *Virginia Woolf* put its finger on the rumbling beneath the polite surface of those suburban marriages, tensions that I felt but that were left unacknowledged. I knew there was something fundamentally true about the movie. It was sexy, which was just beyond my reach, and there were curse words, which my adolescent self appreciated. Over the years, every time I've watched the movie, I've discovered new layers in it. I appreciate the intelligence of Albee's astute observations about marriage, and how faithful Nichols's direction is to the material. I am endlessly entertained and inspired by the brilliance of the dialogue. And I find the bold and unadorned visual clarity of the filmmaking nothing less than magical. Those components make *Who's Afraid of Virginia Woolf?* the singular work I have returned to whenever I think about "movies." While writing this book, I have watched it again and again, sometimes all the way through, other times focusing on individual scenes to parse out particular meanings. After such scrutiny, the film still holds up for me. It doesn't get old. It just gets better.

Watching any couple fight is awkward at best, a too-intimate window onto a marriage. It leaves the witness feeling like a voyeur sneaking a peek at something private, illicit. Watching George and Martha go at each other summons our embarrassment as much as our curiosity. It only adds to the mystique that Taylor and Burton brought their own mercurial real-life marriage to their on-screen roles. We are not supposed to be there, and yet, like rubberneckers passing a car accident, we cannot look away. It is still the truest rendering of love in marriage that I know. Call me a romantic.

New York City, 2023

Cocktails with
George and Martha

Chapter 1

The College of Complexes

If you removed the homosexuals and homosexual influence from
what is generally regarded as American culture you would be
pretty much left with Let's Make a Deal.

—FRAN LEBOWITZ

One evening in 1954, a young, unknown writer sat down in a neighborhood bar and ordered a beer. In the back of the bar hung a mirror on which patrons scrawled comments, in the manner of graffiti written on a public bathroom wall. Because the bar was in Greenwich Village and the clientele was bohemian, the comments on the mirror were more ironic than salacious. That night, Edward Albee's eyes fell on one quip written out with dry soap near the bottom of the mirror: "Who's Afraid of Virginia Woolf?" It's a witty turn of phrase, granting a nursery rhyme the intellectual heft of a famous author's name, the singsong itself making a mockery of the lofty play on words. He made a mental note of it, letting it drift into the vapors of his unconscious.

At the time, Albee was a twenty-six-year-old aspiring novelist. He lived just down the block from the bar, which was in a brick row house on West Tenth Street and would soon be renamed the College of Complexes (Freud being all the rage then). The College of Complexes became a seminal Greenwich Village coffeehouse for beatniks, where poetry readings and heavy drinking set the tone.

Albee had set up in Greenwich Village in 1947, at age nineteen, drawn by the area's reputation as a hotbed of literature, theater, art, and music. "I was told that [the Village] was where all the interesting people were," he recounted in later years. "So, I moved there, and it was true. It was the most wonderful time of my life. Being there completed my education. I saw all the Abstract Expressionist painters; I heard contemporary music; I got to see off-off Broadway plays—Beckett, Brecht, Pirandello. The paperback book market was around, so I read a lot."

By 1952, Albee was sharing an apartment on West Fourth Street with his boyfriend, William Flanagan, a composer and part-time music critic five years his senior. Their circle of friends included the composers Aaron Copland (Flanagan's teacher) and Ned Rorem; the playwright William Inge; and the poets W. H. Auden and Richard Howard. A half-dozen blocks away was the San Remo Café, a gathering spot that drew such cultural icons as James Agee, James Baldwin, William Burroughs, Miles Davis, Allen Ginsberg, Jack Kerouac, Frank O'Hara, Dylan Thomas, Gore Vidal, and Tennessee Williams. By moving to the Village, Albee had put down roots in a neighborhood that, over the 1950s and '60s, would incubate a disproportionate share of the twentieth-century American cultural canon.

A half century later, in his memoir *Kafka Was the Rage*, the literary critic Anatole Broyard would recall the artistic life of the Village in the late 1940s, identifying the presiding attitude of his fellow students at the New School that spilled into the fabric of the surrounding community. "For most of the people in [my] class, art was the truth about life—and life itself, as they saw it, was more or less a lie," he wrote. "If civilization could be thought of as having a sexuality, art was its sexuality."

Amid all this libidinal artistic energy, Albee struggled, as many young writers do, to complete a novel and publish his poetry while taking odd jobs to support himself. First, he was hired at WNYC radio, where he spent a year writing notes for the station's musical programming. "I had an awful lot of jobs," he remembered. "A $40 a week office boy for the ad agency Warwick and Ledger; salesman in the record department at Bloomingdale's; salesman in the book department of Schirmer's; luncheonette counterman at the Manhattan Towers hotel." He worked for several years as a Western Union delivery boy. He liked the mindlessness of the job, and it gave him an opportunity to walk around the different neighborhoods of the city. "If you were really clever, you could earn tips easily," he said impishly, suggesting that he wasn't above turning the occasional trick on his rounds.

At night, Albee and Flanagan socialized with their friends—the writers, composers, and playwrights who would later become voices of their generation. The two of them could drink heavily, often going on binges. "There were a lot of saloons we all frequented," Albee said. "All the painters would go to Cedar Bar; the writers would go to the San Remo. We all knew each other. It was all very friendly." A typical evening would begin around eleven P.M. and continue until four in the morning. Howard, later to distinguish himself as a Pulitzer Prize–winning poet, considered Flanagan to be brilliant: "He had this wonderful Jesuit-trained mind, and he was very quick and sharp and funny." Yet Howard acknowledged that Edward and Bill were "not pleasant together when they were drunk. . . . there was a lot of jockeying for power in the relationship."

Early on, Flanagan introduced Albee not only to a world of composers and writers but also to a way of thinking about art and literature with a critical eye on form. Albee looked up to him and stood in awe of his accomplished friends. "It was part of the learning experience," Albee explained. "Looking, learning, seeing, hearing. Being hectored at and lectured by Flanagan all the time, every sentence beginning with 'You see . . . ,' or 'Do you understand. . . .' He was terribly bright and a great teacher. He molded and shaped my aesthetic." They were clearly lovers, as Albee described the relationship; at the same time, it was imbalanced, with Flanagan in the role of mentor and Albee his protégé. "He pointed out to me very clearly that this is the way one should be exploring one's life with the arts."

Robert Heide, an aspiring playwright, often cavorted with Albee and Flanagan from one Greenwich Village bar to another. After the bars closed at four A.M., he would go back to their apartment with them and continue drinking. Gay relationships did not adhere to conventional norms, even in those days. "There was no sense of monogamy," Heide said. "Flanagan was very promiscuous. He would go to tea rooms. He was obsessive." At the same time, he could be intensely jealous of Edward. "I would sometimes end up in bed with Edward, who would lock the door," Heide remembered. "Bill would end up pounding on the door in a rage." Rorem described their circle in euphemistic terms as "the family." "People slept out of the family," he said, "but when I think back on it, the amount of promiscuity and the amount of drinking that went on in this milieu was astonishing."

While Howard perceived in Albee a streak of meanness, beneath it all there was a sensitivity that made him deeply sympathetic to Albee's plight. "He was very much an orphan of the storm at that point. There was no family. There was only Bill [Flanagan] and the home they made together against the world." Howard recalled vibrant and entertaining late-night conversations with Flanagan and Albee, adding that Edward always had decisive opinions. In the late 1950s, Howard wrote a poem about his friendship with them titled "Duet for Three Voices," published in his first book of poems, in which Flanagan was "the failure," Howard was "the phony," and Albee was "the feral."

By day Albee would work on his poetry and try to make progress on his novel. When they went out at night, he drank for pleasure, but eventually it became his "writer's habit," as he referred to it. "Flanagan and Albee shared a weakness for alcohol and melancholy," writes Christopher

Bram in *Eminent Outlaws*. "They were known in the downtown gay bar circuit as the 'Sisters Grimm.' The Sisters Grimm were regulars at the San Remo, at Julius's, and at The College of Complexes." At one hangout, Lenny's Hideaway, Albee and Flanagan were known as "the two owls, because they stared straight out," said Heide. "When I think of Flanagan and Edward, I think of all that anger and rage." While Heide believed that the tension was due, in part, to jealousy on both sides as a result of their promiscuity, Albee maintained that the reason he never smiled in those years was because he had such bad teeth. Nevertheless, Rorem agreed that the element of anger between the boyfriends created "a feeling of danger" for the people around them.

Albee was lucky to have friends like Auden and Howard, who read his poetry and gave him comments. Once, he and Flanagan met with the playwright Thornton Wilder, by then the Pulitzer Prize–winning author of *Our Town* and *The Skin of Our Teeth*. After a tepid critique of Albee's poems, Wilder suggested that he write plays instead, changing the course of the younger man's life.

∼

Albee was in some ways the poor little rich boy. He grew up in a household of baronial opulence, yet the emotional life of his childhood was impoverished. Born on March 12, 1928, in Washington, D.C., he was adopted by Reed and Frances (Frankie) Albee within weeks and brought to New York. "I have no idea who my natural parents were, although I'm sure my father wasn't a president or anything like that," Edward later said. Reed Albee was heir to an empire of vaudeville theaters. Stars Ed Wynn and Groucho Marx were among the Albees' many dinner guests over the years in their stately mansion in Larchmont, just north of New York City, with its deep wraparound porch flanked by a Doric-style colonnade. The grand foyer opened onto a solarium at the end of the hall. To the left stood a walnut-paneled formal living room with sixteen-foot ceilings and, on the right, a dining room of equal height. In the bookshelf-lined library, "I used to make old-fashioneds for my grandmother at cocktail time," Albee said. It was from this library that Edward once took a book upstairs to read in his bedroom—a leather-bound volume of *Virgin Soil* by Ivan Turgenev—only to be scolded by his mother the next morning. Books were part of the decor and not to be removed from the shelves.

Young Edward was the envy of the children he played with because of his many varied and desirable toys. "I was given all the things that money can buy," Albee said. "Electric trains, private schools, a nanny, as well as a man named Zerega who was my athletic trainer and paid companion." On the property was a stable with saddle horses, and Edward was taught to ride on a horse of his own. He was given tennis lessons at the Westchester Country Club. During the week, the family chauffeur drove him to the Rye Country Day School. Sometimes, the chauffeur drove Edward and his nanny in one of the family's two Rolls-Royces into the city for a Broadway matinee. In the winter, the family traveled in their own private railroad car to Edward's grandparents' house in Palm Beach, next door to the Kennedy compound.

But his parents were cold and remote. He spent very little time with them other than the perfunctory moments when his mother might allow him to say goodnight to her before bed. Frankie Albee was a grande dame with a commanding presence and a sense of style that was utterly correct and perpetually ceremonial. Her social standing was more important to her than her relationship with her son. When her temper flared at Edward, she would remind him that he was adopted, leaving him to infer that "if I did not behave, if I did not measure up, I could be returned to the orphanage" like an unwanted possession. "I will never forgive her for that," he told Mel Gussow, his biographer. Edward's childhood friend Noel Ferrand, who spent a lot of time at the Albee home, observed Frankie Albee's bigotry: "It was not just her casual racism, her cracks about ethnic minorities, but her dismissiveness about homosexuals, or about any behavior she considered aberrant."

Meanwhile, Reed Albee "rarely spoke," sitting silently as his wife predominated, Ferrand said. Edward denied having any semblance of genuine contact with his father. "He was such a negative quiet person that I never even got to know the man."

The absence of affection at home would weigh on his performance at school. "I was pathologically shy when I was a child," Albee said. "Really. I didn't talk much." He was disaffected enough to refuse to do his schoolwork or even to abide by the rules. "No sooner would my well-intentioned family get me into one boarding school—Lawrenceville, for example, in Princeton, New Jersey—when I would get myself thrown out," Albee explained. "I think it was nothing more complex than my desire to be at home and my family's desire to have me away." By the time he was fourteen, his parents had enrolled him at Valley Forge Military Academy. J. D. Salinger, who predated him there by six years, later modeled Holden Caulfield's school, Pencey Prep, after what Albee referred to as "Valley Forge Concentration Camp." "I did not write *Catcher in the Rye*," Albee said, recognizing some of Holden's qualities in his own petulant teenage years. "I lived it."

When he was thrown out of Valley Forge, his mother attempted to enroll him at Choate, the ultimate pedigree for the son of someone with her social ambition. The assistant headmaster there, dubious about Edward's academic record but curious about the status-y Albees, made a surreptitious inquiry to the headmaster at Lawrenceville. The communication he received back was the miracle that altered Albee's entire adolescence. After acknowledging Edward's excellent reading habits and undeniable promise, the headmaster ventured a conclusion about his poor academic performance with unusual psychological probity: "Ed is an adopted child and, very confidentially, he dislikes his mother with a cordial and eloquent dislike which I consider entirely justified. . . . She is, in my opinion, a selfish, dominating person, whereas Ed is a sensitive, perceptive, and intelligent boy. . . . I can think of no other boy who, I believe, has been so fully the victim of an unsympathetic home background or who has exhibited so fully the psychological effect of feeling that he is not wanted." Edward was accepted at Choate, where, finally, his curiosity eclipsed his alienation, and he thrived academically. He became the managing editor of the school literary magazine, graduated with good grades, and was admitted to Trinity College in Hartford. Yet, there, once again, he grew restless and bored, his grades deteriorating to the point of flunking out. "Maybe I thought I was punishing [my parents] by not doing well," he said. "It's like suicides. I'll kill myself and then they'll be sorry."

Despite his parents' harsh rebuke about his failure at Trinity, he moved back home and commuted daily to a job they arranged for him in the city. Soon enough, he and a friend decided to join the Army Reserve to avoid being drafted, but when the interviewer asked him if he was homosexual, he did not lie and was peremptorily rejected. He remained at home and commuted to his job, but the question lingered about what Frankie suspected regarding his Army rejection. They never discussed anything remotely emotional at home, much less sexual, but her denunciations about homosexuality were always pointed and emphatic. He and his mother argued bitterly, persistently, about incidental things. Once, she took a crystal ashtray and threw it at him. Another time, he took the car to the city and stayed out all night. When he got home, he left it parked in the driveway with the lights on and went to bed. When he awoke, he was summoned to the dining room for a formal dressing down. "How dare you come home at five in the morning?" his parents scolded. "How could you leave vomit in the car for the chauffeur to clean up?"

He felt no connection to the people everyone referred to as his parents. "I'd learned to hate their politics, their morality, their bigotry," Albee said. "I was really very unhappy in that whole environment." When his father gave him an ultimatum—either straighten up or get out—he went upstairs, packed one suitcase, and left home that day for good. "Was I thrown out or did I leave?" he later mused to his biographer, weighing the likelihood that both were true. He was nineteen years old and fled like a refugee from the stately—if asphyxiating—upper crust to a world of possibility in bohemian Greenwich Village.

~

It would be ten years later, long after his meeting with Wilder, that Albee wrote his first one-act play. He completed *The Zoo Story* in February 1958—one month shy of his thirtieth birthday. It took him less than three weeks to write it, pecking away at the kitchen table of his walk-up apartment on a standard typewriter he had "liberated" from Western Union, using yellow copy paper he had also stolen from his employer. He called the process of writing the play an "explosion," the dialogue just flowing out of him from the very first line. "I have been to the zoo," one character, Jerry, says to a stranger on a park bench, who ignores him. "I said, 'I've been to the zoo,'" he repeats. "MISTER, I'VE BEEN TO THE ZOO," he yells, finally getting the stranger's attention. One critic with a cynical eye later described the one-act as a play about "a homosexual who, despising the square world and unable to live in his own, tricks an inoffensive stranger into killing him." While there is a modicum of truth in that assessment, *The Zoo Story* cannot be so offhandedly simplified. Albee wrote *The Zoo Story* the same year that *The Human Condition*, by Hannah Arendt, was published, and the latter's sweeping thesis about the dehumanization of the individual in society is more consistent with what *The Zoo Story* is about. Arendt warned against "our diminishing human agency and political freedom, and the paradox that as human powers increase through technological and humanistic inquiry, we are less equipped to control the consequences of our actions." In *The Zoo Story*, Jerry rants on and on in this vein, too, indignant, disconsolate, until he arrives at an even more pointedly existential conclusion about our helplessness in society, which he delivers with the thud-a-dud actuality of fact. "I have learned that neither kindness nor cruelty by themselves, independent of each other, creates any effect beyond themselves; and I have learned that the two combined, together, at the same time, are the teaching emotion. And what is gained is loss."

Flanagan was the first person to read the play. "There was no preparation for that sudden emergence of a full-blown talent," he said. "He arrived with nothing coming before . . . as if he didn't exist creatively before he was thirty." But this was not quite true; Albee was hardly a tabula rasa. "You must remember I'd been watching and listening to a great number of people for a long time," Albee later reminded Flanagan in an interview for the *Paris Review*. "Absorbing things, I suppose." Albee claimed to have wanted to be a writer as early as age six, when he started producing poetry. "When I was fifteen, I wrote seven hundred pages of an incredibly bad novel," he explained, and described a second novel he wrote at nineteen that was not much better. "I was still determined to be a writer. And since I was a writer, and here I was twenty-nine years old and I wasn't a very good poet and I wasn't a very good novelist, I thought I would try writing a play, which seems to have worked out a little better." He was also drawing details from his experience. When Albee worked as a messenger boy, "there were a lot of people living in rooming houses on the Upper West Side," he told his biographer; the things he saw while delivering telegrams likely informed Jerry's description of his cramped and squalid accommodations in just such a building.

Albee described writing *The Zoo Story* on the eve of his thirtieth birthday as "a kind of present to myself." His anxiety about entering a new decade of life fueled the play's lightning-fast composition process. But Albee felt another source of urgency too: an inheritance of one hundred thousand dollars (close to one million dollars in today's currency) from his grandmother's trust due when he turned thirty. It would free him forever from the weekly allowance he had been receiving—a financial umbilical cord administered through the family business. Once a week, tail between his legs, he would trudge uptown to his father's office at 630 Fifth Avenue and pick up a twenty-five-dollar check, placed in his hand by a secretary. He was hoping to prove that he could make it as a writer before he became an heir.

Flanagan sent *The Zoo Story* to his friend David Diamond, the composer, who had hosted him and Albee in Italy several years earlier. Diamond liked the play enough to send it on to a producer in Berlin, where it had its world premiere in 1959. For Albee, this debut represented a symbolic graduation, as it were: completing the play meant earning artistic autonomy from Flanagan's tutelage.

In this respect, Albee succeeded all too well. Flanagan's star was on the wane. Performances of his song cycles at Carnegie Hall would receive respectful notices in the *Times*, and he would continue to write music reviews for the *New York Herald Review* and *Stereo Review*, but in the coming years, his prospects as a composer would only diminish, whereas *The Zoo Story* was about to launch Albee to extraordinary heights. Unwittingly, the younger man's early success had precipitated a rocky and protracted breakup that would linger in a purgatory of recrimination before their relationship settled into an on-again, off-again, equally troubled friendship. In the end, what remained were Albee's impressions of his ex's failure to fulfill his artistic potential and his tragic fall from intellectual grace, combined with excessive drinking—all of which would be glimpsed in one of the main characters of what was soon to be Albee's first three-act play.

∼

In 1959, Edward Parone, an ambitious young literary agent at William Morris, delivered a stack of scripts to an independent producer named Richard Barr at his garret-like apartment on West Eleventh Street in Greenwich Village. One of them, *The Zoo Story*, by the still-unknown Edward Albee, had been workshopped at the Actors Studio; Norman Mailer (by then a successful novelist and cofounder of the *Village Voice*) had happened to be visiting that day and proclaimed it to be "the best fucking one-act I had ever seen." Barr read *The Zoo Story* and loved it. Parone arranged for Barr and Albee to meet.

Richard Barr was born to produce Edward Albee's plays. In 1938, fresh out of Princeton, he landed a job at the Mercury Theatre on Broadway, run by John Houseman and Orson Welles. There, he assisted on one of the company's first and most notorious radio broadcasts: H. G. Wells's *The War of the Worlds*, presented as a live news flash, reporting that Earth was being invaded by Martians. That program set the tone for Barr's early career and led him increasingly toward experimental theater, which he considered more honest than the standard run of evening entertainment on the commercial stage. The more challenging to conventional preconceptions, he thought, the more inspiring.

The Princeton connection would serve him well. In the late 1940s Barr began collaborating with the actor-director José Ferrer, a fellow graduate, who was then running the New York City Center, a performing arts organization. Barr earned a pittance working on several City Center plays, so to save money, he lived with Ferrer and his wife, the actress Uta Hagen. While enjoying high-toned suburban comfort in Ossining, Barr watched his hosts' marriage slowly deteriorate, reaching its ugliest moments during a 1948 revival of Patrick Hamilton's *Angel Street* (the play that had inspired the movie *Gaslight*). Hagen, the star, was fully aware of sharing the stage with her husband's mistress, but she was so consummate a professional that the run of the show survived their messy divorce. After the director Elia Kazan attended one performance, he called Hagen immediately and cast her as Blanche DuBois in his already iconic production of Tennessee Williams's *A Streetcar Named Desire*, first as Jessica Tandy's replacement on Broadway—opposite Marlon Brando—then to assume the role in the national tour.

In the mid-1950s, Barr coproduced an unusual evening of theater called *All in One* with several short dramatic pieces, including another portrait of a tormented marriage, Leonard Bernstein's chamber opera *Trouble in Tahiti*. Following that small triumph, Barr produced the national tour of the wildly successful *Auntie Mame*, but the compromises necessary to appeal to popular audiences in commercial theater swore him off that kind of production for good. "I wanted to do that which was not possible to do on Broadway," he said. "Give authority to the playwright. Turn the theater back to the playwright."

Barr's apartment was only blocks from Albee's, and at that first meeting, Barr was left with an impression of "a remarkably shy young man with extraordinarily expressive eyes." Albee could be rather stiff and formal, but he was redeemed, according to Barr, by "an occasional glimpse of humor in his eyes." Albee, for his part, had approached his first meeting with a producer guardedly. He was intrigued by Barr's "bizarre theory that playwrights were the most important people in the theater" and allowed himself to conclude that Barr was "an intelligent human being"—a compliment Albee rarely granted. They agreed to work together, and in those early days, Albee followed Barr's lead. "He let me have the illusion of making my own mistakes and maybe making my own decisions," Albee said, while in fact Barr was steering a steady course with a knowing hand.

Barr contacted a neighbor, Whitey Lutz, who had expressed his admiration for avant-garde theater in several editorials in the *Village Voice*; conveniently, he was married to the heiress of the Eli Lilly pharmaceutical company. "There is a whole crop of American writers waiting to be heard and I feel it's about time to do something about it," Barr wrote to Lutz. "I consider it disgraceful that Edward Albee's play had to get a hearing in Berlin first. He wrote *The Zoo Story* and is walking off with raves in many spots of Europe. The play is superb, and I have it." Lutz put up the money. In January 1960, Barr produced *The Zoo Story*'s New York premiere, in an off-Broadway double bill alongside Samuel Beckett's one-act *Krapp's Last Tape*, at the Provincetown Playhouse on MacDougal Street.

The Zoo Story drew substantial attention from the press but also got a boost from some unlikely forms of promotion for an off-off-Broadway production. "Edward was able to parlay a large sum of money inherited from his family . . . which helped make his forays into the theater successful," his friend Robert Heide explained. "I was amazed one afternoon on the beach at the Jersey shore to see a plane flying by trailing a huge flag advertising *The Zoo Story* at the Provincetown Playhouse."

~

Three components shaped Albee's sensibility. One was the dissonance he experienced throughout his emotionally barren childhood in a household of abundant material luxury; he managed to coax the perversity of his upbringing into a frame of observation that was distinctly absurdist. "The Albees at home were amusing, if unintentionally so," writes Mel Gussow, citing the way Edward spoofed them behind their backs whenever his childhood friend Noel Ferrand was around. In *The American Dream*, his second one-act play, Albee portrays "a couple who once adopted a son, whom they crippled with psychological torture of a classic Freudian kind," writes John Skow in the *Saturday Evening Post*. The characters in *The American Dream* are the generically named Mommy, Daddy, and Grandma. "We were very poor!" says Mommy to Grandma. "But then I married you, Daddy, and now we're very rich." Grandma proceeds to denounce Mommy, her own daughter. "If you'd listened to me," she says to Daddy, "you wouldn't have married her in the first place. She was a tramp and a trollop and a troll to boot." It's true that Frankie, Albee's mother, came from humble beginnings; when Reed Albee married her, she had been a shopgirl in New Jersey. And yet, even though *The American Dream* is filled with references to Albee's home life as he reveals the hypocrisies that seep through the pretense of abiding decorum, he disclaimed any autobiographical inspiration at the time. "*The American Dream* is the substitution of artificial values for real values, the acceptance of appearance for content, the slow drift of accommodation," Albee told the journalist Edward Kosner in 1961. "People try so hard to escape being touched by unpleasantness that they wind up being unable to feel anything or communicate anything."

Second, Albee's coming of age in Greenwich Village further cultivated his ironic remove, adding a seasoning of aestheticized disdain for the bourgeoisie. The "keeping up appearances" brand of conformity in the Eisenhower era was anathema to his community of artists and intellectuals. They challenged it in both word and action with their own abiding mantra: "The unexamined life is not worth living."

Finally, Albee and Flanagan were surrounded by gay composers, writers, and poets who personified not only the disaffected artist but, equally, the stigmatized urban queer. For most of the twentieth century, homosexuality was the ultimate cultural taboo—and, until the early 1970s, *illegal*. Albee and his cohort inhabited a roomy gay closet in downtown Manhattan, yet the fear of being exposed outside it was something they had to endure. Irony was the lingua franca they relied on, utilizing a lexicon of words with double meanings to signal their secret identity to one another in "straight" company. Susan Sontag, who resided in Greenwich Village among the same community of artists and writers, would later popularize this paradoxical language—and its exaggerations—to the wider reading public as "camp." The term embodies the irony and hyperbole imposed on a word, phrase, gesture, or object that was hiding in plain sight in the conventional world, yet implicitly understood by the initiated for its symbolic alternative implications.

A safe way to find out if someone was gay, for example, was to ask if he was a "friend of Dorothy," referring, of course, to Judy Garland's character in *The Wizard of Oz*. Dorothy loses her innocence upon discovering that the Wizard is not a magical deity but a small ordinary man; she is transported home by *fairy magic*, the click of her glittery red heels. These camp overtones—intensified by the passionate fandom many gay men felt for Garland herself—reverberated from within the invisible homosexual closet, infusing Dorothy's lost innocence with coded mockery and sexual innuendo, the ultimate "wink-nudge" of one fellow traveler about another.

In 1960, when Barr, a "friend of Dorothy," read *The American Dream*, he recognized not only the Absurdist style pioneered by European playwrights such as Eugène Ionesco but also the eerily playful tone of puppeteer Burr Tillstrom, whose *Kukla, Fran and Ollie* television show Albee had admired as a child and readily acknowledged as an influence on his work. Barr wanted to produce an evening of two Albee one-acts and, once again, sought financial backing. He contacted another Princeton classmate, Clinton Wilder, also a "friend of Dorothy"—a stylish, free-spirited, and wealthy bon vivant. Wilder had recently produced Marc Blitzstein's *Regina* at City Center (the musical adaptation of Lillian Hellman's *The Little Foxes*), as well as *A Visit to a Small Planet*, by Gore Vidal. Barr and Wilder were among a growing, if clandestine, brotherhood of talented gay composers like Blitzstein, writers like Vidal, and playwrights like Albee that would prove as useful in navigating the cultural hierarchies of New York as the Princeton connection.

Their quiet cabal worked in mysterious ways. While Albee was writing *The American Dream*, Barr was traveling in Europe. The young playwright sent him a letter with sotto voce suggestions about nightlife activities he might enjoy in Berlin. "I do think you would be amused by the Kleist Casino—a bar-brothel where the boys dance 1935 jitterbug, and the bar stools are six feet high," Albee wrote. "Around the corner from this Sally Bowles-type saloon there is the Robbie-bar full of loverly but not especially safe like [young men], over from East Berlin (sometimes) with dollars signs where their pupils ought to be. Fetching, but perhaps not for the nice likes of us." This brand of coded information traveled through their secret society, securing not only a network of social and professional relationships but an entire ethos. Out of the bonds they formed would spring legendary projects that became era-defining in the twentieth century, among them *A Streetcar Named Desire*, *West Side Story*, and *Breakfast at Tiffany's*.

"I like that little play you showed me," Wilder told Barr over lunch at Sardi's. He agreed to put up the money and coproduce the two Albee one-acts, *The American Dream* and *Bartleby*, at the York Theatre. The production company they formed—Theater 1961—would become a lifelong alliance between Barr, Wilder, and Albee and speaks to Barr's sincerity in generating playwright-driven productions. "That's how our whole partnership began," Wilder said. "We never had a contract. We don't have one with Edward (Albee). We simply ask each other first."

∾

The Zoo Story had just opened off-Broadway and been reviewed in the *New York Times* when another major presence entered Albee's life. At a party in the actor Michael "Mendy" Wager's house uptown, in January 1960, Albee spotted a cute young gatecrasher. "The first time I laid eyes on Terrence McNally, it was the most beautiful face I've ever seen in my life," Albee recalled. McNally was barely out of Columbia University, and interested in the theater; in his eyes, Albee, ten years older, was an accomplished playwright.

When Edward and Terrence left the party and realized they both lived in Greenwich Village, Albee suggested they share a cab. Once downtown, he invited the young man up for a drink. "Your wife won't mind?" Terrence asked innocently. Albee threw his head back and laughed. That evening commenced a passionate romance between Albee and McNally that lasted five years.

Albee's community was receptive to McNally not only as the beneficially attractive boyfriend but also because of the younger man's own intellectual curiosity and creative ambition. And at the time, Albee's circle of friends was in full expansion, deepening his connection to the forces of the zeitgeist. One such acquaintance was Morris Golde, a patron of the arts who lived in Greenwich Village and surrounded himself with talent. "The parties of Morris's that I attended in the 1960s were occasions for Urbane Greatness to strut its stuff," the poet Bill Berkson wrote in a letter that was read at Golde's memorial in 2001. "These amounted to the preeminent New York artistic salon of the epoch, where theater and music people mixed with smatterings of poets and painters. Conversationally, there were intense assertions pro and con, prolonged gushes, quick slaps, and suavely orchestrated quips crackling in sequence around the room." Besides Albee, the party regulars included the composers Leonard Bernstein, Aaron Copland, and

Virgil Thompson; the painter Jane Freilicher; and the poets Frank O'Hara, Kenneth Koch, Ted Berrigan, and John Ashbery.

In the summer of 1961, Albee rented Golde's house in Water Island, a remote and idyllic beachside hamlet on Fire Island, with a minimum of electricity and no distractions. A sliver of a sandbar ninety minutes from Manhattan, with access only by ferryboat, Fire Island is just wide enough for a dozen or so small communities to line up side by side, each one divided by sand dunes and stretched out from the beach to the bay. The only vehicles to be seen upon arrival were little red Radio Flyer wagons used to cart groceries along the pedestrian boardwalks that snaked through the lush and leafy beach shrub from one house to another. From the rooftop deck of Golde's house, the glistening reflections of the sun on the ocean on one side and the glassy waters of the Great South Bay on the other would create a unique and astonishing kind of light.

McNally was with him all summer, and they were in love, and it was paradisial. "Edward was the first boyfriend I ever had," Terrence said. "We were drunk all the time. We had a lot of fun. And we had a lot of fights. And a lot of sex." While Albee and McNally were drinking and fucking and frolicking in the ocean, Albee's now-officially-ex-boyfriend, William Flanagan—the other Sister Grimm—spent most of that time in and out of Bellevue hospital being treated for alcoholism. In a letter to David Diamond, Albee reported on Flanagan's decline: "Bill's collapse, as Bill will have it, came not so much from Terrence's presence in my life as from the loss of me in his. But who knows?" At any rate, Terrence was not the only thing keeping Albee busy that summer.

Six months earlier, at the end of 1960, Albee had begun working on a new full-length, two-act play he was calling *The Exorcism*. As he had been writing, the half-forgotten bit of barroom scrawl at the College of Complexes—"Who's Afraid of Virginia Woolf?"—resurfaced in his memory. He thought it would make a good line of dialogue. Soon, though, the phrase graduated to the work's subtitle. And, when the play got longer, he decided to take "The Exorcism" as the title of the new third act. It was then that *Who's Afraid of Virginia Woolf?* rose to the title of the still-evolving play. At that point, the rearrangement of titles created a sea change in concept, and he had put the play aside, where it gestated. When Albee got to Golde's house on Fire Island, he picked up where he had left off. He made the best use of the idyllic circumstances, relying on the fuel of his romance with McNally to propel an impassioned story about marriage. "I must tell you that we artists cannot tread the path of Beauty without Eros keeping company with us and appointing himself as our guide," writes Thomas Mann in *Death in Venice*.

The way Albee would conceive a play, by his own account, was vaguely mystical. He described how *Who's Afraid of Virginia Woolf?* came to him in stages. "I will discover one day that I am thinking about a new play, which means that it's been in my unconscious," he said. The idea would drift in and out of his consciousness over several weeks before the characters began to surface. "Hello, here we are . . . In effect they say, '*write us*.' I will make experiments with my characters before I trust them in a play of mine. I will do a form of actors' improvisation. I will take a long walk on the beach with the characters who I plan to have in the play that I haven't written yet. I will put them in a situation that won't be in the play, and I will improvise dialogue for them to see how well I know them."

He worked on *Who's Afraid of Virginia Woolf?* throughout the summer. The play that emerged has a simple plot. George, a college professor, and Martha, the college president's daughter, are a brainy and sophisticated middle-aged married couple. The play opens as they return home late one night after a faculty party. Despite the midnight hour, and to George's consternation, Martha has invited a younger couple from the party over for a nightcap: a handsome, up-and-coming biology professor, Nick, and his flighty wife, Honey. When they arrive, an array of escalating antagonisms unfolds well into the drunken wee hours of the morning, with character-destroying mind games and vengeful infidelity—among other social, emotional, and psychological infractions. Throughout the play, George and Martha exploit their guests with appalling behavior and acerbic phrasemaking as shockingly hurtful as it is brilliantly funny. Equally, George and Martha go at each other with vengeance, wounded pride, sadistic wit, and misguided intelligence, and it is painful to witness their domestic minefield. Yet what endures is a portrait of a marriage stretched inside out to reveal a set of feelings that reside, consciously or not, at the core of any attachment between spouses, ranging from loyalty to betrayal, tenderness to contempt, regard to rejection.

Among the evening's most poignant betrayals—and there are quite a few—is the singular revelation of George and Martha's son. Before the guests arrive, George warns Martha not to bring up "the little bugger," but when she does, it is all-out war, and the result is heartbreaking. In front of Nick and Honey, George announces that while Martha has been in bed upstairs with Nick, a telegram arrived with news that their son has been killed in a car accident. Martha wails in agony. It will soon dawn on Nick that the "son" doesn't exist, that the entire exercise is a perverse charade. For George and Martha, the shared fantasy of their imaginary son is a metaphor for their love—sacred as long as the secret had remained theirs alone. The guests leave, fed up and exhausted from the entire noxious odyssey, but the evening will be redeemed—for the audience and the marriage alike—when George and Martha, dazed though they are by the cruelty of their own ritual hazing, come back together with tenderness, absent all illusion, and confirm their genuine love for each other in the pure light of dawn.

The sources for *Who's Afraid of Virginia Woolf?* in Albee's life are varied, unlike the obvious source of *The American Dream* in his own family. Albee had been teaching at Wagner College on Staten Island when he started contemplating a play about two faculty couples. His friend Charles Strouse, a composer, also on the faculty at Wagner, remarked to his wife after reading the play, "It's like all of us talking"— meaning that it sounded like every couple they knew. Later, several other associates at Wagner asserted that George and Martha were based on one married couple there—only they couldn't agree on which couple.

Albee would sometimes speak in riddles, and once, deflecting a question about whether there was any single source for George and Martha, he alluded to Willard Maas, a poet and experimental filmmaker, who taught in the English department, and his wife, Marie Menken, a painter-cum-filmmaker. They were faculty liaisons to the New York City Writers Conference, to which Albee had been appointed as head of the playwrighting program. "Willard and Marie were the last of the great bohemians," recalled their friend Andy Warhol. In 1965, Warhol would make a film called *Bitch*, about them bickering on a Sunday afternoon. "Menken and Maas were at the center of a social scene of considerable interest to Warhol," according to the film historian Marc Siegel. "In addition to poets such as Frank O'Hara and Kenneth Koch, their celebrated parties and weekend salons attracted writers like Charles Henri Ford, Richard Wright, and Arthur Miller (who lived for a number of years in the same Montague St. building) and film makers [such as] Stan Brakhage." They were ideal subjects for Warhol, who regarded the novelty of their activities with affection. "They wrote and filmed and drank—their friends called them 'scholarly drunks'—and were involved with all the modern poets," he said. "Everybody loved to visit them."

Maas was faculty advisor to the *Wagner College Literary Magazine* as well, and he convinced his prominent friends to contribute, such as Norman Mailer, the poet Marianne Moore, the theologian Paul Tillich, and the critic Lionel Trilling, as well as the Beat poets themselves— Gregory Corso, Allen Ginsberg, Peter Orlovsky. Albee liked to visit Willard and Marie at their apartment in Brooklyn Heights, whether for dinner alone or to attend their many storied parties. "He used to come here every time to eat and just sit and listen while Willard and I argued. Then he wrote *Who's Afraid of Virginia Woolf?*" Menken recalled. "That's supposed to be me and Willard arguing about my miscarriage."

The filmmaker Kenneth Anger, a one-time roommate of the Maases, offered a description of them that could easily double for George and Martha. "They would begin drinking on Friday and would continue to drink all weekend, and then on Monday morning, they'd both go back to work and be on time for their jobs. Each weekend was like a lost weekend—well, a found weekend for them, because this was how they could be themselves," Anger recalled. "Watching their arguments was a little like watching Punch and Judy. If I had been able to film their fights, I would have had quite a film because they did the most extraordinary things."

As the summer of 1961 rolled into fall, Albee was still writing. The play kept getting longer and longer. At one point, Albee complained to his friends that the first act alone was 102 pages. He was concerned that audiences would be bored by intermission. But then, while McNally was away, traveling in Europe, Edward got drunk with Ned Rorem one night, invited him home at three A.M., and read him the entire play. "I'm bored when people read aloud to me," said Rorem, "but the minute Edward started, I was taken, grabbed by it. He read and read—and you know how long the play is—and one climax followed another, and another wave of theatricality would come over it. Then he told me how the third act would end. To make me attentive—*drunk* at three in the morning—means the play has to have strength." At the same time, Rorem, the composer, recognized the musicality of it. "There's a rest here, a comma there. A composer would not change his words," he said. McNally, too, said that Albee wrote like a composer.

In a letter from Venice later that fall, Terrence inquired about Edward's progress using their camp argot. Always in the back of Albee's mind as he conceived the character Martha was an image of Bette Davis; now McNally was referring to the play as " 'Miss Wolfe' aka 'Betty Wolfe,' " his affectionate shorthand for their shared intimacy while Albee was writing it and reading him passages aloud. McNally had been thinking about the play and insisted to Edward that it had to be on Broadway: "The dilemma of George/Martha will not leave me. You have written brilliantly before but not like this. There is a quality of razor blades here. Clean slices come up one after the other." McNally's vision of Albee's play slashing through the staid, decorous world of uptown theater was about to prove more accurate than either of them could have predicted.

Chapter 2

Marquee Dreams

Albee's star had risen rapidly because of *The Zoo Story*, and within a year of its 1960 downtown premiere he found himself being considered a new voice in the theater. His work was taken to exemplify the "Theatre of the Absurd," a term coined by the eminent theater polymath Martin Esslin in a landmark 1961 book of the same name, which placed Albee in the company of Eugène Ionesco, Samuel Beckett, Jean Genet, Harold Pinter, and other European playwrights. Their plays, according to Esslin, disrupted the comfortable certainties and orthodoxies of mainstream society, shocking the audience out of a delirium of normalcy and waking them up to the harsher realities of the human condition. The Theatre of the Absurd, in Esslin's words, "tends toward a radical devaluation of language, toward a poetry that is to emerge from the concrete and objectified images of the stage itself. The element of language still plays an important part in his conception, but what *happens* on the stage transcends, and often contradicts, the words spoken by the characters."

With Albee's growing fame from his one-act plays, articles about him started appearing with greater frequency. The name of his next play began surfacing in magazine stories long before the work itself was completed. "Albee . . . is currently . . . writing a two act play that seems unlikely ever to appear on a midtown marquee," *Time* magazine wrote provocatively in early 1961. "Its title is *Who's Afraid of Virginia Woolf?*"

At the same time, in a snappy 1961 profile of Albee in the *New Yorker*, he told Lillian Ross that the play he was working on is "about a two-in-the-morning drunken party of two faculty members and their wives." When asked about his influences, he laughed. "There are anywhere between 500 and 1000 good plays, and I'd have to go back to the Greeks and work my way right up," he replied. "After Brecht, I admire Beckett, Jean Genet, Tennessee Williams, and Harold Pinter. In fiction, I have a special preference for Salinger and Updike."

William Flanagan described Albee's manner of presenting himself to the press as "barbed, poised, and elegantly guarded." When Ross asked Albee about his creative process, his answer was gnomic. "I'd like to preserve an innocence, so that what I do can surprise me," he said, adding a vague complaint about being asked to articulate how he goes about writing: "It makes you self-conscious about trying to remain unself-conscious." Finally, after a little prodding, this is as far as his interviewer got: "When I sit down to work, four or five hours at a time is all I can manage. Then I have to go out to the San Remo and have a couple of beers with friends. . . . It's a pleasant agony."

He was already settling comfortably into the role of a public intellectual, striking a posture as contemplative as it was irreverent. "Angry? No, I'm not angry," he told Ed Kosner for a 1961 profile in the *New York Post*. "I think [James] Baldwin has the right idea. You meet Jimmy at a party and you find him to be a quiet guy with good manners and a nice sense of humor. He doesn't come on angry. The anger comes in his writing. I write angry plays, but I don't come on angry."

While still at work on *Virginia Woolf*, he wrote an essay about the Theatre of the Absurd for the *New York Times Book Review*. "When I was told, about a year ago, that I was considered a member in good standing of The Theatre of the Absurd I was deeply offended," Albee wrote. "I had never heard the term before, and I immediately assumed that it applied to the theatre uptown—*Broadway*." While the essay was complimentary about Esslin, and the other playwrights with whom he had been grouped, Broadway held for Albee the most pejorative connotation of razzmatazz commercialism, even though it was also the playwright's (secret) goal—the ultimate destination for his work. Albee went on to disparage the state of American culture by pointing to the high standards of foreign audiences. "The health of a nation, a society, can be determined by the art it demands. We have insisted of television and our movies that they not have anything to do with anything, that they be our never-never land; and if we demand this same function of our live theatre, what will be left of the visual-auditory arts . . . ?"

The name of Albee, Barr, and Wilder's production company had just turned over from Theater 1961 to Theater 1962—it would change every calendar year—when Albee completed the script of *Who's Afraid of Virginia Woolf?* Barr and Wilder, two producers in service of the playwright, were eager to produce it even before they read it.

While waiting for Albee to finish the script, Theater 62 mounted several evenings of works by new playwrights, including *This Side of the Door*, by McNally, at the Cherry Lane Theatre. McNally later claimed that an ongoing pattern in his relationship with Albee had begun the previous summer in Water Island: "Edward was very supportive of the next generation of playwrights, but he wasn't, I don't think, very supportive of me—his partner." This is not unlike Edward's feeling that Flanagan, so long occupying the role of mentor, had not liked being eclipsed by his protégé. "[Bill] was very, very important in my education. Aesthetic education. We were very good lovers together," Albee said in later years. "That relationship collapsed when I started having a career. He just sort of deflated in an odd way." In fact, despite McNally's complaint, he nevertheless benefited from Albee's support in his own climb to theatrical heights. In the summer of 1962, McNally, then twenty-three years old, would win the Stanley Award for playwriting from the New York City Writers Conference for *This Side of the Door*. Who was on the jury? Actors Studio luminaries Geraldine Page and Kim Stanley, TV host David Susskind—and Albee.

In early 1962, Albee, Barr, and Wilder all agreed that Alan Schneider, who was associated with the new Theatre of the Absurd movement, was the one to direct *Who's Afraid of Virginia Woolf?* Throughout the 1950s, Schneider was resident director at the experimental Arena Stage in Washington, D.C., but his route to *Who's Afraid of Virginia Woolf?* really began in 1955 when he was asked to direct a production of *Waiting for Godot* on Broadway. "Intrigued as I had been by that play," Schneider said about the offer, "I could not imagine a production in Broadway terms." Schneider was sent to Paris to meet with Beckett. "Who or what is Godot?" he asked the playwright, who stared into space for a moment and said, "If I knew I would have said so in the play."

Schneider would direct *Godot* everywhere but on Broadway. (That job went to Herbert Berghof, Uta Hagen's second husband.) In 1959, when Schneider was asked to direct *Krapp's Last Tape*, Barr had offered him *The Zoo Story* to read as a possible companion piece. "I decided that it was the most original and powerful American work I'd come across in years," Schneider recalled. Barr set up a meeting with Albee. "Edward was both taciturn and shy, emitting only a handful of words in our few brief meetings," as Schneider described those early encounters. "Even then I sensed below his surface a tremendous inner intensity, like molten lava, waiting to break out." While *The Zoo Story* ended up being directed by Milton Katselas, Albee watched Schneider direct *Krapp's Last Tape* and liked the way he seemed to "respect the author's words and intentions." For that reason, he had asked Schneider to direct *The American Dream*, which opened in early 1961. "I found *Dream* a charming and well crafted 'cartoon,'" Schneider said, "detailing the decay of American virtues and values, and amazingly prophetic in its insights."

In the fall of 1961, while still working on *Virginia Woolf*, Albee was asked to be interviewed for a series called *Playwrights at Work* for National Educational Television. They wanted to shoot footage of a work in progress, and Albee decided to "workshop" the opening scene of *Virginia Woolf*. He asked Schneider to direct it. That was Schneider's first awareness of the new play. He had by then directed a repertoire of plays on stages throughout the country, not only Beckett but also Bertolt Brecht's *The Caucasian Chalk Circle*; Anton Chekhov's *Uncle Vanya*; Ionesco's *The Bald Soprano*; Shirley Jackson's *The Lottery*; and Wilder's *Pullman Car Hiawatha*.

In the spring of 1962, Schneider, eager to size up *Who's Afraid of Virginia Woolf?*, sat with Barr in the producer's Greenwich Village kitchen, reading the full script for the first time. "I remember vividly the hand-to-hand passage and piling up of these papers in the ever-darkening room, page after page of Edward's lightning-like words exploding in my brain," Schneider wrote. "I felt as though I were being hit over the head with a succession of concrete blocks, and yet didn't want them to stop hitting me. . . . I kept thinking of Strindberg and O'Neill—and Edward Albee, who was piercing the darkness with these unexpected pulsating flashes of light." Turning over the final page, Schneider gathered up the entire script and followed Barr out of the kitchen and into the living room, where they sat down as if in shock, neither of them able to speak.

Schneider had written notes in the margins of the *Virginia Woolf* script, aware that all the characters were wounded. "Martha is hurt and wants to lash out to hurt back," he had scrawled. "George is hurt and has to fight back in order to survive. Nick wants to hurt others before they hurt him—he's out to get all he can. And Honey just tries not to get hurt anymore." There was no doubt in his mind that he wanted to direct *Who's Afraid of Virginia Woolf?* Schneider called Albee to tell him that he loved the play and was excited about doing it. "Evidently, I was going to direct it," Schneider later recalled, "although no one ever told me directly."

∾

Barr arranged a full reading of the script in his apartment—the unofficial Theater 62 office—casting himself as Martha, Albee as George, Clinton Wilder as Honey, and the actor Ben Piazza as Nick. Several young staff members were present, and their reactions, according to

Barr, were not encouraging: "No one liked the play!" The staff were put off by a script riddled with "fucks" and "motherfuckers." While Barr, too, was concerned that the "sensationalism of breaking the 'word-barrier' would disgust Broadway audiences," he was nevertheless undeterred. Despite his own reservations, he said that he hoped to take at least one "fuck" uptown. Wilder's belief in the play remained inviolate, but he conceded it needed several more months of work.

Since Albee was willing to revise the script and agreed to sacrifice some of the more incendiary language, the Theater 62 team wondered if *Virginia Woolf* might have a real shot at Broadway. The idea of challenging convention held for them a quiet glee, yet underlying their impulse toward provocation was a simmering indignation about American society's refusal to shed its prudery, never mind its failure to live up to its own utopian ideals. To underscore this point, the names of the lead characters in *Who's Afraid of Virginia Woolf?* were derived from George and Martha Washington, the first couple of American democracy. "Indeed, I did name the two lead characters George and Martha because there is contained in the play—*not* its most important point, but certainly contained within the play—an attempt to examine the success or failure of American revolutionary principles," Albee said in one interview.

The Theater 62 team understood that an intricate calculus was involved in hitting the jackpot—Broadway—and they knew that the relatable marital bickering in *Virginia Woolf* was the key: If they could just straddle the right balance between shocking transgression and rapier wit (along with an ultimate redeeming love between husband and wife), then they might have a hit. They wasted no time contacting Billy Rose, a famous impresario of glitzy, highly successful theatrical entertainment, who had recently bought and refurbished the old National Theatre (today the Nederlander) on West Forty-First Street, ostensibly as a tax write-off. While its location south of Forty-Second Street worked against its "Broadway" circuit status, Rose intended to elevate the theater's profile on the Great White Way. When Barr and Wilder, who represented a brand of elite respectability, floated *Who's Afraid of Virginia Woolf?* as a dark, provocative, sophisticated comedy with succès de scandale potential, they were speaking Rose's language. He agreed to rent the theater to them—but only if they cast marquee-worthy names, such as Katharine Hepburn and Henry Fonda. While Uta Hagen and Richard Burton had been the team's ideal cast, they were not averse to offering the roles to Hepburn and Fonda to secure a Broadway theater.

Hepburn had just completed filming Sidney Lumet's version of *Long Day's Journey into Night*, for which she would receive an Academy Award nomination. She read the *Virginia Woolf* script promptly but declined, claiming that she was "not good enough for this role." The play was sent to Fonda's agent, who found it too unsavory to forward to his client. Eventually, when Fonda got word that the script of *Who's Afraid of Virginia Woolf?* had been withheld from him, he fired his agent. Years later, he wrote a letter to Schneider avowing his single greatest regret: "I never got to play George." Burton, who had just completed a stellar run as King Arthur in Richard Rodgers and Oscar Hammerstein's *Camelot* on Broadway, had to decline the role of George, as he was heading off to Rome to play Marc Antony in the film *Cleopatra*—a twist of fate that would later come to serve *Who's Afraid of Virginia Woolf?* in ways no one could possibly have anticipated.

As the casting was taking place, Albee—who had been a member of the Actors Studio's Playwright's Unit since 1956—knew that the Studio was thinking about starting a production arm. The Studio was at the height of its influence and glamour then, with members like Marilyn Monroe and Paul Newman. The Theater 62 team felt a coproduction with the Actors Studio would attract the right investors. Barr sent *Who's Afraid of Virginia Woolf?* to the actor Michael Wager, who by day was executive administrator of the Studio and responsible for finding plays that the Studio might produce. Wager read it in one afternoon and called Lee Strasberg, director of the Actors Studio, to say "I have just read the best American play since *Long Day's Journey into Night*." That was all Strasberg needed to hear to anoint it as the Studio's first Broadway production. Strasberg wanted Studio members Geraldine Page and Eli Wallach to play Martha and George. But when Page read the play, she thought it was "intensely ugly" and refused the role. She went further in claiming that *Virginia Woolf* was a disastrous choice for an Actors Studio production on Broadway. Whether she was offended by the extent of the drinking, the vicious bickering, George's disdain for the guests, Martha taking Nick to bed, or Honey passing out more than once, more resistance soon rained in from several members of the Studio's Board, who were also put off by *Who's Afraid of Virginia Woolf?*

The saga dragged on throughout the summer, attracting media attention not only because of the stature of the Actors Studio but, equally, due to the growing curiosity about the avant-garde playwright. BACKERS OF THE PLAY BY ALBEE IN DOUBT, read a *New York Times* headline. The article mentions that "negotiation difficulties" had arisen, but the producers described the situation as still "fluid." Soon after the article, Barr and Wilder decided to produce *Virginia Woolf* on their own. "If we had opened with that play," Wager declared, years later, "the Studio would still have a theater today."

Meanwhile, Schneider was confronted with an obstacle of his own. Before committing to *Virginia Woolf*, he had signed a contract to direct an evening of Harold Pinter one-acts, *The Dumb Waiter* and *The Collection*. The timing of the *Virginia Woolf* production would have fallen in place nicely after the scheduled opening, but the Pinter project fell behind: *Virginia Woolf* was moving rapidly, and the producer of the Pinter one-acts refused to amend the terms of Schneider's contract. Schneider wanted to direct *Virginia Woolf* but feared the legal risk of violating his commitment. Then, Schneider gave Pinter the Albee script to read. The playwright confessed being "totally in awe." It was Pinter himself who convinced Schneider "not to give up something as powerful—and potentially successful—as *Virginia Woolf* for his own one-acts."

~

Schneider had seen Hagen in everything, from *Streetcar* and *The Seagull* to *Othello* and *Saint Joan*, and he believed she was born to play Martha. Hagen was everyone's first choice. "She was a great actress," Schneider said. "She was ideal for the part. Edward had practically written the play for her—without even knowing it."

Playing Blanche DuBois in *Streetcar* had secured Hagen's reputation as a Broadway legend. When that tour ended, a profile in the *New York Times* described her as living a high-minded bohemian life in a spacious old apartment overlooking Washington Square. Bookcases were filled with prestige authors. A Bach score was open on the piano rack; two excellent Paul Klee paintings—gifts from ex-husband José Ferrer—hung on the wall, alongside a drawing of her in *Streetcar* by her friend, the *New Yorker* illustrator Saul Steinberg. "There is no maid, no chaise longue, no temperament, no hostess gown," reported the author about Hagen's lack of pretension, "simply a big-boned, ash-blond girl with short-cropped hair, wearing a wash dress and sandals, who, in rare moments of repose, is reminiscent of Ingrid Bergman."

Barr had put out feelers to Hagen months before the *Virginia Woolf* script was finished, and she was primed to read it when it finally got to her on July 10, 1962. "I had the reputation for being unbelievably choosy," she said. "I don't mean this to be true without exception, because mostly I can tell within ten minutes whether a play is going to interest me. . . . In the first four pages of *Virginia Woolf*, I knew I wanted to play Martha." Hagen kept detailed journals of her work during the early 1960s and recorded her reaction when she first received Albee's script. "After class I ran home and organized a lot of things in the house and then started reading *Who's Afraid of Virginia Woolf*," she wrote. "Albee is an extraordinary writer." She described reading to the end, counting 265 pages. "I was so gripped by the play, and moved, it took me quite a while to recover."

The following day she invited Albee, Barr, and Wilder to her apartment, confessing that she was "floored that Albee was so young (34—looks 24)," but feeling an immediate rapport with him. And, yet, while expressing wholehearted enthusiasm for the role of Martha, Hagen had personal reservations. During the end of her marriage to Ferrer—a painful period that left permanent scars—Barr's continued friendship with her ex-husband-to-be had felt like an emotional betrayal. It took a concerted effort for her not to let the discomfort Barr brought up cloud her interest in the play he was producing. And yet that was nothing compared with her patent refusal to work with Alan Schneider.

"If I hesitated, it was about Alan, not the script," Hagen said. "When I got interested in the script, I called Fritz Weaver and I said, 'They like me a lot and they haven't got a George. Do you want me to push you for this?'" When she told him who was directing, it was the end of the discussion. "If Alan Schneider is directing, I don't even want to know the script exists," he told her. Apparently, Weaver had been tortured by Schneider during rehearsals for his 1957 Broadway production of *Miss Lonelyhearts*. "Those kinds of stories were rampant among theater people," Hagen said. "Alan was wonderful with producers and very often with playwrights, but with actors he was a sadist."

Schneider knew about his reputation. "I was more insecure than I am now," he later acknowledged. "I think I was tougher [on some actors] than I had to be. After dealing with community- and university-theater people for so long, I wasn't used to talking to Broadway stars."

A week after that first meeting between Albee and the producers with Hagen, Schneider called her at her house in Montauk. "We had a long talk, and he was wooing me, being overly pleasant, and it embarrassed me," Hagen wrote a friend several days later, adding that "the play is so GREAT," if she could get past her trepidation about the director. Schneider's memory of events differs from Hagen's. "I spent five hours talking her into accepting the part," he wrote in his memoir.

Albee described yet another sequence of events. "I thought it would be interesting to cast Uta Hagen in the play. She lived in Montauk, and I was coming out to persuade her to be in it." He remembered this trip specifically because it was when he fell in love with Montauk, a seaside town on the easternmost tip of Long Island, three hours by car from the city. "I was driving along the highway and discovered that I had to live out here. I was hoping that *Virginia Woolf* would become a commercial success." Albee spent a breezy afternoon with Hagen talking about the play. When it became clear to her that Theater 62 had no intention of replacing Schneider, "I had no choice," she said, agreeing finally to take the part and to tolerate—or *tame*—the director.

When Burton's commitment to *Cleopatra* forced him to pass on *Virginia Woolf,* Hagen offered a list of suggestions for the role of George, including Jason Robards and even Ferrer (with an "*eek*" next to her ex-husband's name). The role was offered to several other actors, but without much traction. It was Schneider who proposed Arthur Hill, a lesser-known actor, for George. He had been impressed with Hill's performance opposite Colleen Dewhurst in the Pulitzer Prize–winning play *All the Way Home,* by Tad Mosel. Schneider called his friend Arthur Penn, who had directed that play, to inquire about "how deep an actor" Hill was. Penn described his "surprising range," believing he "could do anything," and added that, having directed Henry Fonda in *Two for the Seesaw,* he thought Hill was a much better choice for George. The others, including Billy Rose, were not enthusiastic, but Barr admired Hill's work, too, and the script was sent to him in London, where he was making the film *In the Cool of the Day* with Jane Fonda.

As Hill later described it, "a script the size of the London telephone directory" arrived from his New York agent. "I had the afternoon free, and I sat down to wade through [*Who's Afraid of Virginia Woolf?*]—one of the most astonishing afternoons I'd ever experienced. I can remember thinking to myself, 'This thing will never make a dime commercially, but this play has to be done. Actors are just going to love getting themselves right up into the armpits in this play, but nobody will come to see it.'" He shot off a telegram to his agent with an unqualified yes.

By the end of the summer of 1962 the full cast was set, and Albee was relieved. He felt that Hagen and Hill would realize the characters as he imagined them. They had cast relative newcomer Lane Bradbury as Honey. But George Grizzard, who was cast as Nick, had by no means been the unanimous choice. The part called for a beefy athletic bruiser, and Grizzard, while a strong actor, was not very tall. He didn't feel "butch enough, jock enough, tough enough," Albee remembered, acknowledging his own doubts about Grizzard's ability to fulfill the role. Later, though, Albee admitted that "once George got into rehearsal, I saw the subtlety and the aggression, and I had no problem with him as Nick."

The funding had come together more easily than they had expected. Aside from the $10,000 that Albee, Barr, and Wilder together put up through Theater 62, and another $3,500 Wilder put in, they raised a total of $55,000 from twenty or so investors, including Milton Sperling, a Hollywood producer and screenwriter, the single largest investor, putting in $15,000. They had budgeted $75,000 for the production, but the costs turned out to be under $50,000. One expense they were able to cut was the use of the song "Who's Afraid of the Big Bad Wolf?," the rights of which would have come to $200 a week. It was Wilder who realized that when the script calls for Martha to sing "Who's Afraid of Virginia Woolf?," the words could just as easily be set to the tune of "Here We Go Round the Mulberry Bush," which was in the public domain.

As everything fell into place, a new problem—or, perhaps, a mixed blessing—confronted the team. Because of a cancellation, the Billy Rose Theatre was available earlier than expected. Rose insisted on opening the play in October, even though Hill would not be finished shooting in London until early September. This left barely a month to rehearse. It would turn out that Hill's film dragged on several days longer than expected, squeezing the rehearsal time even more and leaving a danger-ously narrow window.

During that summer of 1962, Albee wrote a letter to the eighty-two-year-old Leonard Woolf—author, publisher of the distinguished Hogarth Press, stalwart of the Bloomsbury group legacy, and widower of Virginia Woolf—to ask permission to use his wife's name in the title of the play. Albee offered to provide a copy of the script through his London agent, if Mr. Woolf was so inclined to read it. It was a symbolic gesture, a courtesy. But, equally, Albee was hoping for a consecration of his new play before it was released into the world:

> I am writing you in reference to my intention to use your late wife's name in the title of my new play, which opens on Broadway this coming October. The play is to be called *Who's Afraid of Virginia Woolf?* It is a paraphrase of the song Who's Afraid of the Big Bad Wolf? And the play is neither about your wife's work nor her life. . . . The play is set in a university community—at a party—and the paraphrase is made by one of the professors in the play. . . . Virginia Woolf meaning big bad wolf meaning life. The play is not a frivolous work, and the use of your wife's name in the title will not, it seems to me, do dishonor to her name or position. . . . Would you be good enough to write me, either granting me permission to use your wife's name, or refusing it?

Mr. Woolf's nod of approval arrived two days before rehearsals were to begin: "I have no objection to your using my wife's name in the title of your play."

∼

"There are two equal roles in this play—George and Martha—of equal intensity, equal difficulty," Albee said. The rehearsal for *Who's Afraid of Virginia Woolf?* commenced in a read-through in Hagen's Manhattan apartment on September 10, 1962—one month to the day before the play was to open. In her journal, she described with some annoyance that everyone was expected at four thirty but arrived half an hour early. As a woman of that period, Hagen—the *star* of the show—had to rush around preparing snacks, coffee, and drinks. "Barr and Wilder [the producers] made some stupid announcements about a ghastly second cast for matinees etc. . . . Finally, we read while the girl photographer snapped pictures." They got to the end of the second act and, quite suddenly, the producers called it a day, expressing their delight before saying their good-byes. "I felt all suspended, strange, like nothing had been achieved," Hagen wrote, and then recorded her assessment of the reading. "[Honey] is nice & dull. George [Grizzard, who played Nick] hasn't done much more work. Edward [Albee, who was reading the part of George] is no actor, & Alan [Schneider] made no comments. Ah me."

They met again at her apartment two days later, with Albee once more reading George's part "minus Arthur Hill," Hagen wrote. "Edward reading George badly—I think Edward is a genius so naturally I have a crush on him, but he can't act!"

Hill arrived a few days after rehearsal started, "just before everyone could commit suicide," according to Schneider. With Hill, finally, they began rehearsals in full tilt on the empty stage of the Billy Rose Theatre, and there the play started coming to life for the actors. First, they sat around a table and read the play all the way through, the actors trying to find the voices of their characters. Albee, Barr, and Wilder were present at that table, as was Terrence McNally, who sat next to Albee and watched in silence. Hill's memories of those first days of rehearsal were dominated by his anxiety about learning the lines in two and a half weeks. Yet he vividly recalled his immediate rapport with Hagen:

> She was wearing these sort of pulpit glasses sitting across the table from me and kind of eyeing me and enjoying what I was doing. I thought, "My God, she's a great audience." And then when she let loose herself it was such fun. I just remember that we were having fun immediately. We hadn't even got on our feet

yet. But she was so open and generous. Completely accepting of whatever there was that was coming and sort of "Come on, let's have some more." And that's my immediate memory of Uta.

Hagen was a temperamental force to reckon with. At the beginning of rehearsals, she told Schneider that her performance needed six months to really find itself. "Uta worked from inside, but with exceptional control of her physical self," Schneider observed. "She always knew exactly what she was doing on stage, and what effect it was having on the audience—even as she never lost hold of her inner impulses and instinctive grasp of the moment's truth." By contrast, Hill was a "technical" actor. "Each move, each gesture, came from outside, studied and deliberate," Schneider said. "Arthur would, for example, literally spend hours working out exactly on what syllable of a word he would pick up a glass, fondle an ice cube, or hand someone a completed drink. . . . Always, however, he seemed to be doing it spontaneously and freely, no matter how rigidly he had worked to get to that feeling. His sense of reality was as sure as Uta's—sometimes even surer—even though it came entirely from outside."

Within ten days of rehearsal, they brought in the set furniture and did the blocking. They were able to set up the lighting, and, occasionally, if a costume was ready, the actor would wear it for a day as they rehearsed. Hagen described the importance of having the set, props, and costumes so early in the production: "To me, that was not only precedent-setting [but] one of the unique experiences of my entire life in the theatre, starting with the things that are food for the play being alive on the stage—every little ice cube, every little clinky glass. I found this the most useful circumstance of any production I've ever been in."

While Hagen assumed the role of Martha with intelligence, intuition, and the passion of her conviction, her real-life emotions could get in the way of her judgment. In the middle of rehearsal, she would repeatedly pull either Albee or Schneider aside to complain about

Hill's performance. It is possible that she was unhappy that Hill, the technical actor, was so solicitous of Schneider's attention at every turn. "He begged for help, he demanded help, he needed help, seemingly for every moment, every line, every move," Schneider said about Hill's process of finding George. "I spent hours in and out of rehearsal guiding him, encouraging him, making him feel that he was a match for Uta." Herbert Berghof, Hagen's husband, fielded her complaints about Hill every night at home, but finally, after attending the first invited preview, Berghof told her that Hill's George perfectly complemented the cunning intensity she brought to her Martha. Only then did she accept her costar as her equal partner. Despite her well-documented complaints during the rehearsals, Hagen, perhaps with a bit of selective amnesia, would much later speak respectfully of Hill's performance as George and, even, affectionately about the entire production. "I loved working with Arthur Hill," she told Mel Gussow, Albee's biographer. "He's a wonderful colleague and to the end we played together like crazy."

Regarding her director, "the best thing Schneider did is that he didn't interfere," Hagen later said, with grande dame condescension. "He didn't help. He didn't have any ideas." Schneider once told a reporter that, early in his career, the doyenne actress Helen Hayes had urged him, "*Edit* me, Alan. Don't *direct* me." It brought him to an understanding about the role of a director as "a necessary evil . . . a means to an end . . . a kind of midwife." It was from that perspective that Schneider was much more generous—and, perhaps, even more objective—in his memory of Hagen during rehearsals. "Hagen's preparation was terrific," he said, describing the way she marked up her script all the time, "naming the scenes," and writing down possible "character objectives." He remembered her constantly asking him or Albee for clarification of the character's intent, coming at it with her own imaginative reconstruction of Martha and George's life up to the moment the play begins. "Never have I worked with anyone more talented than Uta Hagen, or more capable of greatness," Schneider said in later years.

In fact, the parallels between her own life and Martha's circumstances gave Hagen quite a bit to draw from. While Uta was growing up, her father had established the art history department at the University of Wisconsin and served as its chair; Martha's father is the president of the small, elite New England college where George is on the faculty. Hagen implicitly understood the tyranny of the intellectual standards set by Martha's father, the hegemony of his domain, and the significance of his approbation. She grasped all of this as a woman of that era, subjugated by his authority regardless of her own intelligence and abilities. "She was working the way an actress of great understanding and sensitivity and experience would work," Schneider said. "She understood what the problems were much better than Edward or I did at that point, because she had had to deal with them."

An experience deep in Hagen's past caused her to struggle with Martha's need to hold on to the imaginary child, despite George's decision to kill him. "Uta just would not go far enough in opening herself up," Schneider remembered. Only after the fact did he learn that Hagen herself had had miscarriages "that nearly broke my heart," she later told a reporter, and to draw on such a tender experience for the intensity of a genuine performance, as in this case, "she could not suffer the pain of revealing herself that openly night after night."

The imaginary child in the play symbolizes the unique and secret bond shared by George and Martha. In Albee's own words, the child is "a 'beanbag' for them to throw at each other, a way of getting at each other indirectly." Given Albee's upbringing, it is little wonder that he could be so flippant about it. While Albee would claim no autobiographical relationship to his characters, he, too, was the phantom "beanbag" in his parents' life, first as the "imaginary" child before they adopted him, and second as the "invisible" child so often away at boarding school. Might we surmise that, in the realm of Albee's psyche, George and Martha—with their intellectual sophistication, razor-sharp wit, and emotional fragility beneath their all-too-clever defenses—are akin to the unknown birth parents he pictured for himself? Albee imbued the "little bugger," as George refers to the imaginary child, with all the potency of George and Martha's heartbreaking love for each other—quite the opposite of a "beanbag." That said, Albee could be circumspect about the artistic purpose of this conceit. "It always struck me as very odd that an audience would be unwilling to believe that a highly educated, sensitive, and intelligent couple, who were terribly good at playing reality and fantasy games, wouldn't have the education, the sensitivity, and the intelligence to create a realistic symbol for themselves," he said, "to use as they saw fit."

While George and Martha had been perfectly cast, there were issues with the "guests." Bradbury, as Honey, was not working out and had to be quickly replaced. Schneider made a discreet call to the actress Melinda Dillon to come in and audition. Dillon did not feel up to the part and expected not to get it, so she arrived overdressed, her hair uncombed—ostensibly sabotaging her chances. Schneider had an instinct about her ability to play Honey and sent her home to pull herself together. She returned and auditioned for Schneider and Albee, both of whom thought she was terrific. They gave her the part.

The producing team later acknowledged that Schneider found his victim in Dillon. He treated her badly, confirming for Hagen, too, his reputation as an autocratic director who picked on his actors. According to Schneider, "Melinda, whose New York debut this was, seemed throughout the proceedings to be surrounded by a slight haze made up of equal parts of admiration for, and obvious crush on George [Grizzard], fear of her own fate, and her usual tinge of creative hysteria."

When Grizzard heard that Bradbury had been fired, he called Schneider in a rage and ceremoniously quit. "We had changed out Honey without asking or telling him," Schneider explained. "And to compound our felony, [Honey] was now several inches taller than [Nick]. Grizzard was the shortest person on the stage. We had injured his deepest self, insulted his self-image, emasculated him." It took all the patience, sensitivity, and stamina Schneider could muster to convince Grizzard to stay, applauding his performance in rehearsal and offering him a pair of Adler elevator shoes. Not only did he stay, but, according to Schneider, he assumed the wholly inappropriate attitude of a leading man, inventing new lines of dialogue for his character and, at one point, demanding that his role be expanded.

Prior to rehearsals, Albee and Schneider had spent many hours and days together establishing a good working dialogue, teasing out ideas about George and Martha, making small cuts to the script, even tinkering with it during rehearsals. Albee was a central force in the production, which fulfilled Barr's intention to privilege the playwright. "Albee let me stage each scene without being around, then he would come in, fresh, to look at it and give me his thoughts," Schneider said. "Most people think that a director is always making a writer cut out something he doesn't want to. In our case, I can take credit for persuading the author *not* to cut George's . . . speech about the pain of growing up, even though Edward confessed he wasn't sure what specific relevance the speech had to the scene. I told him it was too good to cut regardless of its relevance."

Albee considered it "marvelous" to watch Schneider work, "to really, you know, get in the depths and the essence of what you're after." That said, Schneider had some personality tics that annoyed Albee. "Schneider didn't have a sense of humor," he said, describing him as didactic, at times, to the point of being overly thorough about the most pedestrian details and driving everybody crazy. Much later in his life, Albee would reflect on Schneider's insecurities, citing his perpetual defensiveness. "He was very insecure with women. And, so, the Uta Hagens, the Colleen Dewhursts, and the Irene Worths of this world did not like him. . . . He was probably intimidated by them. Sexual insecurity. I always had the feeling that that's what was behind it all with Alan." He added that Schneider lied about his age, claiming to be six or seven years younger than he was. Yet, on another occasion, he summed Schneider up with the kind of high praise he rarely allowed: "As a director he was tough, demanding, thorough and absolutely dedicated. His type doesn't come along very often."

As producers, Barr and Wilder stayed away from the rehearsal, but once the set was in place on the stage, Schneider invited them to a run-through of the show. They sat in the back of the empty theater, quietly "astonished, excited and ineffably moved by what we saw," Barr wrote. "At the end of it we were so shaken that outside of a few mumbled words of conventional necessity, we left the theatre in silence and headed for Wilder's house on East 74th St." There, over drinks, they plotted out a strategy for generating word-of-mouth interest in the play before it opened. Barr quickly organized several "free" preview performances while rehearsals were still ongoing, and several other "low-priced" performances offered to known individuals. "The need for an intelligent and sophisticated audience was imperative—even though an audience of theatre 'wiseacres' could potentially be 'devastating,'" Barr said, describing the risks involved. Having theater people in the house was a way for Albee, Barr, and Schneider to "sense immediately and acutely any sections of the play that sagged or missed their point." They were not only heartened by the audience reactions during these previews—the laughter at just the right moments and the enthusiastic applause—but confident, too, that the potential for success was in their grasp.

Chapter 3

Wild Applause

If you take the cha cha out of Duchamp you get what a dump.

—RAY JOHNSON

Who's Afraid of Virginia Woolf? opened on Broadway at the Billy Rose Theatre on October 13, 1962. The curtain rose on an empty living room. A cackling Martha could be heard before she barreled through the front door onto the stage. "Jesus H. Christ," she barks, stumbling into the room. "Martha, *Shhh*, for Chrissake, it's 2 o'clock in the morning," George says, closing the door behind them. "Oh, George, what a *cluck* you are," she scoffs, reaching for the lamp and turning on the light. She shakes off her coat, throws it on the couch, and surveys the casual disarray of their well-worn living room. "What a dump!" she sneers with boozy disgust. Then, suddenly, a glimmer of amusement animates her face, and she swings around to George. "Hey," she blurts out, poking him. "What's that from?" She repeats the phrase with the exacting elocution of Bette Davis—"WhaT a DumP"—and looks at him expectantly. "How would I know?" George says, turning away with an air of impatience and hanging up his coat.

"Oh, come on, what's it from, for Chrissake?" Martha persists, her salon-coiffed hair losing its shape after their long evening out. He looks at her, seemingly lost in a haze of inebriation. "What's *what* from?" he says. "Dumbbell," she snaps. She thinks for a moment. "It's from some *goddamn* Bette Davis picture," she says, "some *goddamn* Warner Brothers epic." George is clearly not interested in the conversation. "*Mar*tha," he says. "I can't remember *every* picture . . ." She glares at him, exasperated. "Well, no one's asking you to remember *every* single *goddamned* Warner Brothers epic," she says, shaking her head. "Just *one*, one single little epic." Martha walks across the room, her gait slightly askew, the movie in question now slowly coming back to her. Excitedly, she embarks on a description of Davis as a housewife coming home with several bags of groceries to a modest little cottage. Davis plunks the groceries down on a table and looks around disparagingly. Assuming the air of the character, Martha again performs the line with the actress's signature hauteur. "Wha*T* a Dum*P*," she says with perfect staccato precision, then looks at George, as if expecting him to clap—or at least to name the movie. "Hmm" is all he can muster. Martha walks up to George with her hands on her hips and states defiantly: "She's *dis*-content."

Martha's own disappointment in life is established in that scene as if she were drawing the evening's first line in the sand. Throughout the arc of the tumultuous hours to follow, she and George will cross that line in behavior that is intermittently tender, acerbically witty, drunkenly vengeful, increasingly monstrous, and bitterly sadistic—if not necessarily in that order. Yet, as the sun is rising after the volatile wee hours of a late, late Saturday night, George and Martha will come back together—vulnerable, affectionate, and redeemed by their love for each other.

Who's Afraid of Virginia Woolf? is over three and a half hours long; the drunken behavior of George and Martha in front of their guests is uncomfortably transgressive; the emotional content is raw and harrowing; on top of that, the disarmingly clever dialogue is painfully double-edged. In 1962 a night like that in the theater posed a confrontational challenge to the standards of American society that had been set to an all-purpose, sanitized good cheer. At that moment, *Virginia Woolf* was—and remains today—an existential provocation that serves up a range of fundamental truths about marital attachment usually, and necessarily, lurking, safely hidden, beneath the rituals of everyday life. It would have been impossible then to imagine the same kind of George-and-Martha skirmishes taking place behind the closed doors of the best-known married couples in the collective consciousness of the time: the zany Ricardos—Lucy and Ricky—of *I Love Lucy*; the even-keeled Nelsons of *The Adventures of Ozzie and Harriet*; the upstanding suburban Cleavers—Ward and June—of *Leave It to Beaver*; or the comedic George and Gracie of *Burns and Allen*. And let's not forget the Kennedys, the glamorous, young president of the United States and his first lady—beautiful, stylish, cultivated, cosmopolitan, and telegenic—who had come to represent the apotheosis of the ideal American couple, stepping into the legacy of George and Martha Washington and setting the tone for a more modern—if not also more genteel—set of common American values.

George and Martha in *Who's Afraid of Virginia Woolf?* shattered the polite expectation of their Kennedy-era audiences. It was a bold gamble for Albee, Barr, and Wilder to stage the play for a Broadway crowd that could so easily have construed the display of nasty marital brawling on so proper a public stage as an assault on the institution of marriage, an insult to their values, a repudiation of their common decency. The question lingered right up to curtain time whether the audience would storm out because of the off-color language, the sloppy drunkenness, the unabashed infidelity, and the interminable test of their patience. Or was it possible, as the producers had hoped, that theatergoers would recognize something fundamentally true in the play and take it seriously on its merits? Surely, the audience response and the critical reaction—the play's success or failure—teetered here on the winds of fate.

In a savvy move, the producers had sent opening night invitations to every newspaper and magazine publisher in New York, every editor in chief, theater critic, book critic, and any prominent journalist they could think of to paper the house. And they all came because, in the two short years since *The Zoo Story* was first staged, Albee had become an intellectual curiosity; they came because the name of the play carried its own sophisticated kind of provocation; and because Hagen's reputation had the pull of a Broadway legend. Mel Gussow, then a young theater reporter at *Newsweek*, was in the audience that night, and, in his biography of Albee, he described the crackling exuberance all around him: "Opening night was a nail-biting ordeal for everyone involved in the production—except for the actors, who were focused on the performance." He remembered the bursts of laughter from the audience followed by collective gasps at the insults hurled across the stage. "When the play ended at 11:40 PM, there was a moment of silence, then thunderous applause, followed by curtain call after curtain call for the actors, who were high on the adrenaline of the evening."

This characterization was echoed by Schneider, who stood at the back of the theater throughout the performance. "Opening night— Saturday, October 13, 1962—was the most exciting night I've ever had in the theater," he wrote in his memoir. "The audience seemed to have a sixth sense that they were in for something special. . . . With Uta's 'Jesus H Christ' entrance, I felt the audience fused into rapt attention, punctuated by machine-gun bursts of New York laughter. And two minutes into the performance, the actors onstage were unable to produce anything other than perfection. I knew—from my usual pacing position beside the playwright at the very back of the orchestra—that nothing could stop us."

The audience called for the author during the standing ovation, but Albee declined to come to the stage, turning to Schneider, who was standing next to him at the back of the theater: "Tonight belongs to the actors." It was well after midnight by the time Hagen arrived at the party she was hosting upstairs at Sardi's restaurant. Albee threw his own celebration downtown. "We had a party afterwards at our apartment on 12th Street," McNally said. "Abe Burrows (a Broadway legend) walked up to Edward and said, 'Welcome to the American theater.' And I thought: 'where the hell do you think he has been the last few years?'"

Because the opening was on a Saturday night, the reviews would not appear until Monday. Clinton Wilder had a small Sunday evening gathering for drinks and dinner at his elegant townhouse on the Upper East Side—Albee, Barr, Schneider, Rose, and several press agents—to await the Monday reviews that started trickling out later that evening. Their spies were strategically placed at the various newspaper printing plants to deliver word of their fate hot off the presses. "With the first reviews, the atmosphere in Clinton's warm living room suddenly became extremely chilly," Schneider remembered, as everyone's anxiety grew. The *Mirror*'s review was the first one to be read to them over the phone: "Edward Albee's *Who's Afraid of Virginia Woolf?* is a sick play about sick people." The next was the *New York Daily News*, with the headline, A PLAY LIES UNDER THE MUCK IN *WHO'S AFRAID OF VIRGINIA WOOLF?* It described the play as "3 1/2 hours long, four characters wide, and a cesspool deep. . . . If only somebody— the producers or the gifted director or even Uta Hagen—had taken young Albee out behind a metaphorical woodshed and spanked him with a sheaf of hickory switches, he might have grown up to the responsibility which should come with his being an uncommonly talented writer."

Barr was so dispirited that he downed several more drinks before taking a walk around the block alone. He came back and took a nap upstairs, until he heard Albee reading aloud from the influential critic Walter Kerr's more positive review in the *New York Herald Tribune*: "*Who's Afraid of Virginia Woolf?* is a great many things. It is a horror play written by a humorist. . . . It is an evening in the parlor with people who play nothing but games, war games. It is a brilliant piece of writing, with a sizable hole in its head. It need not be liked, but it must be seen." While Barr considered it a backhanded review, Rose, a Broadway stalwart, was reading a different set of tea leaves. He believed that the review would bring audiences flocking to the show and, without saying as much, offered to buy the producers out on the spot. They declined, and it was a good thing, too, as the next morning, when they arrived at the theater, a line of more than one hundred people stretched down the block waiting for the box office to open.

Perhaps the Monday morning review by Howard Taubman, the theater critic for the *New York Times*, is what drew people to the box office: "Thanks to Edward Albee's furious skill as a writer, Alan Schneider's charged staging and a brilliant performance by a cast of four, *Who's Afraid of Virginia Woolf?* is a wry and electric evening in the theater." Taubman continues with a lucid observation of the play that is both philosophical and mature. "You may not be able to swallow Mr. Albee's characters whole, as I cannot," he writes, and then urges readers to hasten to see it anyway. "*Who's Afraid of Virginia Woolf?* is possessed of raging demons. It is punctuated by comedy, and its laughter is shot through with savage irony. At its core is a bitter, keening lament over man's incapacity to arrange his environment or private life so as to inhibit his self-destructive compulsions."

Tennessee Williams attended one of the preview performances and concluded that the play is "one of those works that extend the frontiers of the stage." Gore Vidal's sister, Nina Steers, sent Wilder a note after the opening to say that both she and Gore adored the play, and offered to throw an opening night party should it come to Washington. Elizabeth Ashley, the Broadway actress who won a Tony that year for *Take Her, She's Mine*, attended the opening night performance. "I remember being enthralled and overwhelmed by it," she said. "Uta Hagen was this acting legend; finally seeing her was just extraordinary. Rarely do you see a great actor strip off the skins to where you see raw, naked, primal power." Colleen Dewhurst, who had been offered the role of Martha for the matinee cast, and had to decline because of a previous commitment, was there on opening night, as well. "There was an air of excitement in the audience that went beyond my wildest expectations," she

said. "This was not just a special opening night. Both the playwright
and the cast made theater history that night." Among those who saw it
in the opening weeks was the playwright A. R. Gurney. "I was teaching
at M.I.T. at the time," Gurney said, "an introductory course to Western
Culture—Sophocles, 'The Confessions of St. Augustine'—and I added
Who's Afraid of Virginia Woolf? to the list as soon as I got back."

Perhaps the most meaningful response came from John Steinbeck,
who had just won the Nobel Prize in literature. He was present on
opening night and, afterward, sent a note of congratulations to Albee:
"The flash of the moment of truth is blinding. . . . When Walt Whitman
sent his home-printed copies of *Leaves of Grass* to the so-called giants
of his time, only Emerson deigned to reply. He said—and I want to
plagiarize—'I salute you on the threshold of a great career.' Isn't it interesting that only the vulgar papers found your play vulgar? But that was
inevitable, I guess." He added, "I want to see it again and again."

Who's Afraid of Virginia Woolf? paid its investors back in only thirty-
one performances. "Broadway did make a difference," wrote Gussow.
"Albee was put on a pedestal, occasionally knocked down from that
pedestal; repeatedly interviewed, he was quoted, courted, and invited."
Barely a month after the opening, Albee was honored with an invitation to the White House as part of a delegation of tastemakers to meet
President John F. Kennedy.

~

The success of *Who's Afraid of Virginia Woolf?* exposed a chasm in the
cultural life of America. The media was finite then, with only three
national television networks, two major newsweeklies, and a handful
of national feature magazines. There tended to be only one predomi-
nant public conversation, and it was calibrated to a narrow frequency
of white middle-class Babbittry. Yet there were plenty of educated people
of different ethnic and racial backgrounds starved for reflections of
themselves in a more honest and intelligent social dialogue about actual
human experience. The historical conditions that determined the

midcentury cultural mood varied widely. Cold War threats of nuclear annihilation were brought dangerously close to home by the Cuban missile crisis—where nuclear-armed Soviet missiles were pointed directly at the U.S., ninety miles offshore—which erupted three days after the opening of *Virginia Woolf* on Broadway. The production was also shadowed by the apparent suicide of the thirty-six-year-old Marilyn Monroe two months prior—the iconic power of her international stardom cutting deep into the American psyche, as the entire culture mourned the loss of the postwar symbol of sexualized optimism she personified. Despite the shattered illusions left in the wake of those disparate events, the media set a steady, anodyne pitch of everything-will-be-fine fortitude—an illusion of its own.

At the same time, in an instance of the stars aligning (in every sense), Richard Burton, who passed on the role of George in *Virginia Woolf* just months before, had begun an affair with Elizabeth Taylor on the set of *Cleopatra* in Rome. Both were married to other people, and, immediately, it catapulted the couple onto the world stage at a scale unprecedented in the scope of media obsession. Pictures of the two of them in costume as Cleopatra and Marc Antony were splashed on the covers of newspapers and magazines all over the world. Overnight, "Le scandale" became interchangeable with "Dick and Liz" in headlines. Media coverage had become ubiquitous enough to get the attention of Jacqueline Kennedy, who asked the publicist Warren Cowan, "Do you think Elizabeth Taylor will marry Richard Burton?" One chronicler wrote: "They had moved off the show biz pages and into the hard news. They were right up there with Kennedy and Khrushchev and the Cuban missiles." Infidelity had never looked so glamorous, but the shock to the institution of marriage itself reverberated all the way up to the United States Capitol, where Georgia representative Iris Faircloth Blitch called on Congress to make "Miss Taylor and Mr. Burton" ineligible for reentry to the United States on the grounds of "undesirability." Several other congressmen agreed, blaming the nation's "moral slide" on the Burton-Taylor affair.

In the early 1960s, two very different watershed books underscored some of the reasons why *Who's Afraid of Virginia Woolf?* struck such a deep chord. *The Feminine Mystique*, by Betty Friedan, was published in early 1963, soon after *Virginia Woolf* opened. Women recognized themselves in Martha, identifying in her "discontent" the feeling that Friedan, in her book's opening paragraph, called "the problem that has no name." "The problem lay buried, unspoken, for many years in the minds of American women. It was a strange stirring, a sense of dissatisfaction, a yearning that women suffered in the middle of the twentieth century in the United States."

At the time, both the law and social mores bound American women as, in effect, indentured servants to their husbands. "In 1963, when *The Feminine Mystique* was published, only eight states gave stay-at-home wives any claim on their husband's earnings, even if they had put their husbands through school and then devoted themselves to raising the children," writes the historian Stephanie Coontz. "'Head and master' laws gave husbands the final say over financial decisions, whether a wife could get a credit card, and where the couple should live. Rape was legally defined as 'forcible sexual intercourse with a woman other than one's wife,'"—giving women little recourse should sexual abuse occur within their marriage.

Friedan challenged the belief that women were biologically destined to be domestic and subordinate, and her book helped women begin to define for themselves the contours of their own destinies and set the terms for their own fulfillment—regardless of the predeterminations of a patriarchal society. Today the book is understood to have precipitated the women's movement in the 1960s. "For many women, and not a few men, the publication of Friedan's book was one of those events which seem, in retrospect, to have divided the sixties from the fifties as the day from the night," observed Louis Menand in the *New Yorker* fifty years later. No wonder Martha was angry. She was unfulfilled and trapped, not only within her own psyche—never mind within her marriage—but also by the conditions of her time.

The same year *Who's Afraid of Virginia Woolf?* opened, Richard Yates's novel *Revolutionary Road* was nominated for the National Book Award. "This novel locates the new American tragedy squarely on the field of marriage," wrote Alfred Kazin in a blurb used on the original book jacket. The novel is about the Wheelers, a couple who first meet at a party in Manhattan. April is an aspiring actress, and Frank, a longshoreman with a college degree, talks of his ambition to become a writer. Both express the desire to live unique and original lives. They marry, one thing leads to another, and we find them settled in conventional suburban Connecticut with a house and two kids. Frank commutes daily to his job in the city as a junior executive in a large corporation, and April fulfills the domestic obligations of a housewife and mother—so quickly have they conformed to a version of the American dream that was not what they intended.

Yates puts his finger on the existential heart of the novel in a conversation between Frank and a lunch guest. Frank condemns "the hopeless emptiness of everything in this country," and his visitor eagerly agrees: "Now you've said it. The hopeless emptiness. Hell, plenty of people are on to the emptiness part; out where I used to work, on the Coast, that's all we ever talked about. We'd sit around talking about emptiness all night. Nobody ever said 'hopeless,' though; that's where we'd chicken out. Because maybe it does take a certain amount of guts to see the emptiness, but it takes a whole hell of a lot more to see the hopelessness."

April, discontent with the ordinariness of their lives, proposes a big change: "Let's take the kids and move to Paris." She has done the research. She can take a job to support them, which would give Frank the time to study and think and write. Frank is swept into April's excitement about the change, and, together, they pursue the necessary arrangements. But when they break the news to their friends, the reaction is not what they expect. "Why would you want to move to Paris?" their neighbors ask, pointing out the Wheelers' perfectly wonderful life here in the suburbs, and judging them as foolhardy. For April, that judgment is proof of why they need to escape. As fate would have it, Frank is offered a promotion at work with a handsome raise. Confronted with the pride of his success and the security it affords, he faces the truth that, all along, his ambition to be a writer had been hollow. As his courage to move to Paris erodes, he loses April's respect. Soon enough he will lose April, too, in a tragedy that destroys the family and shatters his spirit. "I meant the title to suggest that the revolutionary road of 1776 had come to something very much like a dead end in the 1950s," Yates later said about the book.

In 2009, Sam Mendes directed a film of the Yates novel that hews very close to the spirit of the book. "*Revolutionary Road* comes out of a tradition of marital literature, in that it's a sister of *Who's Afraid of Virginia Woolf?*" he told the interviewer Charlie Rose not long after the film was released. April's disappointment in Frank echoes Martha's disappointment in George. In both cases, as the women struggle with "the problem that has no name," their husbands face a crisis of masculinity as they fail to live up to their wives' expectations. In George's case, as the associate professor in the history department of a small prestigious college, he is berated by Martha—the college president's daughter—for not "running" the history department but, even more to the bone, for not becoming the *writer* he wanted to be—just like Frank in *Revolutionary Road*. "I'm loud, and I'm vulgar, and I wear the pants in the house because *somebody*'s got to," Martha bellows in one of the many rat-a-tat-taunts she levels throughout the bumpy night. In the terms of the era, George has failed Martha by not being a man worthy of her love, a man equal to her father.

The film version of Eugene O'Neill's play *Long Day's Journey into Night*, directed by Sidney Lumet, opened in movie theaters the same week as *Who's Afraid of Virginia Woolf?* on Broadway. Albee claimed that *Virginia Woolf* owes a thematic debt to O'Neill, the older playwright, who wrote characters that cannot survive without their illusions. Both Friedan and Yates are among Albee's generation of writers and intellectuals who questioned those illusions—the pretenses of society that function as emotional armor. "*Virginia Woolf* says get rid of them," Albee said, in contrast to O'Neill. "My play is about people of more than average intelligence getting to the point where they can't any longer exist with a whole series of games, tricks, and false illusions, and then knocking down the entire untenable superstructure. The end result? Something may or may not be built in its place."

Nancy Kelly, who would later star as Martha in the national tour of *Who's Afraid of Virginia Woolf?*, remembered Walter Kerr passing the Billy Rose Theatre every day and hearing couples in line to buy tickets bickering about which one was dragging the other to see the play. "He said that the play comes to life outside the theater," she recalled. "Albee always said that Act Four of the play was when the audience leaves the theatre, and the couples argue all the way home."

~

The momentum that established *Who's Afraid of Virginia Woolf?* as an era-defining play had begun. Several days after it opened, an episode of the WNET program *Playwrights at Work* aired on national television and included footage of the opening scene of *Virginia Woolf* shot a year earlier with actors selected by Schneider. This marked the slow dissemination of the play into the greater public consciousness. "This is excellent TV," wrote the *New York Daily News* television critic about *Playwrights at Work*, citing the program's "capital use" of *Virginia Woolf*, which added to "the charged excitement that attends a controversial but explosively creative drama." This television review, by the way, was a mere twenty-four hours after the same newspaper's theater critic, John Chapman, had disparaged the play as being "four characters wide, and a cesspool deep."

Only one week later, Chapman doubled down, publishing a follow-up review of *Virginia Woolf* in the weekend section of the *Daily News* with the headline FOR DIRTY MINDED FEMALES ONLY. This did not prevent his own wife from ordering tickets to *Virginia Woolf* for the members of her Westchester Garden Club. Billy Rose used this tawdry review to full advantage, taking out a *New York Times* advertisement for *Virginia Woolf* designed to appeal specifically to women, titling the ad "The Literate Are Seldom Rich" and offering special low-priced tickets to the intelligent but wallet-strapped stenographers of rich bosses.

"People who wouldn't come to see *Who's Afraid of Virginia Woolf?* as a play of ideas about the failure of American marriage, or a philosophical drama dealing with the ambiguous conflict between truth and illusion, came to see us because they thought we were a 'dirty' play or because someone told them there were sexy scenes—Uta Hagen touching the inside of George Grizzard's thigh," Schneider said. He remembered how carefully they had worked on the wording for that advertisement, and how successful it was. The morning after it ran in the paper, he added, "I journeyed down to 41st Street to discover a line stretching out a fair distance from the Billy Rose Theatre."

In the summer of 1963, Hagen and Hill temporarily stepped off the Broadway stage to star in a London production of *Who's Afraid of Virginia Woolf?* Again, controversy fueled the success of the play; reviews with backhanded praise seemed to draw the crowds. The opening gambit in the *Guardian*'s review is exemplary: "Hateful is the proper word for *Who's Afraid of Virginia Woolf?* by Edward Albee at the Piccadilly. Hateful and shamefully funny and hideously watchable. It is too long; it repeats." The critic ultimately considers the play a guilty—if complicated—necessity: "And there is weight and anger and pity in it, with none of the monolithic grandeur of O'Neill maybe, but none of the lurid squalor for squalor's sake or misreading of sexual character which throws not a few Tennessee Williams plays off centre." While acknowledging the general distaste for American plays among London audiences, the review ends by saying, "But times are changing."

The same year, Ingmar Bergman—who had already directed more than twenty films, including *The Seventh Seal*, *Smiles of a Summer Night*, and *Wild Strawberries*—was appointed director of the Royal Dramatic Theatre of Sweden, known as the Dramaten. There was a clamoring to stage a production of *Who's Afraid of Virginia Woolf?* in Europe, and

Bergman, who won the rights, directed it. The play had its continental European premiere at the Dramaten in Stockholm on October 4, 1963. The reviews in Sweden were mixed. "What a hangover on the day of reckoning!" wrote one critic in *Aftonbladet*, a leading Swedish newspaper. "Edward Albee's—when he has to motivate this ideological trash; Ingmar Bergman's—when he must explain why he exerted himself to show this artistically sterile package ahead of everybody else in Europe." But in *Arbetet*, the more liberal Swedish paper, the critic called the performance a scenic knockout, "a shaking, spiritual striptease-act and a deep critique of civilization."

As for guiding and pacing the actors, Bergman later suggested that *Virginia Woolf* did not even need a director. "If they are very good actors, they will find it," he said. "They will find a rhythm of their own. I'm sure of that. I am convinced. It's not so difficult. You can read [the play]—and it's all there." Ten years later, Bergman would write and direct *Scenes from a Marriage*, initially produced for Swedish television and, eventually, presented as a film in the United States. It is not hard to see the DNA of *Who's Afraid of Virginia Woolf?* written all over it: *Scenes* anatomizes what is by all appearances an ideal marriage as it slowly deteriorates. As the frustrated wife becomes less tolerant of her husband's egotistical buffoonery, the couple's arguments grow increasingly bitter and more honest until, eventually, they divorce.

In New York, *Who's Afraid of Virginia Woolf?* played a total of 644 performances, all of them sold out. The production won a Tony Award in 1963 for Best Play, and Hagen and Hill each won Tonys for Best Actor and Best Actress, as did Schneider for his direction. The New York Drama Critics' Circle awarded it the best play. Then came a big slap in the face: in May 1963, the Pulitzer Prize Board of Trustees announced that there would be no prize for Drama that year. This was a direct and intentional snub of *Who's Afraid of Virginia Woolf?*—the only play nominated that year in a season that included the Broadway productions of *A Funny Thing Happened on the Way to the Forum*, *A Thousand Clowns*, and *Beyond the Fringe*.

John Mason Brown, a renowned drama critic and veteran Pulitzer juror, had written one of the two nominations for the play: "With his unblinking view of life, [Albee] slashes savagely into his characters' innermost selves. Some critics have described him as being a new Strindberg or O'Neill. Like O'Neill, he shrinks from no horror; like Strindberg, the war he declares between men and women is brutally fierce. But Mr. Albee already has an identity of his own. . . . In terms of dialogue that is at times hilariously funny and at times abrasively revealing, it is a study in hatreds and frustrations, of impotence and jealousy, and with doing away with illusion." John Gassner, another juror, was even more positive in his verdict: "Although Mr. Albee's play has easily detectable flaws, it is a slashing and penetrating work by the most eminent of our new American playwrights. . . . I see no insuperable objection to the work on the grounds of immorality, lubricity, or scatology once one reflects that we cannot expect the vital plays of our period, whether we like this period or not, to abide by Victorian standards."

Various committee members explained their votes opposing *Virginia Woolf*. One, an editor of the *Providence Journal Bulletin*, said the play "was pretentious, did not conform to the terms of the award and was not a good play," and added peremptorily: "We did not vote against it because it was controversial or shocking." But the editor of the *Chicago Tribune* minced no words when he asserted that it was "a dirty play." And the editor of the *Cleveland Press* lumped it in among all plays that "reek with obscenity" and "offend good taste." An editor of the *Washington Evening Star* voted against the play without even having seen it, which critics of the committee believed to have compromised the integrity of the prize.

On May 6, 1963, thirty minutes after the announcement that no prize would be given for Drama, Brown called the Pulitzer Prize committee to say that he and Gassner were resigning. To the press, Brown announced their resignation in terms of protest: "This is a case of advice without consent. They have made a farce out of the drama award."

The playwright Arthur Kopit remembered what a big deal it was to see Albee turn from a rebel to "a rebel on Broadway." He believed that *Virginia Woolf* transcended all the criticism because of its sheer impact. "It made you uncomfortable, and I think that scared the Pulitzer committee. I think it actually did the play a favor when Columbia was stupid enough to deny it the Pulitzer. It made the play dangerous."

~

Who's Afraid of Virginia Woolf? was written at a moment of heightened creative productivity in American literature and arts. New York was the cultural capital of the world, and artists, writers, playwrights, and musicians were trying to put their fingers on the truth of human experience. The zeitgeist was informed by the existentialist philosophies of Martin Heidegger and Sartre, and by Freudian—and Jungian—psychology. "There was an inevitability about psychoanalysis," writes Anatole Broyard, for years the book critic of the *New York Times*, in his memoir about that period in New York. "Psychoanalysis was in the air, like humidity, or smoke. You could almost smell it." Broyard described his own brief psychoanalysis not in terms of "a condition or a situation" but, as he writes, " a poetics. I wanted to discuss my life with [my doctor] not as a patient talking to an analyst but as if we were two literary critics discussing a novel."

Albee was after a "poetics" in *Who's Afraid of Virginia Woolf?*, rendering husband and wife in existential terms—that is, with stripped-to-the-bone conversations and arguments that register actual lived behavior, playing out in dynamics that are psychologically informed, in language that pierces through decorum with brutal honesty, all the while arresting the audience with its intelligence and wit. This is a play about marriage—a decidedly twentieth-century one. In the more distant past, love-based marriage had not been the norm. Rather, marriage had been meant to serve the structure of society; increase the labor force; improve a family's social or financial position; facilitate a parent's political gain; secure property for generations to come; or fulfill religious obligations. "Marrying for love instead of for economic and political calculation remained rare and socially disapproved until the late 18th century, when radicals such as America's founding fathers insisted that people had a right to 'the pursuit of happiness,'" writes Coontz. "Almost immediately, youths began to defy their parents and marry or not marry as they wished. Individuals also began to demand the right to divorce rather than remain in an unhappy marriage." Divorce would remain stigmatized well into the twentieth century. Even today, it is considered a last resort.

Though it manifests in various ways—inflected by class, race, ethnicity, culture, geography—the modern, love-based marriage has at its core a matrix of emotional attachment. Anyone who observes marriages for long enough will notice how this attachment between spouses draws from the same wellspring as our original attachment feelings in infancy. Marriage pulls on the same string that links a child to its parents; couples play out dramas that were scripted in each partner's earliest years of being (adequately or inadequately) nurtured. While it is true that, in *Who's Afraid of Virginia Woolf?*, George and Martha go at each other with vicious cruelty as they draw from a grab bag of ill intentions, their display of hideous behavior can be easily traced to the panoply of regard, desire, rejection, resentment, disappointment, frustration, and self-doubt composing the matrix of attachment central to every marriage. That their behavior is inexcusable is entirely beside the point. (It is theater, after all.) The play offers a kind of under-the-microscope examination of marriage itself, for better or worse, for richer or poorer, in sickness and in health, till death do us part.

In its psychological acuity, the play is a mirror that shows us things about ourselves—about the species—that are as painful to acknowledge as they are edifying to grapple with. It is a bitter pill, albeit one that makes us laugh out loud repeatedly, and then leaves us closer to the core of our emotional selves—a place, alas, that many people prefer never to visit. Fundamentally, Albee is challenging his audience to recognize that marriage has an emotional foundation, where the matter and the marrow lie, and from which the messy psychological complexities of both individuals intertwine like a helix and manifest in their domestic routines, their real-life obligations, their day-to-day interactions, and their public presentation. That is what underlies the saga of George and Martha—and the realities of every marriage. Albee is peering beneath the surface of one marriage to reveal a set of fundamental truths about marriage itself.

While a majority of the reviews acknowledged the play's significance, sometime in 1963 critics began to turn on *Virginia Woolf* because of Albee's homosexuality. "It happened slowly, imperceptibly: a growing unease with both the play and Albee," writes Christopher Bram in *Eminent Outlaws*. "A trickle of critical remarks became a mudslide, falling not just on Albee but on all gay playwrights." The first homophobic salvo in this attack appeared in the Spring 1963 issue of the *Tulane Drama Review* (later the *Drama Review*), a small but influential theater quarterly. Its editor, Richard Schechner, who would go on to found the experimental troupe the Wooster Group in New York, writes that "the American theater, our theater, is so hungry, so voracious, so corrupt, so morally blind, so perverse that *Virginia Woolf* is a success . . . I'm tired of morbidity and sexual perversity which are there only to titillate an impotent and homosexual theater and audience. I'm tired of Albee."

A more public swing at *Virginia Woolf* below the belt appeared in the *New York Times* that August. Joseph Hayes, the author of *Desperate Hours* (first a novel, then a play, and then a film) wrote an essay in the Sunday Arts section accusing contemporary playwrights of misrepresenting—distorting—the fundamental beliefs, feelings, convictions, or aspirations of the American people. Hayes berates the New York theater for its depiction of "man's hopelessness, lack of significance or value under an empty, scowling sky, his self-deluded stupidity, cupidity, contemptible puniness—his utter worthlessness." While Hayes's treatise purports to be about the theater in general, soon enough he zeroes in on two culprits who "seem to be glorying viciously in their own contempt for others (and for themselves) and their own self-oriented sickness": Edward Albee and Tennessee Williams. Hayes faults the playwrights for their "neuroticism" and "nihilism," and for imposing "their own sick views on the public," all the while contradicting himself about the crisis of the American stage by highlighting as vital and redeeming the works of Arthur Miller and Eugene O'Neill— (heterosexual) playwrights who are exempt from his thesis. "There is the possibility of course that we are living in a sick time in a sick world and that such a time and world are best described and symbolized by sick minds," Hayes laments. "Does the waspish bitchiness of the dialogue in *Virginia Woolf*, for instance, correspond to a recognizable pattern of the speech in a marriage, or to some other relationship out and beyond the experience of most of us?"

While in 1963 the antigay implication of Hayes's diatribe might have sailed by most readers of the *Times*, any remotely literate homosexual would have picked up on its coded disdain for "their kind" with clear-eyed distress—if not outright indignation. Hayes couched his attack on Albee's (and Williams's) sexuality with euphemisms like "neuroticism" and "sick vision" as an attempt to discount the validity of Albee's observation about marriage. Albee was asked by the *Times* to write a rebuttal, which appeared with appropriate invective in the same spot the following Sunday under the headline WHO'S AFRAID OF THE TRUTH?

Albee begins by describing the idyllic summer he is having on Fire Island—except for the pests. "If there is a strong breeze from the north, swarms of green stinging flies are liable to be carried from Long Island. One curses and swats at them while they are about." He compares them to another kind of pest that "nestles in the entertainment sections of the Sunday editions of the *Times* and the *Herald Tribune*," identifying one as "the amateur essayist" who writes in place of the real critics away on vacation. "While they are about, one must curse and swat at them, for they can ruin an otherwise sane and lovely day."

Without directly calling Hayes a bigot, Albee refutes the attack that he is subversive, ripping into "men like Mr. Hayes who will truly and finally corrupt the taste of our theater audiences, destroy our theater, undermine the national morality, and bring things to a point where it will not matter if the bombs fall. (Mr. Hayes accuses Mr. Williams and me of all of the above, and it seems only fair to toss the old hat right back at him.)"

Albee, in high dudgeon, denounces Hayes for the "escapist commercialism" he puts on the stage, which maintains the status quo at all costs, and challenges him to explain how a "sick vision" by a "sick individual—*me*" has brought about the sold-out success of *Who's Afraid of Virginia Woolf?* in an ongoing yearlong phenomenon. "If the theater must bring us only what we can immediately apprehend or comfortably relate to, let us stop going to the theater entirely," Albee writes. "Let us play patty-cake with one another or sit in our rooms and contemplate our paunchy middles."

If, according to the likes of Hayes, the theater was to be forced to appeal to the comfort level of mainstream audiences or, more to the point, if open-minded people are forced into silence to protect narrow-minded people from being offended, here is Albee's last word: "Down, then, say I, with Moliere, Ibsen, Shaw, Aristophanes. Down with the theater as an educational as well as an entertainment medium; down with the theater as a force for social and political advancement. Down with the theater!" And in a final gesture, he dismisses the pesky exercise entirely: "Isn't it a sad and telling and, yes, tragic comment on our theater that playwrights such as Mr. Hayes think the thoughts that they do, and then that they write them down? Now, back to the beach."

Albee had won this round, but it would hardly be the last time such critiques would be leveled at his work. Soon after his play *Tiny Alice* opened in December 1964, the recently founded *New York Review of*

Books published a review by a young novelist named Philip Roth. Under the title "The Play That Dare Not Speak Its Name," Roth called *Tiny Alice* "a homosexual daydream." He attacks it for "its ghastly pansy rhetoric and repartee" and compares it to *Virginia Woolf* by pointing out that "a woman defeats a man." Roth concludes his review with this question: "How long before a play is produced on Broadway in which the homosexual hero is presented as a homosexual, and not disguised as an angst-ridden priest, or an angry Negro, or an aging actress; or worst of all, every man?"

Once again, in the summer of 1965, the *Tulane Drama Review* leveled a weighty and lengthy critical denunciation of *Virginia Woolf* in the form of a diagnosis by the psychiatrist Donald Kaplan, who cited it as a prime example of "the infantile sexuality" of "homosexual theater." The subject of homosexuality scored one misdirected point in its favor when, in late 1965, Martin Gottfried came to its defense in *Women's Wear Daily*: "The fact is that without the homosexual American, creative art would be in an even sorrier state than it is now." He goes on to wrongly claim that *Who's Afraid of Virginia Woolf?* is "perhaps the most successful homosexual play ever produced on Broadway. If its sexual core had been evident to more people, it probably would never have run—even though it is perfectly exciting theater."

By January 1966, the debate was entrenched enough that Stanley Kauffmann, the new lead drama critic of the *New York Times*, could assume that "the principal charge against homosexual dramatists is well known." In his now-infamous piece "Homosexual Drama and Its Disguises," Kauffmann writes that "because three of the most successful playwrights of the last twenty years are (reputed) homosexuals and because their plays often treat of women and marriage, therefore, it is said, post war American drama presents a badly distorted picture of American women, marriage and society in general." He was referring to Albee, William Inge, and Tennessee Williams.

Of course, it was naive, if not disingenuous, for the chief drama critic of the *Times* to write that "the homosexual dramatist must be free to write truthfully of what he knows." In that era, a play about gay characters living gay lives would a priori have been dismissed as "sick" and would never have appealed to a heterosexual audience. (One playwright took Kauffmann up on the dare: Mart Crowley wrote *The Boys in the Band*, which opened off-Broadway in 1968. After the production overcame initial troubles finding actors to play gay characters, the play had a good two-year off-Broadway run. It was produced by Albee and Barr.) Kauffmann's attempt to sideline towering gay playwrights overlooked the most fundamental fact: Albee, Inge, and Williams *were* writing about what they knew. They resided in a predominantly heterosexual world; they had been brought up by mothers and fathers who were heterosexual. They breathed the same air on the same planet as their fellow heterosexual countrymen. They had a parallax clarity about the world around them precisely because of their "difference." They could see things that heterosexuals often didn't see about themselves, allowing Albee, Inge, and Williams to write about heterosexual characters with perspicacity.

That same week, *Time* magazine ran a cover story titled "The Homosexual in America." The unsigned essay is replete with stereotypes and patronizing platitudes. "The great artists so often cited as evidence of the homosexual's creativity—the Leonardos and Michelangelos—are probably the exceptions of genius," the essay alleges. And "homosexual ethics and aesthetics are staging a vengeful, derisive counterattack on what deviates call the 'straight' world. This is evident . . . in the 'camp' movement, which pretends that the ugly and banal are fun." As Christopher Bram writes, "Gay writers could not win for losing. If they wrote about gay life, they weren't universal. But if they wrote about straight life, they were distorting what they despised or didn't understand." Soon enough, the attacks on Albee's sexuality died down.

They flared up out of fear, ignorance, and, ultimately, stupidity that continued to fuel homosexuality as a cultural taboo. In the end, though, the collective effect of the aspersions cast on American theater in general, and *Who's Afraid of Virginia Woolf?* in particular, had little more effect than raindrops sliding down the marble columns of a national monument.

That said, the residue of this homophobic blip in critical reaction—which did not affect public reaction or the long-term regard of the play as a masterpiece—was a lingering rumor perpetuated mostly in the gay community that *Virginia Woolf* was a gay play in drag, that is, about two gay male couples. Over the years, Albee found himself swatting this interpretation away whenever he was asked about it. And, on more than a few occasions, he refused the rights to any theater company that tried to stage the play with four men.

Surely Albee did not welcome this battle and considered the entire subject to be irrelevant to his identity as a playwright. Years later, Terrence McNally drew a clear distinction between Albee's closeted self-identity and the circumstances of the community in which he lived. "I wouldn't say Edward ever lived in the gay world," he noted, citing Albee's obdurate refusal to acknowledge his sexuality in public throughout the years of his great fame, despite his coterie of gay friends, the gay neighborhood he once lived in, the gay bars he patronized for years, and the several long-term relationships he had had with men—including McNally himself. "I was part of the gay community critical of Edward for being so indifferent to what we saw as a struggle for acceptance and rights," McNally said, while also acknowledging the reality that "Edward was terrified of being identified as a gay playwright. I agree that he was not a 'gay' playwright, but a playwright, just as Arthur Miller is not a 'Jewish' playwright, but a playwright, or August Wilson is not an 'African-American' playwright, but a playwright."

⁓

Sometime in 1963, the Oscar-nominated screenwriter Ernest Lehman was working on a new script when Abe Lastfogel—his agent at William Morris, the agency that also represented Albee—sent him the script of *Who's Afraid of Virginia Woolf?* "I read it, and I was so disturbed by it that I said I'm never going to see this play," Lehman said. "Never. I don't want it in my life. It was very upsetting to me." Several months later, on November 11, 1963, *Who's Afraid of Virginia Woolf?* opened in Los Angeles for a three-week run at the Biltmore Theatre, starring Nancy Kelly and Shepperd Strudwick. Lehman claimed that he was dragged to see *Virginia Woolf* by his wife. "I was totally destroyed in that audience with people I knew seated around me," he remembered. "It was on opening night. I was trying to conceal sobs that were coming out of me. I was just decimated by that play, and I stumbled out of the theater."

Afterward, Lehman described the effect of the play on him in a phone call to Lastfogel, telling him that he could not imagine it as a movie. "Not in a million years," he added, to drive the point home. In a psychological chess move, Lastfogel told Lehman that there was one other person in town who felt the same way—Jack Warner, the imperious head of Warner Brothers. After a pause, Lastfogel ventured, "Want me to talk to him?" Lehman was at work on a much more uplifting project—*The Sound of Music*—and said no. No, no, no. But not for nothing was Lastfogel chairman of the William Morris Agency. Over the next few weeks, he followed up with several calls to Lehman garnering his interest by avowing to sell the property to Jack Warner. "Would you like me to include you?" he kept asking. No, no, no, Lehman said again. Finally, Lastfogel called to say that Warner wanted it. "It's official," he said to Lehman. "And he has requested you as the producer and writer of *Virginia Woolf.* You have the weekend to make up your mind."

The next day Lehman invited his friend the producer Larry Turman over for a poolside chat. "I told him I hadn't the faintest idea how you do it as a movie. Who the hell's going to go see it?" But Turman convinced him. "Ernie let's face it, you cannot afford to turn down *Virginia Woolf,* it's too important," he said. "To hell with whether you know how to do it, you've got to say yes." And, finally, he did.

Lehman was known as a first-rate screenwriter, but he would be a first-time producer. This did not seem to concern Jack Warner. Lehman had been around Hollywood for years and understood how movies got made. He knew everyone, and he had a reputation for being savvy and level-headed. Lastfogel negotiated a $250,000 contract for him with Warner Brothers (over $2 million in today's dollars) to write the screenplay for *Who's Afraid of Virginia Woolf?* and to produce the "photoplay"— the term of art for "film" in his contract. He was given full control over the casting, the director, and the crew.

Warner Brothers paid Albee $500,000 for the film rights to *Who's Afraid of Virginia Woolf?*, plus 10 percent of the gross once the film earned $6 million—the original budgeted cost of production. Albee secured a gentleman's promise from Jack Warner to cast Bette Davis and James Mason in the roles of Martha and George. Now that he had sold the film rights to Warner, he was uncertain about what Hollywood would do to his work. Regardless, it was now out of his hands.

Chapter 4

Hollywood Bound

P robably no one in Hollywood is getting more unsolicited advice
these days than Ernest Lehman," reported the *New York Times* in
the summer of 1964, three months after the announcement that Warner
Brothers had acquired the film rights to *Who's Afraid of Virginia Woolf?*
Every major newspaper in America had identified Lehman as the
producer and screenwriter attached to the project. The *Times* article
described *Virginia Woolf* as "one of the most powerful and unorthodox
American dramas of the past decade," imbuing it—and the forth-
coming film—with historic significance when the play had only just
closed on Broadway in May. Whether cornered at cocktail parties in
Hollywood, in the parking lot at Warner Brothers, or at baseball games
at Dodger Stadium, Lehman was besieged by people with suggestions
about how to make the movie and whom to cast.

Lehman struck the profile of a quintessential Hollywood "suit."
Trim and balding, wearing dapper clothes and smart fedoras, he might
well have stepped out of any office in *Executive Suite*, the first film he
wrote, released in 1954. He had begun his career in New York as a press
agent, writing copy about theater personalities and productions, and,
eventually, feeding gossip to Walter Winchell. He started writing articles and short stories for magazines such as *Collier's, Cosmopolitan,*

Esquire, and *Redbook*. One story, "Tell Me About It Tomorrow"—a fictionalized morality tale about his experience as Winchell's gossipmonger—later became the 1957 film *Sweet Smell of Success*, starring Burt Lancaster (as the Winchell stand-in) and Tony Curtis (as Sidney Falco, the character based on Lehman). Major box office successes followed, including *Sabrina*, *North by Northwest*, and *West Side Story*—all earning him Oscar nominations. By 1964, in his late forties, the screenwriter was married, with a family, living in Los Angeles in fashionable Brentwood and driving a Cadillac sedan.

Lehman not only looked the part of a powerful Hollywood executive but was also known as one of the saner individuals in the industry—level-headed, methodical, and circumspect. He was seasoned enough to understand what the stakes were as the first-time Hollywood producer of a highly anticipated film, and sophisticated enough to recognize the era-defining nature of *Virginia Woolf* and the phenomenon it had the potential to become. His priorities were in the right place—meaning that he upheld a fidelity to the essential content and meaning of the project, in this case Albee's play—and a serious regard for the quality of cinematic form. Lehman had excellent instincts and he had taste. He had just returned from a scouting expedition in London to see Uta Hagen and Arthur Hill in the West End production of *Virginia Woolf.* "What I hope to do to the movie audience is to wallop them over the head and in the gut with Albee," Lehman told the reporter. "Much of the power of the play I think is communicated directly from Albee's subconscious to that of the audience. I hope I can manage to preserve this elusive quality."

The first draft of the screenplay was due in September. As he worked on the script in his office at Warner Brothers, he was simultaneously making lists of actors to cast for George and Martha, as well as lists of possible directors, cinematographers, and production designers. While Jack Warner had given Albee his word about casting Davis as Martha and Mason as George, Lehman had ideas of his own. He scrawled a list of Marthas on his notepad, in this order: Ingrid Bergman, Uta Hagen,

Nancy Kelly, Anne Bancroft, Patricia Neal, Shelley Winters, Bette Davis, Deborah Kerr, Geraldine Page, and Viveca Lindfors. Not only was Davis far from the top of the list, but the name of the eventual on-screen Martha was nowhere to be found. Lehman alone knew that this was really his "B list."

"I started getting very excited about the idea of Elizabeth Taylor which I kept a deep dark secret because everyone in town was playing the game of casting this picture," Lehman would later explain. "Every actress wanted to play the role," he said. "I was an open target for every agent. I had to barricade myself." He knew that if he floated the idea of Taylor for the role of Martha, everyone would try to talk him out of it. He himself could parrot all the arguments against casting her: She was twenty years younger than the character. She had never played such a psychologically complex role. And, on a purely practical level, her conspicuous sense of entitlement had grown to monarchical proportions. "The opulence of Cleopatra's palace would pale next to the extravagance of Burton-Taylor's life together, with its yacht, its jewels, its furs, its entourages, its champagne, and caviar, the five-star hotels, the Van Goghs and Matisses and Pissarros," write Sam Kashner and Nancy Schoenberger in *Furious Love: Elizabeth Taylor, Richard Burton, and the Marriage of the Century.*

"Why did I think Elizabeth would be right?" Lehman mused. "I sensed certain wavelengths in her personality akin to Martha. I don't mean she is a shrew or tears husbands to sheds, but I think she has a deeply feminine vulnerability. People know how good Uta Hagen played her. They certainly know how Bette Davis would do it. But they would wonder how Elizabeth Taylor would do it."

～

With the possible exception of the recently widowed Jacqueline Kennedy, Elizabeth Taylor was, by the summer of 1964, the most famous woman in the world. She was an otherworldly beauty (known for the lilac radiance of her eyes) whose résumé included roles in *A Place in the Sun*,

Giant, Suddenly Last Summer, Cat on a Hot Tin Roof, and some thirty other films she had already appeared in by then. But her astronomical fame was due, as well, to the lingering effects of "Le scandale." Her on-set affair with Richard Burton had brought added interest to her most recent star turn in *Cleopatra*, released the previous summer, making the film a huge box office success and burnishing her superstardom— despite her own disappointment with the production. "They had cut out the heart, the essence, the motivations, the very core, and tacked on all those battle scenes," she said. "It should have been about three large people, but it lacked reality and passion. I found it vulgar."

Taylor was thirty-two years old and had been married four times. Her first marriage—to Conrad "Nicky" Hilton Jr., the handsome young hotel heir—was set up by MGM Studios as a "publicity event"; the ceremony took place only two days before the 1950 release of *Father of the Bride*, in which the eighteen-year-old Taylor starred as "the bride." The couple looked great in tabloid pictures, but the marriage had been an unconscionable studio charade all along. Even worse, Hilton was cruel and verbally abusive. They were divorced within a year. Her second marriage, to Michael Wilding, a British actor twenty years her senior, was more authentic; the couple had two sons together, but split after five years because of Wilding's infidelities. Then in 1957, Taylor married the producer Michael Todd. He was the first significant love of her life, and father of her third son, but Todd was killed in a plane crash within a year. His best friend, Eddie Fisher—at the height of his popu- larity as a crooner—had been best man at the Todd-Taylor wedding, and comforted Elizabeth after the tragedy. In their mutual grief, an unexpected romance erupted between them. Fisher was already married to Debbie Reynolds—known at the time as "America's sweetheart"— with whom Taylor had grown up as a child actor at Metro-Goldwyn- Mayer, in Hollywood, and who had been matron of honor at her wedding. Fisher abandoned Reynolds to marry Taylor.

The big screen was the most influential and ubiquitous form of enter- tainment in the world, which gave Hollywood a central role in shaping

American culture in the twentieth century. For that reason, the press sometimes took a prosecutorial role in the court of public opinion and fully exploited the ugly Fisher-Reynolds divorce because of the fame of the three stars involved, vilifying Taylor for what was characterized as the bald theft of her "dear friend" Reynolds's husband. The melee would not taint Taylor's career, though: She went on to star in the 1960 film *BUtterfield 8*, along with Fisher, and to win her first Oscar for Best Actress.

When, in 1962, Taylor and Burton met on the set of *Cleopatra* in Rome, the chemistry was immediately palpable to everyone around them—including Taylor's husband, Fisher, whom Taylor's friends secretly referred to as "the busboy," according to Truman Capote. It was the "busboy" himself who eventually alerted Burton's wife of thirteen years, Sybil, about the affair between her husband and his wife. Joseph L. Mankiewicz, the director of *Cleopatra*, first observed the attraction between Taylor and Burton during one scene when Antony kisses Cleopatra; he yelled cut, and they didn't stop. "Elizabeth and Burton are not just *playing* Antony and Cleopatra," he warned Walter Wanger, his producer, in trepidation that a romance between them would further complicate the already overbudgeted production. Bert Stern, a *Life* magazine photographer Wanger had hired to take film stills on and off the *Cleopatra* set, was one of the first members of the press to catch the lingering gazes between Taylor and Burton dressed in costume. "At first the romance struck some people as too campy, too Hollywood to be true," Stern said. When he notified *Life* that there was a love story beyond the set, his editor dismissed it as "nothing more than an affair." But Taylor and Burton were anything but discreet about their budding romance, and it would not be long before "Dick and Liz" and "Le scandale" were synonymous in headlines around the world.

Their attraction for each other was a tempest well beyond their control, evident in one early letter Richard wrote to Elizabeth: "I lust after your smell and your paps and your divine little Money Box and your round belly and the exquisite softness of the inside of your thighs and your baby bottom and your giving hips and the half hostile look in your eyes when you're deep in rut with your little Welsh stallion." She was no less in thrall. "Imagine having Richard Burton's voice in your ear while you are making love," Elizabeth later said. "It drowned out the troubles, the sorrows, everything just melted away." She described him as "an incredibly sexy man," acknowledging his notorious libido and his history of sleeping with his leading ladies. "I was the happy recipient of his reputation as a man who knew how to please a woman. Being unfaithful to Richard was as impossible as not being in love with him."

The college-age daughter of the film's producer, Stephanie Wanger, spent time on the set with her father and could see from her close vantage point that Taylor and Burton were in love. She offered the same kind of glamorized version of their affair that reverberated across the world. "It was the real thing, and everybody knew it," she said. "As a couple they fit well together. They had a rapport, and all of Rome seemed to be caught up in the romance. It became what Camelot ought to have been for Jack and Jackie Kennedy."

Twentieth Century–Fox was putting Taylor and her entourage up in a spectacular pink marble villa on the Appian Way. Behind closed doors, the saga of the affair reached operatic heights in more than a few painful confrontations between Fisher and Burton, in which Burton lorded his raw animal spell over Elizabeth and flaunted it sadistically in front of Fisher. One night early into their affair, Burton was a dinner guest of the Fishers. There were often others at their table—if not invited guests, then one or another from their stable of agents, managers, personal assistants, and children's tutors. Drunk, in his booming Shakespearean voice, Burton demanded that Elizabeth declare herself in front of her husband. "Who do you love?" he asked her. She looked at one and then the other and said to Burton: "You." Later, again in Fisher's presence, Burton planted a kiss on Elizabeth's lips, his tongue deep into her mouth, and she happily succumbed. Their intoxication with each other emanated from somewhere beyond their self-control, beyond decorum, and was given freer rein by the surprising quantity of alcohol each of them consumed from morning to night, which added to their heady euphoria while also distorting their judgment. Burton's cock-of-the-walk bullying of Fisher and Taylor's unabashed participation in front of her husband was classic alcoholic behavior—and a foreshadowing of performances to come as George and Martha in *Who's Afraid of Virginia Woolf?*

That same night, Burton pointed to a framed picture of Mike Todd and demanded to know what it was doing displayed there so prominently. "He didn't know how to *use* her," Burton sneered about her deceased husband, and then scoffed at Fisher with equal disdain, "*You* don't know how to use her, either." Elizabeth fled from the room in tears while the two men sat together at the table with their brandy snifters, Fisher numbed by his rival's audacity. "Burton did most of the talking," Fisher recounted about that night in his memoir, "flattering me, insulting me, laying little traps, charming and apologetic one moment, and abusive the next." Fisher might as well have been describing Albee's George, who turns belittling Nick into a game called "Get the Guests"—only, here, Burton was both the tormentor flinging abuse and the interloper flirting with the mistress of the house. And just as in George and Martha's living room, the truth-serum effects of alcohol unleashed raging manias of love, jealousy, and unbridled contempt.

After *Cleopatra*, Taylor and Burton—each in the process of divorcing their spouses—made another film together in London called *The V.I.P.s.* This would be the first of several films they would appear in together as a couple who drew on their real-life circumstances for the roles they played on-screen. *The V.I.P.s* focuses on Frances Andros (Taylor), a famous actress and unhappy wife of Paul Andros (Burton), a wealthy industrialist who rarely has time for her. The entire movie takes place at Heathrow Airport. Frances is surreptitiously leaving her husband, flying off with her lover, Marc Champselle (Louis Jordan). The film is hardly worth the description, but Terence Rattigan, the screenwriter, cannily added scenes that echoed details of the actors' relationship. At one point, Burton, as the jilted husband, brandishing a gun, bursts into the airport lounge where Taylor's character is holed up with her paramour. In the early stages of the duo's actual affair, Fisher was also known to have acquired a gun, which he kept in the glove compartment of the Rolls-Royce convertible Taylor had bought him when they first got to Rome. He planned to use it on Burton and, once, threatened Taylor's life with it at dinner.

The very first scene of *The V.I.P.s* takes place in the back seat of a Rolls-Royce on the way to the airport; Paul is giving Frances a very expensive diamond bracelet as a small going-away present. Burton, too, learned early in the relationship that Taylor adored exquisite jewelry. Walter Wanger explained to him that Taylor expected her producers to shower her with gifts—a diamond bracelet, emerald earrings, here a bauble, there a bauble—just to keep her satisfied, "like tributes paid to royalty by their subjects," write Kashner and Schoenberger. "Queens are meant to accept tribute, and, having already become the first actress in history to be given $1,000,000 plus salary to play Cleopatra, no less, she was the closest thing America had to royalty." (They posit that Taylor's attraction to diamonds was a way to deflect the rapt gaze of her admiring public.) During an escape from the paparazzi, Burton and Taylor darted into Bulgari on the Via Condotti, where Elizabeth had previously ogled a stunning emerald and diamond necklace with a pendant that could be detached and worn as a brooch. Burton took the hint and bought it for her for well over $100,000. She wanted to wear it as Frances in *The V.I.P.s*, but the insurance premium was too high for the film to cover the cost.

Taylor was fully aware of her growing cultural influence, and she became increasingly savvy about taking advantage of it in the entertainment business. After commanding her unprecedented one-million-dollar fee for *Cleopatra*, she then secured the same for *The V.I.P.s*. Her standards rose, and her calculations were ever more strategic. She wanted to use her fame to help Burton achieve the acclaim she thought his talent entitled him, and she guided him toward more worthy projects. After *The V.I.P.s*, Taylor remained in London while Burton filmed *Becket*, alongside Peter O'Toole and John Gielgud. Then she traveled with him to Mexico for the filming of *The Night of the Iguana*—perhaps to keep an eye on him in the presence of his costar, Ava Gardner, but also because Puerto Vallarta was a tropical paradise, and she needed a vacation. Taylor felt that the quality of both productions suited Burton's career—one based on the work of the French playwright Jean Anouilh, the other on that of America's greatest living playwright, Tennessee Williams. "They would show the world that they were not tarnished celluloid adulterers," write Kashner and Schoenberger, "but artists of the highest order, and they belonged in a realm where ordinary codes of behavior no longer applied. They were beyond bourgeois morality now."

In March 1964, they were in Toronto, where Burton appeared in a stage production of *Hamlet*, directed by Gielgud. The show would soon transfer to Broadway for a four-month, critically acclaimed run, bearing Richard to New York, and Elizabeth beside him. But before they left Canada, there was some business to take care of: Taylor's divorce from Eddie Fisher had come through, and she and Burton were married in Montreal on March 15. They would return home, for the first time, as the Burtons.

∿

It was not until August 1964 that Lehman was able to get Taylor's attention. She certainly knew about the success of *Who's Afraid of Virginia Woolf?*, but she had been so consumed with her own work in Europe—and accompanying Burton on his projects in Mexico and Canada—that she wasn't able to see the play before it closed on Broadway in May 1964. After the run of *Hamlet*, Taylor and Burton were heading to the West Coast to start shooting their next film together, *The Sandpiper*, in Monterey, California. Elizabeth agreed to take Albee's play with her on the Super Chief, the cross-country train from New York to Los Angeles. (They both had an aversion to flying.) She read *Who's Afraid of Virginia Woolf?* and, without any comment, handed it to Burton to ask his opinion. "You've only to read the first lines and you know this is a great play," he later recounted, but he was very specific in his advice to Elizabeth. "I think you're too young," he said about her playing Martha. "I don't think you're enough of a harridan. Maybe you don't have the power, but you've *got* to play it to stop everybody else from playing it."

Taylor was reluctant to play Martha, an aging battle-axe; she would have to gain twenty pounds for the role and be fitted daily with prosthetics to make her look fiftyish on the screen. She wondered how it would affect her Hollywood image, as did her agent, her manager, and her lawyer. Regardless, she sent a message through her manager to Lehman, to let him know that the role was of interest, and before the Burtons left Los Angeles to begin filming in Monterey, Lehman met with them in their bungalow at the Beverly Hills Hotel to discuss *Virginia Woolf.* Elizabeth said that she would think about it.

Lehman had made his list of Georges to consider, as well, which he had typed up in this order: Peter O'Toole, Jason Robards, Arthur Hill, Kirk Douglas, Peter Finch, Maximilian Schell, Christopher Plummer, Marlon Brando, Gregory Peck, Paul Scofield, Peter Ustinov, Richard Widmark, William Holden, Burt Lancaster, Peter Sellers, and James Mason. He had already offered the part to Jack Lemmon, and then, to the noir and western actor Glenn Ford, neither of whom considered *Virginia Woolf* suitable for the trajectory of their careers. Then, Lehman got word that Taylor would agree to take the part of Martha, but only— once again looking for roles worthy of her husband's talent—if Burton was cast as George.

Lehman had his doubts about Burton. George—residually handsome—was a beaten-down character whose authority was dimming behind his tattered dignity. That's why Lehman had thought of Lemmon or Ford for the role. Burton, on the other hand, was a force of nature, his virility too compelling for the mild-mannered professor. Hume Cronyn, who had starred with Taylor and Burton in *Cleopatra*, and shared the stage with Burton in the Gielgud production of *Hamlet*, claimed that Burton was one of the very few actors he had known "who was truly touched by the finger of God: his appearance, despite the pockmarked face; his quick intelligence, beautiful voice, and above all, a Welsh lyricism of spirit that only money, notoriety, and an overweening ambition to be a film star could waste."

Lehman agreed to give Burton a screen test, and, as he suspected, the Shakespearean actor came across with a masculine intensity that was too bold for George. But if attaching Burton were the only way to secure Taylor as Martha, Lehman knew it was worth it. He had seen the lines around the block for Burton's just-released *The Night of the Iguana* and thought to himself, "Imagine the lines around the block in every city of the world if Elizabeth Taylor and Richard Burton were to star together."

In November, Lehman flew to Paris to meet with the Burtons, who were there to shoot interiors for *The Sandpiper*. The production had accommodated their request to complete the shooting overseas because Burton was not a U.S. citizen, and the tax obligation on his income would have left him with only half of his contracted earnings from the film. With Taylor's one-million-dollar fees for *Cleopatra*, *The V.I.P.s*, and *The Sandpiper*—as well as royalties from her movies—the Burtons had learned how to dodge taxes by spending a requisite amount of time out of the country. They were staying with their entourage in the posh Hôtel Lancaster on the Champs-Élysées, and, on November 19, Lehman invited the Burtons to his suite at the same hotel. Over two and a half hours that evening, they consumed two bottles of champagne and plenty of caviar as they discussed topics ranging from the need to shoot the film in absolute chronology to Burton's concern about his appearance. Lehman scribbled notes on hotel stationery. "Richard strong on need for cameraman who will keep his face (seen after and in extreme close-ups on film) from being distractingly pockmarked," Lehman noted. "Wants camera and makeup tests to ensure this. Said he cannot perform to his utmost ability unless he feels absolutely secure about this." Burton also suggested ways in which he might tone down his strong presence through costume. One idea he had was to wear eyeglasses. Elizabeth thought that she might address the age difference by playing Martha as thirty-eight instead of fiftyish. "Thinking of wig with relatively short hair—over lacquered. She wants hair and makeup tests." The Burtons were curious about who would be cast for Nick and Honey, and Lehman floated Robert Redford and Colin Wilcox, who were unknowns to them at the time. "What about George Grizzard?" Lehman suggested, but they thought that he would seem too old if they were playing George and Martha as thirty-eight and forty-two, which, fortunately, turned out to be a short-lived idea.

Lehman summarized the meeting with a satisfied belief that "they both seem seriously devoted to an attempt at artistic triumph with this film." He wrote that "Liz gets passionate, even a bit angry, at any suggestions that she personally doesn't know exactly how she's going to do the role. She says she does, and says it forcefully," but then "Richard called her 'lazy bones,' said she's never really worked hard enough, said she damned well better work harder in this one. She resented his statement, but I think she got the message." But Burton was already learning how to manipulate Taylor by oscillating from denigration to worship: During the evening, he thanked Lehman twice for accepting him for the picture, and, finally, he hinted to Lehman "that Elizabeth's last producer just gave her a diamond and emerald pin." Lehman replied in his own dry-as-a-martini defense: "Wonderful—because she'd never want two of those."

~

It was agreed that Burton and Taylor would have veto power over the director. Lehman's notes on the meeting (cosigned by Burton's agent, Hugh French) record the five names under consideration. One was Robert Wise, with whom Lehman had worked on *West Side Story*. Another was Fred Zinnemann, director of *High Noon*, *From Here to Eternity*, and *Oklahoma!* Zinnemann had been rumored to be under consideration for *Virginia Woolf* as early as eight months prior, when the *New York Times* mentioned him in its first article reporting the sale of the play's film rights. But when Lehman finally approached him, Zinnemann declined. As Lehman reported to French, "Fred flatly will not ever again make a picture based on a Broadway play. That is why he is not interested." (Ironically, Zinnemann then went on to direct the film adaptation of Robert Bolt's Broadway hit *A Man for All Seasons*, which would have a memorable role to play in *Virginia Woolf*'s on-screen life.)

The three remaining names on the list belonged to theater directors who had never before helmed a film. One was Alan Schneider, who had steered *Virginia Woolf* to Broadway success; another was Tyrone Guthrie. The final name was a complete surprise to Lehman, but both Taylor and Burton insisted that he be in the running: Mike Nichols, a man they considered not only a good friend but an undeniable genius.

~

Nothing could make a cosmopolitan New Yorker feel more sophisticated, in or around the year 1957, than to say that he or she had just seen the comedy act Nichols and May at the Blue Angel, a nightclub on East Fifty-Fifth Street. Mike Nichols and Elaine May, newcomers in their midtwenties, had become an instant word-of-mouth phenomenon among the taste-making set for their wry, often-improvised dialogues on taboo subjects that had never been addressed before in so legitimate a public venue—sexual behavior, adultery, American mediocrity. The duo could make a mockery of highbrow self-importance with the simplest dismissive colloquial phrase, or push familiar setups to outrageously absurd ends. One skit begins with a stereotypical Jewish mother phoning her son, a literal rocket scientist:

MAY: Arthur, this is your mother. Do you remember me?
NICHOLS: Mom, hi. I was about to call you. Is that a funny thing? I had my hand on the dial.

MAY: You were supposed to call me last Friday. I sat by that phone all
   day long, all day Friday night, all day Saturday. And all day Sunday.

NICHOLS: Mom! We were launching *Vanguard*.

MAY: And your father said to me, "Phyllis, eat something. You'll faint."
   And I said, "No, Harry, no. I don't want my mouth to be full when
   my son calls me."

NICHOLS: Mother, I was sending up a rocket. I didn't have a second.

MAY: Well, it's always something, isn't it? I read in the paper how you
   keep losing them.

NICHOLS: *I* don't lose them.

MAY: I nearly went out of my mind. I wondered, what if they're taking
   it out of his pay?

NICHOLS: Stop. Now I feel terrible.

MAY: Oh, Arthur, if I could believe that. A mother's prayer.

   By the end of the call, Arthur has regressed so much that he is speaking
in baby talk: "Okay, Mommy. I wuv you, Mommy. Ma ma, wee wah."
The emotional blackmail had the audience laughing in recognition.

   In a 1996 PBS documentary about Nichols, Tom Brokaw, with his
plainspoken newscaster logic, offered a simple explanation for the duo's
success in New York. "Because their act was so intelligent," he mused,
citing their use of language, their appearance, and their style, "they had
snob appeal." While their verbal sketches could pivot on a series of
ironic twists, they did not rely on definitive punch lines, which distinguished them from the more obvious comedy acts on the radio or in
early television. At the same time, they could draw an audience that
might have balked at attending one of Lenny Bruce's incendiary,
profanity-laden shows—there was no risk of Nichols and May's act
being raided by the vice squad.

   In 1960, Nichols and May opened their show on Broadway, which
catapulted them into a new stratosphere of notoriety, with access to just
about anyone. Opening night was a gala, preceded by a buffet at Sardi's.
Among the guests were Carol Channing, Sidney Lumet, Gloria

Vanderbilt, and Nichols's best friend, Richard Avedon. As perks of the festivities, the producer arranged for an armada of Rolls-Royces to shuttle guests the one block from Sardi's to the theater, where a Ferris wheel was set up in front to celebrate the opening; fans danced in Shubert Alley after the curtain fell on the first night. The production was a huge success and ran for almost a year—although it would be the last time Nichols and May would appear together as an act.

During that run, Nichols met Edward Albee, and they had dinner together one night before curtain. It makes sense that they would find each other. They were close to the same age; both were considered intellectually fashionable and outré. *The Zoo Story* had opened off-Broadway that January. Albee had already seen *An Evening with Mike Nichols and Elaine May* once and offered suggestions about several scenes—notes that Nichols respected but did not honor. He later reflected that he did not think either of them was influenced by the other, yet, from the first, he sensed a certain empathy with Albee: Both of them had "outsider feelings." For Nichols, those feelings could be traced back to his childhood as a German immigrant (born Igor Mikhail Peschkowsky) who arrived in America at age seven not speaking a word of English. On top of that, when he was four, an allergic reaction to medication brought about a lifetime alopecia-like affliction, which left him unable to grow hair. Nichols wore wigs his entire life. Meanwhile, Albee, as an adopted child, felt like an immigrant in his own family. He and Nichols shared a sense of alienation and unhappiness about their respective student years at boarding schools. While Nichols found Albee austere and socially restrained, "I felt a real connection to him and almost an affection, obviously because of his mind and his work, but also because of his wry cordiality."

Around the same time, Nichols also got to know Richard Burton, who was starring in *Camelot* in the adjoining theater. They became friendly at Sardi's, where actors gathered for postcurtain drinks, and soon Nichols was a fixture at the nightly parties Burton hosted in his dressing room for his Broadway pals. In 1962, when Burton went to

Rome to star in *Cleopatra* and the ensuing affair between "Dick and Liz" became an international scandal, he invited Nichols to come visit. "I'll be on the *Cleopatra* set most days," he told Nichols. "Perhaps you wouldn't mind escorting Elizabeth around to see the sights while I'm shooting? The press is driving her crazy."

In Rome, Nichols suggested to Taylor that she don a babushka, and during that week, he walked with her incognito through the streets of the Eternal City, going to chapels to look at frescoes and eating at little trattorias, thankfully unrecognized by the paparazzi. "One time," at the Villa d'Este, Nichols later recalled, "someone actually pointed at us and said, 'There's Mike Nichols.'" Mike endeared himself to Elizabeth on that trip, and they would become great friends.

Nichols couldn't wait to share news of his Roman visit with Avedon. His tales sparked the photographer's idea for a ten-page fashion feature, "Mike Nichols and Suzy Parker Rock Europe," that he conceived for the September 1962 issue of *Harper's Bazaar*. "With Suzy and Mike, I decided to do a satire of Elizabeth Taylor and Richard Burton who were making *Cleopatra*, having all their fights in public, but also saying 'Why doesn't the press leave us alone?'" Avedon said years later. "So, I took Mike Nichols, who was then a comedian, and Suzy Parker, who was my favorite model at that time, and we did this elaborate fashion feature while pretending to be making a film of 'Napoleon and Josephine in Paris.'" The fashion shoot reached comic proportion when, at several locations during the production, Parisians began flocking around Mike and Suzy for autographs, believing that they were real movie stars—art imitating life imitating art.

Nichols was a special combination of a performer—who, together with May, could improvise skits onstage—and a director who instinctively understood how the material of a story needed to be drawn out by actors. By 1964, his career was soaring, and his social orbit was expanding. He had directed the hit Broadway production of Neil Simon's *Barefoot in the Park*, earning himself a Tony Award. He was acquiring the kind of clout that satisfied his avaricious urgency to be at the center of things.

Nichols was a "brainy" individual, as people called intellectuals then. He had attended—but did not graduate from—the academically rigorous University of Chicago, where he met not only May but also Susan Sontag. ("We talked about books, about feelings, about how to get free of our pasts," Sontag remembered about Nichols then; they would remain friends throughout their lives.) Nichols could be erudite without even trying, commanding respect with his sonorous voice, crisp elocution, and incisive—if also sardonic—observations. He was known to keep up with Burton, quoting from Shakespeare and beating him at word games, like Anagrams, which annoyed the actor but earned his esteem. While Nichols was not one to suffer fools, a delighted child lurked just beneath his contemplative demeanor, waiting to burst into hysterical laughter at the drop of a bon mot or an absurd moment. His delight was infectious enough to make the people around him laugh, too, just because he was laughing.

When Nichols learned that Taylor had been approached to play Martha in the film version of *Virginia Woolf*, he immediately called her agent and stressed that he wanted to direct the movie. Nichols had never directed a film before, but he had "Cleopatra's" ear, and a Tony to boot. Taylor, who already considered him charming and brilliant, loved the idea when her agent mentioned it. That's how the name "Mike Nichols" came to be on Taylor's tongue that evening in Ernest Lehman's suite at the Hôtel Lancaster, echoed by Nichols's good friend, Richard Burton.

∼

In late November 1964, Nichols was on a working vacation in Jamaica when Lehman reached him from Paris—a phone call that cost an astronomical $250 at the time. Lehman made notes during the conversation, the gist of which he summarized for the Burtons' other agent, Robert

Lantz: "Essentially, Mike thinks the project and whole idea is marvelous. Also, he now sees how and why the Burtons can play the roles. However, he is in some very serious disagreement on certain changes in the story. Would be very helpful if we could talk for a few days."

Nichols hung up from that phone call with Lehman, looked out at the sea, and thought, "How can I turn my back on this piece of material? To turn it down out of fear it would be cowardice." The zany comedy *Luv*, which he directed, had just opened on Broadway, starring Alan Arkin and Eli Wallach; *Barefoot in the Park* was still drawing crowds in its second year. Nichols had several movie projects lined up, including *The Public Eye*, which had been delayed until the spring, and *The Graduate*, which didn't yet even have a screenplay. He had gone to Jamaica to work on his next theater project—*The Odd Couple*, also headed for Broadway.

His career was evolving as a director of agile comedies, but it did not reflect the depth of his regard for serious theater. When Nichols was sixteen years old, he saw *A Streetcar Named Desire* with the original stars, Jessica Tandy and Marlon Brando. "I saw it on the second night," recalled Nichols. "There had never been anything like it. It was, to this day, the only thing onstage that I had ever seen that was 100% real and 100% poetic." He had taken a girlfriend with him to see it, and "we weren't exactly theater buffs, but we couldn't get up at the intermission. We were just so stunned. Your heart was pounding. It was a major experience."

He had a similar reaction when he saw the original production of *Who's Afraid of Virginia Woolf?* on Broadway. "I thought it was the most exciting play in production that I'd ever seen, with the exception of *Streetcar*. I always thought that it was Shakespearean in that the two main characters compete in recruiting the audience to their side, in a manner not dissimilar to *Taming of the Shrew*. Kate says: 'You see what he does to me? Watch *this*' . . . Petruchio says: 'Are you kidding? *Look* at her. She's a nightmare.'" Similarly, in one of his own most celebrated skits with May, "Pirandello," the audience bounces back and forth between the characters: "I'm on her side. I'm on his side. I'm on her side," as Nichols once described it. He believed that the intensity of the volley depended on "who was playing the characters and how lovable each of the actors is," but, equally, "on the power of the dialectic of the jokes, if they are—as they are by Edward Albee—brilliantly balanced." In effect, he saw *Who's Afraid of Virginia Woolf?* the way Albee himself did: "There are two equal roles in this play—George and Martha—of equal intensity, equal difficulty." And the jokes were key to Albee's calibration of the script too. The playwright sometimes complained about Schneider missing the comedic intentions throughout. "And that's one of the things I'd keep having to remind him about during rehearsals. Funny. Humor. Funny."

Yet theater was one thing; film was quite something else. A theater audience responds to characters in real time. At its best, the theater creates an ambience where the emotions generated by the characters onstage are alive to the audience in the room. The mood is created by the set, the lighting, the rendering of material by the actors, the physical dynamics between one character and the other, and the illusion of believability created by all of it—that is, the live emotion palpable in the performance. By contrast, the construction of emotion, mood, and believability in movies is achieved in two dimensions and lives in an afterlife on-screen. Everything is geared to the camera. Actors are not speaking to a live audience but to a mechanical instrument.

At twenty, Nichols saw Montgomery Clift and Elizabeth Taylor in the film he would come to call his Bible—George Stevens's *A Place in the Sun*. The experience was as revelatory about movies as *Streetcar* had been about theater. It is a mournful film about a poor yet appealing young man thrust into a glamorous circle he cannot resist. His inexperience is challenged, his moral compass goes haywire, and his life is destroyed. At the time, Nichols identified with Clift's character, feeling himself to be a rube, too, and wondering how he would find his own way into a more cultivated world. The film is shot in a lush black and white that underscores its moodiness. Stevens luxuriates in long takes that, like still photographs, allow the eye to linger and the viewer to contemplate the characters, as well as the details of their circumstances. Nichols later claimed to have seen the film about 150 times, mostly when he was in his twenties. Throughout his life, *A Place in the Sun* would be the movie he would mine for inspiration. As Mark Harris writes in his biography of Nichols, "It was his core text when he prepared to direct Taylor himself in *Who's Afraid of Virginia Woolf*, and the length of each shot in the stillness of Stevens' camera strongly influenced his approach to [his next film], *The Graduate*."

$\sim$

While Nichols wrestled with his hesitations about Hollywood's version of *Virginia Woolf*, Lehman's next step was to get the screenplay to him in Jamaica, a task that would require the kind of careful choreography more often associated with Cold War espionage. The screenplay was a top-secret document that had to change hands several times to get to its destination. First, Lehman flew to New York himself with the screenplay in hand. He had set it up with Warner Brothers for someone in the office to meet him at the airport at two P.M. The studio liaison would take the screenplay to the terminal and personally hand it to the pilot or a stewardess on the flight to Montego Bay leaving at five P.M. Intricate instructions on the package directed the stewardess to take it off the plane in Jamaica, since that was not the flight's destination. A local liaison at the airport in Jamaica was to receive it upon arrival, then wait for Nichols to pick it up later that evening.

Lehman's screenplay had been completed only two months earlier, on September 11, 1964. It opens with "VERY LOUD PIERCING, HIGH-PITCHED, SAVAGE CRIES OF PAIN," then a close-up of "TWO VERY LARGE DOGS (A MALE AND A BITCH)" locked in terrifying combat, fangs and claws tearing away at each other's throats before, suddenly, they race out of the shot.

The fornicating dogs' departure reveals a view of a college campus at night and a building at the far end, its front door opened and people trickling out. As George and Martha amble in the direction of the viewer, the camera closes in on a young couple in the foreground—students—embracing against a tree along the campus pathway. We hear them moaning and cooing and avowing their ardor for each other before the sounds of George's footsteps and Martha's clicking heels get louder and louder and the couple run away. Then the focus is on George and Martha as they walk home from the late-night party.

Lehman had added that opening, and made several other changes to the content of the play as well. For example, because of the criticism about the imaginary child in the play, Lehman made the child real. In his screenplay, the secret between George and Martha became their son's suicide at eighteen. Nichols, however, believed the imaginary child to be the central metaphor in the play, a symbol of how much George and Martha care for each other. "They actually love each other very much," Nichols said, not long before he died, in an interview with Steven Soderbergh. "When I used to say that, people thought I was nuts."

The idea of making George and Martha's imaginary child "real" was the equivalent of giving the play a "heart transplant," according to Soderbergh, and Nichols heartily agreed. That was one of his reservations about taking on the project, which he expressed to Lehman before accepting the offer to direct *Virginia Woolf.* Preventing that "heart transplant" turned out to be prelude to an ongoing tug of war between Lehman and Nichols over the screenplay that would last throughout the entire production.

Finally, on December 10, Lehman dictated a telegram to the Burtons at the Hôtel Lancaster: "Hallelujah. We've got Mike. Happy Holidays. Ernie."

Chapter 5

If You Give Me Chocolate,
I'll Give You Flowers

Abstruse! In the sense of recondite. Don't you tell me words!

—MIKE NICHOLS'S FAVORITE LINE IN THE PLAY THAT
GOT CUT FROM THE FILM

Mike Nichols rode into the new year 1965 on a gust of critical acclaim. *Luv*, which he had recently directed on Broadway, was an unlikely runaway hit. Harold Taubman of the *New York Times* gave it the kind of review that made people flock to get tickets. His highest accolade went to the director for his "unerring instinct for fusing far-out techniques of avant-garde theater with the raffish resources of low comedy, farce and vaudeville." In December, a *Times* item had reported that Nichols—"one of Broadway's most popular directors"—was set to make his debut as a film director with *Who's Afraid of Virginia Woolf?*, beginning production early next summer. And, in the days before the new year, Nichols began rehearsals for *The Odd Couple*, which was scheduled to open at the Plymouth Theatre on Broadway in March, right next door to *Luv*. On top of that, his off-Broadway hit *The Knack*, which had opened earlier in the year, was still selling out every night. All of this only fueled Edward Albee's disdain when he first heard that Nichols would be directing the film version of *Virginia Woolf.* "My play is not a farce," he lamented.

Nichols was, indeed, venturing into an alien, if parallel, universe. While rehearsing *The Odd Couple* on Broadway, he was simultaneously thinking about how to turn *Virginia Woolf* into a movie. There was some security in knowing that Elizabeth Taylor and Richard Burton were attached, but he was at a loss when it came to casting Nick and Honey. Quicksand was something akin to fertile soil for Nichols; the terror of uncertainty gave his imagination free rein. Whether he discussed the casting options with Ernest Lehman or not—in one early note, Lehman listed the names Yvette Mimieux and Piper Laurie for Honey— Nichols wasted no time asserting his directorial authority by casting Nick and Honey himself. He had directed Robert Redford in *Barefoot in the Park* on Broadway the previous year and, like Lehman, thought he would be the perfect Nick. But Redford turned him down flat. "I was never a fan of the play," Redford told Mark Harris, Nichols's biographer. "At that point I felt this is not an honest play, and I didn't want to be in it. I was wrong on many levels, but that was my standpoint at the time."

Nichols's second choice was George Segal, who was starring in *The Knack.* He certainly looked the part of the "young god he needed to be for Elizabeth's Martha," Nichols said. "And he was witty enough and funny enough to deal with all that humiliation." Segal had his own brief history with *Virginia Woolf;* he had auditioned for the role of Nick on Broadway when George Grizzard was leaving the original production. "I did a reading at the Cherry Lane theatre for Edward Albee and a few of the show's producers," Segal said. "I *nailed* it. Sometimes, you just know when you've nailed it. I felt so comfortable and relaxed coming off that reading. I thought to myself, *if I don't get this, then I don't know what I'm doing.*" But the role went to Segal's roommate, Ben Piazza, who, it turned out, was having a very clandestine affair with Albee at the time.

Since Taylor had casting approval, Nichols set up a private performance of *The Knack* for her and her ex-husband, Michael Wilding, who
was still one of her agents. Segal was movie-star handsome; he had a
compelling stage presence; and Taylor liked what she saw. Segal shared
an agent, Abe Lastfogel, with Lehman; and now, with a nod from
Taylor, Nichols would have an easy victory garnering Lehman's and
Jack Warner's approval.

Honey was another story. Nichols had his eye on Sandy Dennis, who
was currently starring in *Any Wednesday* on Broadway and had won a
Tony for her role in *A Thousand Clowns* the year before. She was talented,
but her manner was quirky, halting; onstage, she would repeat lines if
she didn't think she had gotten them right the first time. The twenty-
seven-year-old was an acquired taste—the antithesis of Hollywood.
Decidedly wholesome and midwestern in her affect, she left home in
Nebraska for New York when she was barely twenty, attending the
Actors Studio and then studying with Herbert Berghof (Uta Hagen's
husband) at HB Studios. She starred in several off-Broadway productions before landing the small role of Kay in *Splendor in the Grass*,
directed by Elia Kazan, in 1961. She could look, at times, like a Hitchcock blond—prim, innocent, and attractive, but her toothy smile gave
her a goofy fragility. Regardless, she was taken very seriously as an
actor. Over the years, she would be called out by critics for her eccentric performances: Walter Kerr of the *New York Times* cited her "habit"
of speaking onstage as though sentences "were poor crippled things that
couldn't cross a street without making three false starts from the curb."
And Pauline Kael of the *New Yorker* once complained that she "has made
an acting style of postnasal drip." Yet Nichols had an inkling about her
vulnerability for the role of Honey and got tickets for Taylor to see her
in *Any Wednesday*. Her apparent "mousiness" worked in her favor, as
she posed no threat to Taylor's beauty. With Taylor's nod, Nichols
thought a screen test would be the best way to solidify his case for
Dennis to the "suits" in Hollywood.

To shoot the screen test, he brought in Haskell Wexler, the brother of an old Chicago friend of Nichols's. Fresh off the set of Kazan's *America America*, the young cinematographer also came with a strong recommendation from fellow director Norman Jewison. Wexler shot a series of luscious, tonal black and white scenes of Dennis—as much an audition for him to become the cinematographer of *Virginia Woolf* as it was a screen test for her to play Honey. In the first close-up scene, she takes several sips from a brandy snifter, then, eyes closed, emanating a shiver of pleasure, she lets slip a moan of delight. "I love brandy," she says. "I really do." She is convincing in just ten seconds. In another scene, she is standing in the middle of a living room, a blonde in a simple black cocktail dress. "I dance like the wind," she says suddenly in a drunken whisper before removing her heels and taking flight with her arms, prancing around the living room slightly off balance, *dum-de-da-dumming* to the music, intentionally off-key.

Dennis manifested a quality that Nichols often described in his own attempt to direct actors: "It's a matter of tapping your unconscious and the actor's unconscious and ultimately the audience's unconscious. You can't just work with the unconscious but there are ways to encourage it a little bit." When Lehman and Warner saw Dennis's screen test, they consented to cast her as Honey, albeit with some reluctance. This was only the first time that Nichols challenged their seasoned judgment with his unlikely choices. It would not be the last.

Though Nichols often professed bafflement about his own success, he projected a knowing certainty. The unique glamour of his public profile made him that much more convincing. He had become a bold-face name in the press, and his status as a man about town granted him a cone of immunity from professional resistance or social judgment. And his reputation with women only added to his stature. Separated from his second wife, Margot Callas, Nichols was always seen squiring an alluring woman on his arm. "He was incredibly smart and fun to be with," Gloria Steinem said, remembering her affair with Nichols during this period. Beautiful, intelligent, sophisticated, Steinem was an up-and-coming journalist who had just written a profile of Dorothy Parker to be published in the March 1965 issue of the *Ladies' Home Journal*. "He got every joke, and that was important to me," she said. "And he was appreciative of talent, so he always had interesting friends." Mike regularly attended sing-along evenings with songwriters Betty Comden and Adolph Green in Green's apartment, where he introduced Steinem to his pals Leonard Bernstein and Stephen Sondheim. "I was entranced by the world that he provided a window on," Steinem said. "I remember wandering around the Village singing on the street with Julie [Andrews]." That lofty, glamorous New York inner sanctum was new to Steinem then, and also instructive about the channels of power. It must have been heady, indeed, when Nichols took her to Lyndon Johnson's inauguration in Washington.

Nichols's friends encouraged him to wed Steinem, but while she enjoyed his company, she did not want to marry him. Before she broke up with him, though, her influence on the production of *Who's Afraid of Virginia Woolf?* would prove to be of some consequence. First, she introduced Nichols to her friend Richard Sylbert, an art director with several Kazan films under his belt, including *Baby Doll*, *A Face in the Crowd*, and *Splendor in the Grass*. Nichols and Sylbert hit it off immediately, and Nichols hired him as the production designer for *Virginia Woolf*. Steinem's other contribution was her suggestion to shoot the exterior scenes for *Virginia Woolf* at Smith College, her alma mater, in Northampton, Massachusetts. Since the play was about a college professor and his wife, the daughter of the college president, a New England campus of charm and distinction, like Smith, would add authenticity to the film. And Nichols's embrace of the idea would prove to be the most extravagant enterprise in the entire production.

∾

Nichols understood that he would have to take up full-time residence in Los Angeles during the production of *Who's Afraid of Virginia Woolf?*, and it didn't take long for him to adapt to the splendor of Hollywood. In the spring of 1965, he rented the glamorous Brentwood estate of the recently deceased Cole Porter. The house was hidden behind a tall privet hedge, the driveway entrance on North Rockingham Avenue protected by a pair of imperial wrought-iron gates. On the front lawn, right where Porter had left it, was a life-size male nude statue, now clad by Nichols's secretary in a pair of sunglasses and a red-checked bikini. Once inside the central foyer, arriving guests could look beyond the spacious living room to a set of French doors opening out to a leafy brick patio. Visitors might catch their breath at the view of several classical Greek statues amid the bougainvillea, their reflections shimmering in the glassy water of the oval swimming pool.

Nichols liked to exploit the ways in which conspicuous—if discerning—measures of wealth could at once intimidate and impress those he wanted to hold in thrall, which was just about everyone. By the time he had settled into the palatial comfort of this Brentwood home, the renowned interior designer Billy Baldwin had just put the finishing touches on a renovation of Nichols's triplex penthouse apartment at the Beresford, one of the most elegant residential buildings in Manhattan. At thirty-three years old, Nichols had perched himself on top of the world in New York, hovering where gravity provided less grounding—the air lighter, more effervescent—and now, he was aiming for the same altitude in Hollywood.

Nichols was a man of quick-study refinement, and luxury was undoubtedly to his taste, but, equally, it was a psychological fortress. The splendid address, a swank new black Lincoln Continental convertible, a string of glamorous girlfriends, and the right dinner invitations were all part of a carefully crafted public shield. Behind the glitz, the emotionally peripatetic Nichols could mope and stew and fume and mull. Then, he could recalibrate his equilibrium to a silky-smooth self-possession, the vehicle for his daunting intelligence and his deadpan wit—the whole daily performance of being Mike Nichols. While he had an innate confidence, implicitly trusting his perceptions and his imagination, the scars of his childhood left him with debilitating depressions and a gnawing sense of inadequacy. Living like a pasha mitigated some of that.

The first time Lehman visited Nichols in Brentwood, he walked in, looked around, and said to Mike, "I think I just heard somebody at the piano playing 'Night and Day.'" Mike laughed at the reference to Porter, and Lehman noted it in his journal. For Ernie, it would always be a small triumph to make Mike laugh, as if that were the key to winning his respect. Mike offered Ernie a drink and ushered him out to the patio while excusing himself to make a phone call. "I couldn't help but overhear various telephone calls, like one to Julie Andrews, which indicated that Mike had been to a party at her house last night." That Lehman recorded this detail was not incidental. Very likely, Nichols made the call to Andrews precisely to get Lehman's attention. Andrews, already a close friend of Nichols, was at that moment the star of the newly released *The Sound of Music*, which was number one at the box office—a film for which Lehman had written the screenplay. This kind of social jujitsu was part of Mike's arsenal of self-aggrandizing tactics: He was trying to assert himself as an equal in Lehman's own backyard by making him feel excluded among the select group at Andrews's table.

Nichols had learned how to play these social games on his meteoric journey to the top in New York. In a 1967 memoir, Norman Podhoretz, the editor in chief of *Commentary*, offered a glimpse of the daily anxieties someone in Mike's social orbit might experience as ever-fluctuating tallies were silently calculated about everyone's place in the food chain. "Every morning," Podhoretz writes, "a stock-market report on reputation comes out in New York. It is invisible, but those who have eyes to see can read it. Did so-and-so have dinner at Jacqueline Kennedy's apartment last night? Up five points. Was so-and-so not invited by the [Robert] Lowells to meet the latest visiting Russian poet? Down one-eighth. Did so-and-so's book get nominated for the National Book Award? Up two and five-eighths. Did *Partisan Review* neglect to ask so-and-so to participate in a symposium? Down two."

Nichols had arrived in Los Angeles with several gold-plated pedigrees, but that did not stop him from continuing to burnish them. His most persuasive calling card was his friendship with nouveau Hollywood royalty—the Burtons. His recent Broadway successes also granted cachet: his Best Director Tony for *Barefoot in the Park*, the spectacular reviews and strong box office for *Luv* and *The Odd Couple*. In his first weeks in Hollywood, Nichols found himself dining with Jean Renoir, an éminence grise, who gave him some welcome directorial advice: "Don't worry about the technical stuff. Stick with the story and the actors, and the cameraman will take care of all the rest." Billy Wilder would become a mentor to Mike, inviting him to lunch with Joseph L. Mankiewicz and Otto Preminger soon after his arrival. In other words, Nichols was being introduced among the ranks of old Hollywood and getting a first-rate tutorial while racking up calling cards along the way.

In the early days of pre-production on *Who's Afraid of Virginia Woolf?*, Lehman and Nichols danced around each other as they straddled a complicated line. The balance of power between a producer and a director necessarily shifts back and forth: The director has a vision for the film; the producer makes it happen. Because producers control the budget, final authority leans heavily in their camp. But the fact that Lehman was a first-time producer and Nichols was a first-time director—the blind leading the blind—introduced unknowns into the equation. And further complicating the symmetry was Lehman's added role as screenwriter. The director has authority over the "content," but, with this unusual producer-screenwriter hybrid, the balance of power was skewed even more heavily in Lehman's direction.

Lehman had an acute sense of history and an abiding need to establish his place in it. This would later be borne out in the opening credits to *Who's Afraid of Virginia Woolf?*: After the top billing of Elizabeth Taylor and Richard Burton, "AN ERNEST LEHMAN PRODUCTION" is boldly splashed across the screen in lapidary white block letters, even before the film's title appears. Further proof of Lehman's intentional legacy-building exists in the form of a daily production chronicle he kept during the entire process of making *Who's Afraid of Virginia Woolf?* This methodical account of daily events was aimed clearly at posterity, perhaps in a nod to Budd Schulberg's 1941 roman à clef, *What Makes Sammy Run?*, with shadings of the New Journalism emerging then in the writings of Hunter S. Thompson, Norman Mailer, Tom Wolfe, and Truman Capote. Lehman's documentation is a systematic chessboard-like description of the daily activities, obstacles, minuscule dramas, and protracted sagas throughout the production of the film, commencing soon after the arrival of Nichols in Los Angeles.

At the end of every day, Lehman strode to his Cadillac sedan in his designated parking space on the Warner Brothers lot, and on the drive home to Brentwood he spoke into a Dictaphone, recounting the events of the day relevant to the production, monitoring his role as producer-screenwriter, and expressing his feelings. He had an astute awareness of the mechanics of power; this was, after all, the man who had written *Executive Suite*—a Machiavellian tale about bigwigs vying for the reins of a midwestern corporate dynasty—and *Sweet Smell of Success*—an ends-justify-the-means parable based on his own early experience as a Broadway publicist. The following morning—every morning—Lehman would hand the Dictaphone over to his secretary to make a master typescript of his recordings.

It had not been easy for Lehman to make the midcareer adjustment from screenwriter to mogul, even though he was well suited to his new role. He embarked on a vigilant analysis of his experience producing *Who's Afraid of Virginia Woolf?*, grappling with the issues of any executive—the overarching responsibilities, the financial headaches, the invisible politics, the small daily victories, the aggravating defeats, along with ensuring that "the talent" was happy, fielding tedious personnel conflicts, managing the public relations—accumulating little life lessons along the way. Lehman weighed his own self-importance against his readily acknowledged vulnerabilities with surprising psychological sophistication. The self-reflective Lehman who emerges from the journal is a man learning to assert his authority, always focused on the quality of the movie (but ever in service of his own career).

The truth is that Lehman and Nichols related to each other with a brand of slapstick that was not physical but classically neurotic, and typical of competitive New York Jewish men of that era. There's a hint of psychosexual drives being channeled into unbounded professional ambition—they itch to be adulated for their brilliance, regarded for their importance, and handsomely rewarded for both. Nichols had a paradoxical awareness of his neurotic behavior, amused by it, on the one hand, yet, equally, unable to stop himself from being dick-ish. They could both be surprisingly adolescent about the triumphs they lorded over each other, no matter how minor, whether in brooding silences, closed-door office confessions, or, occasionally, embarrassingly, with petty resentments spilling into public view.

One day early on, Ernie and Mike were working on the script in Lehman's office—a large, clean, and uncluttered space, with white walls, white linen draperies, and a white linen upholstered couch, where Mike always sat. A well-dressed stranger named John Springer appeared at Ernie's door. "Oh, you found me," Nichols exclaimed, greeting him enthusiastically and introducing him as his press agent from New York. Mike explained that Springer was in town to do some preliminary promotion for *Virginia Woolf*—"almost over my dead body," Lehman later seethed in that day's chronicle. The publicist handed Nichols a fat bundle of his media clippings to look through, a scene planned by Mike, no doubt, specifically to flaunt his press coverage in front of Lehman. "Mike studied them with great care," Lehman wrote, "moaning and groaning with that part of him that doesn't like publicity and glowing with that part of him that eats it up." Mike then took the bundle and walked off with the press agent. Lehman overheard them talking about a photographer for Nichols—the name Irving Penn came up—which irked Ernie further as he stewed about it in his daily report: "My impression is that I will be the least photographed person connected with this picture; the Burtons will be the most photographed; and Mike Nichols will be coming up a very close second to them. Go fight City Hall or celebrities."

Several days later, the *Hollywood Reporter* ran a story with the headline ERNEST LEHMAN LAUNCHES *WOOLF* REHEARSALS JUNE 28TH. While Lehman's name appeared three times in the item, Nichols was not mentioned once. Clearly, the article had Lehman's fingerprints all over it, and when he got to his office, there was a note from Jack Warner: "Ernie—the enclosed clipping speaks for itself. You or whoever planted the story omitted the name of Mike Nichols, the director. . . . What we all must do now is to stop worrying about publicity and worry about getting the picture on the screen. Every good wish and no forethought of malice. Signed, Jack Warner."

Lehman was perturbed. "My instant reaction to this letter was a mixture of anger, hurt, humiliation and fear. . . . the first sign that Jack Warner could turn on me and show unpleasantness after having been as nice to me as he has been for over a year," he wrote. "Also, it made me feel that my whole plan to get a normal amount of publicity for myself and not be snowed under by everyone else connected with the picture, was threatened."

Lehman had been so thrown by Warner's reaction that he went to see Max Barkett, the head of publicity at Warner Brothers. While his fretting might seem petty, Lehman was no fool. There were Machiavellian twists to this episode, confirmed by Barkett, who warned him of Warner's resentment over anyone getting more publicity than he did, particularly on *Virginia Woolf*, a film that Warner himself had such high hopes about.

Digging further, Lehman sought out a studio insider, who provided a chilling message: "Don't get into any really serious argument with Jack Warner on this publicity issue because I guarantee you there's nothing Warner would like better than to see you walk off the picture so that he could take over [as producer]. . . . One thing Jack Warner will never lose is his nose and that nose smells the big one with *Woolf.*" He ended his insert with a typical Lehman witticism: "The only thing about that remark that I hope is true is the accuracy of Jack Warner's sense of smell."

Early in the production, after lunch one day, Irene Sharaff, the seasoned Hollywood costume designer working on *Virginia Woolf*, asked Lehman how it felt to be a producer. "I'm learning things I had not known about either myself or the whole business of being a producer," he said. "It's much easier to fight authority, at least for me, when one knows that the person one is fighting has the security of knowing he can win by virtue of his authority. It is more difficult to fight someone when one knows one has the authority and therefore automatically appears to be a threat to the person one is fighting." He was talking about the difference between Warner, who owned the studio, and Nichols, the comrade-in-arms with whom Lehman was in direct competition.

~

One weekday afternoon, Mike returned from a late lunch, barreled into Ernie's office, and closed the door. "I'm absolutely overwhelmed with anxiety," he blurted out. Ernie gestured for him to sit down and explain. "The whole idea of directing this film," Mike confessed. "I think about it and suddenly I want to shout *Help! Help!*" Ernie offered a sympathetic ear and shared what he thought was useful advice. "That's good," he told Mike. "I think it's very normal. I think you should be anxious. I think you should be worrying. I think you should be fearful. If a truck were bearing down on you and you didn't jump out of the way because of fear, you would be killed. This picture is bearing down on you, and if you don't really start worrying about it, but *really* worrying about it, and doing something to allay those worries, it will bear down on you and kill you."

Mike took offense, accusing Ernie of scolding him for being too blithe and unconcerned about the enormous task at hand. Mike read Ernie's tone correctly. In his journal, Ernie later reported that "I have felt that Mike tends to leave the picture behind when he leaves the studio, and I think he goes off to a very happy social life in the evenings. Now, perhaps it will all work out well, but I have worked with other directors. . . . they would be burning the midnight oil trying to find all the answers to all the questions."

In fact, Nichols had been thinking about the movie obsessively. He was consumed with anxiety precisely because he understood the stakes. First, he wanted to give Albee's play its due as nothing less than a national treasure. Then, he was preparing himself to extract the best performance he could get out of his stars—also his friends—the most famous couple in the world; of course, he wanted to make a film worthy of the amount of money being thrown at it; and, ultimately, personally, all eyes were on him. He had been seeking advice from some of the world's most revered directors over lunches and dinners—Renoir, Mankiewicz, Wilder. He had every intention of making a great film with the incisive vision and unique sensibility of an auteur. Mike's directorial preoccupations about the movie should have come across loud and clear to Lehman.

On another occasion, Mike waltzed into Ernie's office and said he had been at a party over the weekend at the home of George Axelrod, who wrote the screenplays for *The Seven Year Itch*, *Breakfast at Tiffany's*, and *The Manchurian Candidate*. (Yet another party to flaunt that Ernie wasn't invited to.) Someone there told Mike that, on *The Misfits*, director John Huston had insisted that Arthur Miller write all kinds of camera angles and shots into his screenplay. Was he passive-aggressively faulting Ernie for not having done the same? Ernie stewed over it, later enumerating in his journal several points that Mike might have overlooked in his backhanded complaint: "There are scenes that take place, let us say, in a living room. It is a living room we have not yet even specifically designed. It would be virtually impossible to state specifically in the screenplay how various portions of those long scenes should be shot by Mike. Even if this were done, Mike would be the first one to say that he doesn't want to be told specifically how to direct the scene."

Nichols could be very manipulative. On one level, the subtext of this drive-by humblebrag about the Axelrod party was to one-up Ernie, but his underlying motivation was much graver and more fundamental: The genuine auteur in Nichols was determined to return Lehman's script for the movie to the original dialogue and action in Albee's play. Nichols held in his mind the first time he had seen *Who's Afraid of Virginia Woolf?* "It just knocked me out," he later said. "Albee's pen was just in flames. You could tell, he didn't stop. It was some kind of burst of inspiration. And in that loony way, I just thought I knew all about it." Nichols wanted the movie to possess the same bald existential truth of the play that knocked him out initially, in the very language of Albee's scathing wit and pinpoint psychological acuity. This would be a slow and delicate subterfuge—chipping away at Ernie's screenplay by making him insecure about it.

Lehman and Nichols both recognized the need to cut the three-and-half-hour play by an hour, not only for budgetary reasons but also to hold the attention of a general film audience. During a writing session several days later, Lehman recalled, "Mike and I have tried desperately hard to shorten the script, but it seems to be a very difficult thing to do. In fact, yesterday Mike asked me to add about 3/4 of a page that wasn't even in the script when we started cutting in the morning." Mike's humor could be almost invisible, his straight-faced delivery often mistaken for sincerity. In this case, adding more dialogue when he knew he would later turn around and remove it qualifies as a Mike Nichols mindfuck, a way to garner Ernie's trust before pulling the carpet out from under his screenplay, a way to keep him on ever-shifting ground. "I was a prick some of the time," Nichols admitted about his behavior while making *Virginia Woolf.* "But then, I felt so sure I knew what to do. I don't know how I got so confident. I do think it was my deep connection to the material."

Some days Lehman was happy with the work they did on the screenplay. They were on the same page, he thought, looking for the clues about human behavior that would "testify to the fact that, even though

George and Martha are at each other's throats verbally through much of the picture, still there is a married life that they share together, that there are times when they are, at the very least, friends." In one writing session, Ernie offered several possible examples of their marital companionship: their names GEORGE + MARTHA carved on the tree outside the house; a message scrawled with lipstick on the mirror from Martha to George that the chicken is in the icebox; Martha knitting a sweater for George even as she is excoriating him. While Ernie was proud of his suggestions, Mike felt they verged on cliché, something he would not abide. They did not find their way into the picture.

"Lehman was very talented," Mike acknowledged toward the end of his career. "He did good work. But I don't think he was really suited to the Albee stuff. I have gotten a little more patient since I started but when I was doing *Virginia Woolf,* I didn't have the patience." Nichols's forbearance was tested over and over in the ongoing debate about the imaginary child. He believed it to be a significant building block of George and Martha's story, but "Lehman decided to make the child real," Nichols said. In Lehman's rewriting of the script, George and Martha's child had hanged himself in the hall closet on his eighteenth birthday. They had sealed up the closet and papered over it. That was their secret. "I, at first gently and then quickly, explained that that wasn't going to be possible," Nichols remembered, adding that he had to temper his moral outrage. "It was immaterial whether [Albee's] imaginary child was criticized or not. The *fact* of the imaginary child and the *fact* that it was their secret . . . what you see when you find out about the imaginary child is how much they love each other." Nichols went on to explain what he thought was the essence of the imaginary child to George and Martha—in effect, the essence of the play: "Erich Fromm defined love as wanting the loved one to be his or her best self. That's why Martha tortures George. That's what they want for each other. They actually love each other very much. People thought I was nuts when I used to say that. But it is the very essence of the play and why it's worth doing."

Nichols believed that the imaginary child is the central metaphor of the play. It is something that George and Martha, alone, share—a secret that is only theirs. "During the course of these two hours George betrays the fact of the imaginary child," Nichols said, and elaborated: "*How could you?* she says. *You started it*, he says. *You broke the rule*, she says. *You mentioned him first*, he says. You can't take all that out and say it was a real kid who killed himself." Nichols was determined to stay with the Albee text.

One day, Lehman was unusually distressed. Acutely sensitive to Nichols's moods, he was so irritated that he reported a litany of Mike's infractions into his Dictaphone later that evening: "I was feeling a little stiff backed because last night Mike had called me at home and applied what I felt was undue pressure to sign André Previn as composer for our picture, as soon as possible." Lehman was preoccupied with this all day, for several reasons. First, it was his prerogative as the producer to select the composer himself, after consultation with the director. Then, he thought it was premature to hire a composer before a good portion of the picture had been shot. "And, as much as I admire André Previn," he reasoned, "I think he's one of the world's great musicians—a very bright man and a very nice man—I still am not sure he is the right composer for this picture. So, I guess both Mike and I started off today from the wrong side of the bed, so to speak."

Early in the day, in a peripatetic moment, Mike popped into Ernie's office to give him news about the media circus surrounding the Burtons during the filming of *The Sandpiper* in Carmel; their presence disrupted not only the production but the entire town. It made Mike anxious about the potential havoc their arrival would cause on the *Virginia Woolf* set. When Ernie shrugged it off, Mike stormed away, avoiding Ernie for the rest of the day. "There were moments where I could tell he was in some sort of unexplained rage, which I couldn't fathom, and it made me very uncomfortable. I noticed that Mike kept walking out of my office, that he never spoke to me," he wrote.

At the end of the day, Ernie had Mike paged on the intercom. Mike came into his office, sat down, and Lehman, assuming the role of an executive who was forced to manage the bad behavior of a senior member of his staff, called Mike on his rage, claiming that it was disruptive. "Well, you seemed entirely too flippant about what was really a concern to me," Mike railed at Ernie, consumed with fear that the Burtons' fame would destroy the production before it even got off the ground. Nichols then insisted that his anger didn't mean anything, that it was always fleeting, and it always passed. "That's all very nice and I'm glad to hear it," Ernie said, "but your rage and your anger make me uncomfortable, and I would like to avoid it, if possible, so I think it's better if you tell me at the time what is bothering you, instead of kind of going off quietly to sulk behind closed doors."

Mike softened during that conversation, enough for Ernie to bring up the Previn issue. "I think you are applying far too much pressure about Previn," Ernie told Mike. "Oh, no," Mike responded. "You're just misreading it as pressure." Then, as if dissecting his own strategies of manipulation, Mike offered this explanation worthy of a dialogue in one of his comic skits with Elaine May. "I welcome the fact that you are willing to argue with me about, let us say, André Previn, if not specifically André Previn," Mike said. "If you simply agreed with me and said, 'Fine, you want him we'll hire him,' I would be the one to say, 'Now wait a minute, let's talk about this first.'" It was classic Mike Nichols gaslighting, and Ernie was having none of it.

Several days later, Lehman arrived at the Warner Brothers commissary and ran into Nichols dining with Previn. Mike invited Ernie to sit down, but he was there to meet someone else. After lunch, Lehman went to see Jack Warner and complained about being railroaded into hiring a composer. Warner assured Lehman that, as producer, he was the boss, and the composer was his decision to make. When Lehman mentioned the name Alex North, who wrote the music for *A Streetcar Named Desire*, *Death of a Salesman*, *The Misfits*, and *Cleopatra*, Warner loved the idea. Lehman wasted no time contacting North's agent.

North, who was in Moscow for several weeks, wired back through his agent that, yes, he was interested and thrilled to be asked. Lehman made it clear that the call was exploratory, and they would be in touch once North was back to set up meetings. Lehman informed Warner and then broke the news to Nichols as a fait accompli.

And yet, while Lehman may have suffered in the wake of Nichols's machinations, to his credit he never let an irritating power game obscure his sense of the big picture. One evening in early June, he made this Dictaphone recording on his way home from the studio: "It is 7 o'clock PM. Nothing on *Who's Afraid of Virginia Woolf?* means anything to me when you consider that today will always be remembered as the day when the first American walked out of a space vehicle into space—I refer to Gemini 4. Down here on earth this was the day on which Mike Nichols returned from his sickbed." Nichols had had an intestinal flu over the weekend that kept him on the toilet eliminating his bowels for two days. He joked that it was the fastest weight-loss program he had ever undergone. From Lehman's perspective, at that moment Nichols was a mere speck amid the majesty of humanity's accomplishment in space. As the producer of *Who's Afraid of Virginia Woolf?*, he was hoping to keep that perspective on his irrepressible director.

Chapter 6

Flies in the Ointment

I don't know why you want to make a movie like this one," Sydney Guilaroff, veteran hair stylist to the stars, said to Lehman and Nichols after reading the *Virginia Woolf* script. The three of them were having lunch on Mike's patio to discuss the sort of hair they imagined for the character of Martha, but Sydney turned up his nose at the idea of Elizabeth Taylor as a middle-aged harridan. Guilaroff was not only a legend in his unique corner of the film world but, equally, a diva to rival all the great stars for whom he performed his hair magic, from Joan Crawford, who initially brought him to Hollywood, to Claudette Colbert, Marlene Dietrich, Greta Garbo, Grace Kelly, Marilyn Monroe, Taylor, and more. (Louise Brooks's signature bob was his.) When Nichols invited Guilaroff to lunch, he expected to see some wigs or, at least, concept drawings to discuss Elizabeth's transformation from a ravishing beauty to an aging faculty wife. Mike countered Guilaroff's condescension with some measured sarcasm of his own, couched in the good-natured voice of a television commentator. "Well, Sydney, we feel that people have such pleasant lives and what they really are seeking when they go to a motion picture theater is a film just like *Who's Afraid of Virginia Woolf?* which will make them forget their terribly pleasant lives."

After lunch, Lehman had a conciliatory moment with Guilaroff in the driveway. "The reason Mike and I seem in very slight disagreement as to how much gray there should be in Martha's hair is that Mike sees middle-aged women from the vantage point of his age, which is thirty-three, whereas I see middle-aged women from my middle-aged vantage point." Sydney took this in politely but reiterated that any conversation about Martha's hair was academic until Elizabeth got there. She was the only one he would listen to about how old she was willing to look.

The actors were due to arrive on June 28, and there was still a great deal to accomplish before the production was on the clock. Lehman and Nichols worked on the screenplay almost daily in Lehman's office during the week and, on the weekends, poolside on Nichols's leafy patio. Not only did they have to cut more than an hour out of the play, but Nichols was still intent on performing a kind of invisible surgery to peel Lehman's screenplay back to the original Albee script without ruffling the producer's feathers (too much). Meanwhile, there were many other tasks demanding their attention in ways they had not anticipated. They gained more traction with Sharaff, the costume designer, than with Guilaroff. She had worked closely with Taylor on *Cleopatra* and other films. The plan was for Sharaff to fly to Europe to familiarize Taylor with the designs for Martha's costumes and to do some measuring, since Taylor was supposed to be gaining twenty pounds for the role. When Sharaff, who lived in New York, could not locate the Burtons in Europe, Lehman ventured into an unexpected wild-goose chase, first sending a lengthy cable to Taylor's agent in London, then to her lawyer in New York, then another to her secretary, before finally learning the general whereabouts of their famous stars.

The Burtons were on an extended second honeymoon, incommunicado, so to speak, touring the Côte d'Azur in the green Rolls-Royce convertible that Taylor had initially bought for Eddie Fisher. They stayed with various friends along the way in several historically important châteaux overlooking the Mediterranean, driving into one town or another for long, leisurely lunches by the sea, and playing Yahtzee on the terrace in the evenings. It was an intentionally meandering idyll after three grueling years in which, between them, they had starred in six films, interspersed with Burton's two stage productions of *Hamlet* in Toronto and New York. No one knew exactly where they were or how to reach them. Yet the most important detail Lehman extracted from Taylor's secretary was the date the Burtons were planning to sail for New York—June 16 on the SS *Michelangelo*—which would not get them to the States before June 24. As they planned to travel to California by train, they couldn't possibly report to the set on June 28, as contractually expected.

"If I have to wait until Elizabeth gets to New York," Sharaff told Lehman, "the costumes won't be ready in time." Lehman would not tolerate a two-to-three-week delay in production because of costumes. He called the Burtons' agent again. "The start date is June 28," Lehman curtly reminded him. "We have been talking about June 28 and passing memos back and forth about June 28 for several months." The agent mused that he recalled somebody asking that the picture be delayed until July 7. "Well, it certainly wasn't me," Lehman snapped. The start date turned into a major conflict as it pinballed from Jack Warner's office in Los Angeles to the Burtons' agents in New York and then London and back to their lawyer in New York, and to their secretary in Gstaad, where Taylor owned a home, and back and forth for another week before it was finally agreed that the production would just have to accommodate the Burtons' late arrival in Los Angeles on July 1. Since that was the Thursday before the July 4 weekend, the official start date would be July 7 after all. Taylor's one-million-dollar contract included an additional one hundred thousand dollars for every week of production that went over schedule, so Lehman complained to Warner that they should deduct one hundred thousand dollars from Taylor's contract for this one-week delay. As it was, that week would cost the entire production tens of thousands of dollars. But they reasoned that changing the start date was the price of ensuring the Burtons' happiness and the goodwill of the cast, regardless of the moral sacrifice of bending the entire production to the stars' every whim.

~

Nichols continued to go about the business of pre-production—revising the script with Lehman, meeting with crew members, never mind tending to his breathtaking social life—all the while consumed with a gnawing and essential problem to solve. How was he going to integrate all that he understood as a theater director into directing a film? In a 1992 interview, he recalled feeling much more at home directing his first play than he felt in preparing to direct *Virginia Woolf.* All along, his life had been aimed toward the theater. "When I was twelve, I read all of Eugene O'Neill," he told the television interviewer Charlie Rose, ticking off a list of his associations with the theater: studying at the Actors Studio with Lee Strasberg; performing comedy with Second City; and his early improv work with the Compass Players in Chicago before that. In the theater, Nichols had an instinctive understanding about the narrative requirements of moving the plot forward. He knew how to create verisimilitude on the stage. "Yeah? So? What's next?" is the question he wanted to sustain from a live audience that forces the actors to deliver a moment-to-moment performance that resonates as if it were really happening. This was all native to Nichols, both as a live performer himself and as a celebrated theater director.

The mechanics of bringing a story to life on the screen were entirely different. In film, so much of the work is visual first. The burden of storytelling is foregrounded by the image before the story unfolds. While the theater relies on the voice, the screen relies on the face. On the screen, film magnifies a face as if it were an entire stage; the infinitesimal adjustments in a facial expression can have the same narrative impact as a character's soliloquy in a play. In film, each scene is created specifically for the camera, often shot out of sequence, and later constructed into an edited series of clips. The film director creates a cohesive narrative from a different set of moving parts, coming together not in a living moment but assembled over the course of time. "It's the director's job to tell the story," Nichols said, but telling the story in film felt like acquiring a new language—an unsettling experience for the German immigrant who'd had to learn English at age seven.

On the set of *Virginia Woolf*, "I certainly wasn't confident," Nichols said during that television interview. "I didn't know how to shoot a movie." Nichols agreed with Lehman about shooting the film in sequence—not unlike a play—and they were setting up the production schedule toward that end. He later reflected that "you can actually watch me learning as I go." In conceptualizing the first scene, for example, Nichols planned to introduce George and Martha as they came through the front door, with the camera positioned inside the house. But he couldn't figure out where the camera was supposed to be to get opening shots that zero in on their faces. "Won't the front door hit the camera?" he asked his good friend Anthony Perkins, who was staying with him before production began. Perkins explained that that's what long lenses were for, a revelation to Nichols. He had so much to learn about the technical aspects of shooting a movie; the even greater challenge, though, was how to conjure a performance out of an actor for the camera versus a live theater audience.

In the weeks before the actors arrived, Nichols embarked on his own tutorial in moviemaking. He took over one of the Warner Brothers screening rooms and summoned more than half a dozen films to watch in a series of afternoon screenings. One, *A Streetcar Named Desire*, had been shot by Harry Stradling, the veteran cinematographer assigned by Warner Brothers to shoot *Virginia Woolf*. Nichols also screened his beloved *A Place in the Sun*, which starred a much younger Taylor. "It depressed Mike because he realized that one cannot become George Stevens on one's first attempt, no matter how hard one tries," Lehman reported in his journal. "What I think he forgets is that he can become Mike Nichols on his first attempt, and that might be more interesting, particularly for this picture." One afternoon, Mike asked Ernie to see if he couldn't get the studio to pay the $350 necessary to obtain several foreign films: François Truffaut's *Jules and Jim* and *The 400 Blows*, and Federico Fellini's *8½*. "Hacks only imitate," Mike explained. "We artists steal." Lehman and others joined him for these screenings. Another film that Mike selected was Alfred Hitchcock's *Rope*, which takes place entirely in a single apartment, just as *Virginia Woolf* takes place almost entirely in George and Martha's living room. Mike wanted to understand how Hitchcock handled such a limited set, which was not unlike shooting an entire movie as if it were onstage.

While watching *Rope*, Mike whispered to Ernie that the film's star, Jimmy Stewart, would have been an ideal George, especially playing opposite Bette Davis as Martha. "It was my fault for having Elizabeth Taylor and Richard Burton rather than Bette and Jimmy," Lehman wrote defensively, as if Nichols had accused him of miscasting the movie. He recognized that Nichols might have been joking but addressed the charge seriously, nonetheless. "Of course, he was seeing Jimmy as he looked 20 years ago. I, too, had thought of Jimmy Stewart for George, who became impossible once I made the decision to go with Elizabeth Taylor, who is so much younger. . . . However, as a character in *Virginia Woolf* says, 'that's blood under the bridge.'"

From the start, Nichols had planned on shooting *Virginia Woolf* in black and white, and all the movies he screened in those weeks leading up to production were black and white films—with the exception of *Rope*, which was Hitchcock's first color film. Color had become a lingua franca for musicals and epics, or fantasy; black and white was starting to feel old-fashioned yet was still considered more "realistic" and was reserved for serious, literary, or controversial films. But in the mid-1960s, there was increasing pressure for film studios to shoot exclusively in color because of competition from the television networks, which were broadcasting more and more shows in color.

Aside from the color-processing inconsistencies that could yield garish and unrealistic results, there were practical reasons for *Virginia Woolf* to be shot in black and white. One was that grayscale tones were less revealing of the heavy makeup and the artificially gray-streaked wigs required to make Taylor look forty-eight years old. (That was the age they had settled on to mollify the thirty-two-year-old actress, who could not abide playing Martha as fifty-two, her stated age in the original play.) For Nichols, though, shooting in black and white was a distinct and intentional artistic decision that seemed integral to the material itself. "Here's the thing about black and white," Nichols said. "It's not literal. It is a metaphor, automatically. . . . And that's the point: a movie *is* a metaphor. If it's in black and white, the film is already saying, 'No, this is not life, this is something *about* life.'"

For Jack Warner, "color" was contemporary. More to the point, it meant revenue. He had hired Stradling to shoot *Virginia Woolf* in color. Stradling had won Oscars for his work in both black and white (*The Picture of Dorian Gray* in 1945)—and, most recently, in color (*My Fair Lady*). Nichols respected Stradling's experience—in particular, his fine camera work in *A Streetcar Named Desire*—but Harry was in his sixties and had opinions and prejudices that didn't suit Nichols. One afternoon Nichols invited both Stradling and Haskell Wexler—the younger cinematographer he secretly wanted for *Virginia Woolf*, whom he had known personally even before Wexler shot his first film for Elia Kazan—to watch Fellini's *8½* with him. When the movie ended, Stradling complained that "the film is a piece of shit." Nichols, who worshiped the film, wanted to fire him on the spot.

The issue of black and white versus color came to a head when Nichols and Lehman met with Warner in his office. "Warner said to me and Lehman—who never spoke—'I'm sorry, boys, but New York says it has to be in color,'" Nichols recounted. "Well, there *was* no 'New York'"—meaning that Warner owned the whole studio and "New York" was a figure of speech about some phantom corporate executives to whom he was conversationally passing the buck. Nichols very politely explained that it wasn't possible to shift to color at this point, as everything was being designed for black and white. "Besides," Mike added, "Elizabeth is thirty-two and color will not carry her make-up." After going back and forth for a while, Warner finally relented: "All right,

black and white." A week after that, however, Nichols ran into Stradling on the Warner Brothers lot. Stradling said he had been thinking
about the color issue and casually suggested a compromise: "We could
shoot *Virginia Woolf* in color and print it in black-and-white." Nichols
knew at once that this idea was instigated by Warner himself. He knew,
too, that if the movie was shot in color, there was no way Warner would
release it in black and white.

Nichols asked Lehman to accompany him to Warner's office and
put an end to the idea of color for the film, once and for all. This time,
Warner, now indignant, ordered the film to be shot in color. Nichols
made the same arguments again for black and white, but Warner held
firm. "Okay, then, go ahead," Nichols said finally, standing up and
speaking in that pleasant newscaster's voice that dripped with white-
hot condescension. "Shoot your film in color. I like it at home. I will
just go back to New York." By now, Nichols, a mere novice, had more
cachet than many veteran directors by nature of his current Broadway
successes, his alliances with Hollywood royalty like Billy Wilder and
Joseph L. Mankiewicz, and his unusual social notoriety. Warner calculated that if Nichols walked, the production could very likely lose the
Burtons, too, and the press would gleefully report the unraveling of a
"Dick and Liz" project. Nichols was playing the stronger hand, and
Warner had to concede. "I was a real snot," a much older Nichols
conceded, reflecting on his behavior during *Virginia Woolf* sagely, but
not without a stroke of amusement.

≈

Gloria Steinem's suggestion about shooting the exteriors of the movie
at Smith College took hold. Mike was enamored of the vérité flavor it
would bring to the story, and the studio machinery went into high gear
to try to execute the first-time director's wishes.

At the end of May, Lehman sent Hal Polaire, the film's production
manager, from Los Angeles to Northampton, Massachusetts, to seek
permission from the president of Smith to allow several weeks of filming

on the campus. At first Polaire reported back that the president had declined the "opportunity." He made it clear that the college did not abide such disruptions to the students, their classes, and the quiet routines of campus life. Lehman and Nichols alerted Jack Warner, who gave Polaire some financial latitude. The next day, they all got on separate phones anticipating bad news from Polaire, but he happily declared that they had permission to shoot for four weeks on the campus at the tail end of summer, providing that they finish by September 20, before classes began. The twenty-five thousand dollars that Polaire offered Smith College on behalf of Warner Brothers had been persuasive.

Since Nichols had been nominated for a Tony Award that season and the ceremony was in New York in mid-June, his trip would overlap perfectly with Lehman's plan to fly to Northampton to look at the campus and make a variety of pre-production determinations. Lehman had written a roadhouse scene into the screenplay that does not exist in the play, and location scouting for a suitable bar or tavern had already begun in Los Angeles. Nichols thought that Polaire should scout some taverns for them to look at in Northampton, as well. On June 11, Ernie and Mike flew with a small entourage—the assistant director, the cinematographer, the production designer—from Los Angeles to Northampton. On the first night, Ernie and Mike walked through the campus to get a sense of how to shoot the opening scene with George and Martha perambulating home across the college grounds at midnight. They were pleased with the location and thought it looked wonderful in the moonlight. They roamed around the campus acting out some of the scenes and, according to Lehman, having themselves a ball. At one point, though, Mike darkened. "The only trouble with all this is that it looks exactly like the back lot of a motion picture studio," he said. "I can just see Dwight McDonald [a film critic for *Esquire* at the time] saying *Mike Nichols has succeeded in taking a real campus and making it look like a Hollywood back lot*."

On Sunday morning, June 13, 1965, Nichols and Lehman flew back to New York, where Mike was to attend the Tony Awards ceremony that evening and where Lehman could watch it live on television from his suite at the Sherry-Netherland hotel. Nichols was up for Best Direction of the Current Season for *two* concurrent plays, *Luv* and *The Odd Couple*. When his name was announced as the winner, there was thunderous applause. For Ernie, watching Mike accept a Tony and give a pithy speech was a mixed blessing. Mike's stock rose even higher, making him that much more insufferable. At the same time Ernie was proud of Nichols and thought his success could only add to the buzz about *Virginia Woolf*. He called Mike at home later to congratulate him. "How did I look?" was all Mike wanted to know. Ernie, always competitive, considered every one of Mike's victories, large and small, a challenge to his own success, and he couldn't help but calculate how Mike's Tony Award stacked up against his own current victory with *The Sound of Music*—still number one at the box office for the third month in a row. (As Gore Vidal once said, "Whenever a friend succeeds, I die a little.")

They were supposed to fly back to Northampton the next day, but Mike called Ernie early in the morning to ask if they could stay in New York another day. "The reason was made quite clear to me when Mike said he received a telephone call from 'the lady across the park,'" Lehman wrote. "She is so famous I cannot mention her name in this journal." Jacqueline Kennedy had invited Nichols to lunch at her Fifth Avenue apartment, and he had no intention of turning her down. This singular moment elevated Mike to a category of untouchability in Ernie's mind that made it even harder for him to assert his own authority over his director. Lehman went out for a walk. "New York City was beautiful. The weather was fine. The people looked great. I went to a few galleries," he reported. Afterward, he visited his parents, who had an apartment on Central Park South. That's how he licked his imagined wounds against the magnitude of Nichols's ever-expanding prestige.

The next morning, in the limousine on the way to the airport, Mike told Ernie that he felt "a few little wisps of bad feeling" going back and forth between them and wanted to clear the air. Mike wondered if Ernie was upset about all the Tony Award publicity he was getting. "I want to assure you that I don't seek the publicity," Mike said. "I don't even want it, it seeks me. It's just that I'm kind of a well-known person, and I'm going to get publicity, even if I do nothing to pursue it." Ernie told Mike he was proud of him but acknowledged in his journal that "it does upset me a bit" despite his awareness that he had no right to be out of sorts. "I told Mike that what he didn't know about me was that long ago, before we even met, I had a long career in Hollywood feeling hurt at the lack of recognition." What Ernie left out was that he had long become a master at generating his own publicity as a result. Over those few weeks before going to Northampton, Lehman had been in surreptitious negotiations with Helen Gurley Brown, the editor in chief of *Cosmopolitan* magazine and the author of *Sex and the Single Girl* (and wife of his old friend, David Brown, the head of creative operations at Twentieth Century–Fox), about a lengthy profile on him—the producer of *Who's Afraid of Virginia Woolf?*—for which she allowed him to handpick the writer. It was scheduled to come out in the October issue of *Cosmopolitan*, when the film would be wrapping up production.

Mike then confessed to some angst of his own regarding the attention Ernie had been getting when they arrived at the airports. "Mike has been feeling slighted because of possibly 5% more attention being paid to me as the person in charge of the logistics." Mike told Ernie he'd been feeling hurt about not being fussed over more. "But maybe it's healthy for me to get poor treatment," Mike mused, "so that I can get over wanting to be spoiled." It is hard to know how seriously to regard these ongoing exchanges between Lehman and Nichols. While their petty feelings of competition can seem so surprisingly adolescent, these conversations have a distinct echo of Nichols's improvisational skits on stage with Elaine May that parody the narcissism and neuroses of educated urban sophisticates. Lehman, who was worthy of Mike's affection and respect, could be amusing at times with his own deadpan wit, but he could also be quite literal and flat-footed in his approach to things. That made him not only a likely target for Nichols's irrepressible need to thumb his nose at the status quo but also a foil for Nichols's own penchant for self-aggrandizement. It is very possible that Nichols, with his matter-of-fact delivery, was often enough simply pulling Lehman's leg.

~

Ultimately Lehman would find satisfaction in the fact that *Virginia Woolf* was an ERNEST LEHMAN PRODUCTION, and, despite the slow recalibrating of his screenplay back to the original Albee script, he could take additional credit for several decisions that proved consequential to the film's success. The first was relying on his instinct to cast Elizabeth Taylor and Richard Burton; the second was hiring Mike Nichols, based on the persuasive recommendation of Taylor and Burton; and the third—relevant to this moment in pre-production—was his success in hiring Alex North as the composer.

Now, two weeks before the actors were scheduled to arrive, Lehman arrived home from Northampton to a call from North's agent to report that North had just closed the deal with Warner Brothers as the composer of *Who's Afraid of Virginia Woolf?* He would be flying out to Los Angeles to spend three weeks with them. Ernie was surprised that Jack Warner had gotten involved and sealed the deal so fast. Lehman called Nichols immediately to inform him, and, fortunately, Mike was in a good mood. "I'm glad you were willing to give up your first choice, André Previn," Nichols kidded, "and I had hoped you wouldn't be too upset at my insistence on using Alex North."

As the production loomed, the conversations between Lehman and Nichols became more practical. There were issues to be ironed out before shooting could begin. As a theater director, Nichols was familiar with production design, and he was now spending many happy days with Richard Sylbert, the production designer, going over ideas for the interior sets of George and Martha's house, summoned in part from his memories of the apartment in which he grew up. "My parents used to fight. It wasn't as searching or as vicious or anything [as George and

Martha]," Nichols said. "I would think it was dumb and just go off to the movies." But like Albee invoking the Maases while writing *Virginia Woolf*, Nichols drew on vivid recollections of a couple he had known in Chicago who were prone to vicious brawls. It was his memory of their house that he wanted Sylbert to re-create for George and Martha. "You gotta have these bookshelves, with the bricks, and the boards on the bricks," Mike would explain to Sylbert. "I want to know the place."

When Sylbert built a perfect replica of the facade of George and Martha's house on Stage Eight in the back lot, everyone marveled at the accuracy in relation to the real house they had chosen on the Smith campus. Sylbert put plants in large flowerpots along the front of the porch and several leafy vines climbing up the trellises on either side of the steps. "For the opening scene on the set, Sylbert put moths on thread to look as if they are swarming around the porch light," Nichols later said. "He was so great with detail. He thought of the moths. They looked so real in the film." Sylbert created the "lived in" disarray in George and Martha's house, choosing every book on their bookshelves, and the mainstream magazines and academic periodicals lying on their coffee table and stacked on their nightstands. "It was an eerie experience," Lehman reported in his journal the first time they set foot on the living room set. "In one's mind, one sees oneself at the actual location, at night, in New England, even as one stands in a half-built set, with carpenters all around hammering nails into place."

More and more, Lehman and Nichols would find themselves in impromptu daily conferences. One afternoon, Mike stopped by Ernie's office with Sylbert and asked the producer to walk over to Stage Eight with them. Adjustments had to be made to the interior living room set to accommodate specific camera angles. Additionally, by the end of the day, Nichols had rounded up his cinematographer, film editor, and the sound engineer to discuss his intention to shoot scenes with a lot of crosstalk, since, in real life, when people are drinking, one person is always talking over another, or two conversations are occurring at the same time. Mike wanted to be able to capture that kind of authentic behavior without losing the actual dialogue propelling the story. That day, the entire crew spent an hour on the set discussing ways to tailor the living room to shoot scenes to accommodate the director's vision. Nichols was in heaven.

As the machinery was falling into place—the producer maintaining the schedule and budget; the production designer building the sets; the cinematographer advising on the look of various scenes; the editor anticipating the editing options; the costume designer and the hair stylist and the script doctor all busy doing their handiwork; and, now, the composer considering the emotional tenor of the film—it became increasingly apparent to Nichols that he could rely on his team to do some of the heavy lifting for him. No longer did it feel that his ideas were beyond his reach. He had the substantial backup of a competent crew, which made his decision process so much easier, his intentions more inevitable. If it meant moving a mountain to revise an idea, the personnel was there, the money was there, and the expectations for the film at Warner Brothers were so high that even an expensive mistake made because of his inexperience could be accommodated without repercussion. The alchemy was in place for him to make movie magic—which meant one thing for Nichols and another for Jack Warner. Nichols wanted the film to be a profound existential metaphor about one marriage—original and recognizable and insightful and cinematic—in order to represent all marriage. Warner wanted a smash hit that would make millions. Their goals did not have to be mutually exclusive, but Nichols felt Warner's old-school Hollywood calculus to be a burden, just the same.

~

On June 25, Mike called Ernie at home first thing in the morning to discuss several lines in the script. But before that, while still yawning the sleep out of his voice, he reminded Ernie that the Burtons had arrived in New York. "Did you send flowers and champagne to Elizabeth at the Regency Hotel?" he asked. "And *jewelry*. You know how she likes her jewelry." Ernie countered, "Don't you know I have no style?" Then he assured Mike he had taken care of it—all but the jewelry.

Sharaff met with Taylor in New York to take measurements, then flew to Los Angeles to show fabric samples for Martha's wardrobe to Nichols and Lehman. After that meeting, as they were walking out, Lehman confessed to Sharaff, who had worked closely with Taylor on other films, that he was worried about the star's demeanor. He told her that when he met the Burtons in Paris, "Elizabeth seemed to go at me with too many guns when she was arguing with me." Sharaff offered this rather uncomfortable insight: "Elizabeth has this tremendous need to shatter any man who appears to be a father figure—to shatter him into many pieces and then to pick up all the pieces and put them back together again into a real relationship." This was plausible enough given the profound humiliation Taylor had endured from abusive treatment by Nicky Hilton, her first husband, and the infidelities of Michael Wilding, her second husband, who was old enough to be her father. Certainly, as a child star, Taylor had been directed by older men, and, in Hollywood, directors were both autocrats and deities. Her stardom was based not on her acting ability so much as her camera presence, and many roles she was given early in her career consisted of single lines of dialogue uttered in a kind of pro forma "doing as I'm told" style—compliant performances, deferential to her directors. Now she had grown into a deity in her own right, whose rebellious spirit was part of her allure, and after following the rules for so many years, she was in a position to show anyone in authority that she was the real boss. Sharaff pointed out that, in Taylor's eyes, Ernie was an older man in a role of authority as the Producer, so it was not likely that he would escape her occasional wrath. Whether this was an accurate reading of Taylor or not, it was a bitter pill for a man like Lehman, who thrived on winning everyone's approval. The thought of hostility directed at him from a star of Taylor's magnitude made him dyspeptic.

Yet later that day Lehman was heartened by a report from Polaire, the production manager, about the dressing room that the studio provided for Elizabeth and Richard. "It is nothing less than sumptuous." The next day, Lehman was visited by a delegation of the Burtons' representatives: Elizabeth and Richard's secretary, Dick Hanley, and his friend John Lee; Michael Wilding, one of Elizabeth's former husbands and now one of her agents; and Hugh French and his son, Robin French, who were the Burtons' official agents. Lehman led them on an inspection of the Burtons' dressing rooms, which Lehman described as adjoining suites. Each one had its own kitchen and its own piano. Elizabeth's was done in yellow and white; Richard's was wood paneled with an old English feeling. "Everyone, including myself, approved of them," Lehman wrote. "In fact, Elizabeth's dressing room was so beautiful that most of her agents said they would like to stay there and live in it themselves." Then it occurred to him that they had given no thought at all to dressing rooms for Sandy Dennis and George Segal. "So far they are really getting lost in the shuffle."

As production neared and events began to unfold more rapidly, Alex North arrived in Los Angeles. First, he and Ernie spent some time bandying about ideas, and then Nichols and North took an afternoon together discussing the underlying emotions in the film. On June 30, Lehman finished the sixth draft of the script, which was going to the printing department and would be called the "Estimating Script." This version would be given to the four actors and used in rehearsal, while he and Nichols would continue to refine the screenplay and the dialogue until the Final Script was printed a month later for the actual shooting.

July 1 loomed, and with it, the Burtons' arrival. Everyone began to feel as if they were anticipating an audience with two heads of state or, more to the point, the towering historic figures of "Cleopatra" and "Marc Antony" themselves. Electricity crackled everywhere. Lehman was second-guessing himself as his mind spiraled, recording into the Dictaphone that he spent the entire day trying to figure out what to send to the Burtons at their house for their arrival; what would Segal and his wife like to see in their Beverly Hills Hotel suite when they arrived Monday night; what to send to Dennis's house for her arrival on Tuesday. And then, what to send to all four stars' dressing rooms? It was a vicious riddle: He could not send the same gift to everyone, nor repeat a gift anyone else had sent. He learned that Jack Warner, for example, had sent the Burtons a huge floral arrangement, six bottles of champagne, a case of Scotch, and a case of gin. Lehman flinched when he heard that Nichols was sending a pound of caviar to their home.

Finally, he consulted Hanley, the Burtons' secretary, who suggested that Lehman, as the producer, send a simple spring flower arrangement to the house Elizabeth and Richard had rented in Bel Air. For Richard's dressing room, a bottle of Rémy Martin, a bottle of Johnnie Walker Red Label, and a nice bowl of fruit. For Elizabeth's dressing room, he said that Elizabeth preferred flower arrangements of moderate size and in good taste, so an arrangement of white lilies of the valley with either white roses or some white cymbidium sprinkled throughout. He was quite specific about not overdoing it. He added that a lovely touch would be a bottle of Dom Perignon in her dressing room too. "I could have written half of a screenplay with the creative energy that went into all of that," Lehman concluded, "plus what went into writing the notes that I enclosed with each of the fruit baskets or champagne gifts or flower arrangements to each of the people involved. *And* each of the notes had to be different."

At one point, Mike, punchy from the mounting pressure, came into Ernie's office, plopped down on the couch, and announced that he wanted real brand labels on all the liquor bottles in George and Martha's house. Ernie laughed and said that would not be possible. But Mike insisted, so Ernie called his bluff, asking his secretary to call Jack Warner's office. Warner said that it was not remotely possible for a thousand reasons, not least of which was the impossibility of licensing approval—no liquor company would agree to be associated with the quantity of alcohol consumed in George and Martha's living room, and the ensuing drunken behavior. Mike got on the extension. "If you let me have real liquor labels, I promise not to shoot them," Nichols said, in a playful, if adolescent, fuck-you back to Warner. Mike hadn't forgotten how the studio head had used Harry Stradling to float the idea of shooting the film in color and printing it in black and white.

Just before the July 4 weekend, Ernie and Mike each received hand-written notes from Jack Warner, who had read the Estimated Script and said that it was just too long. They needed to cut it further before having it printed and distributed to the actors. So, over the holiday weekend, Ernie and Mike went to work, parking themselves by the Greek statues on Mike's patio and whittling twenty more minutes out of the script. Mike's house assistant, Luis, served them lunch under the umbrella and brought them iced tea and, later, drinks throughout the afternoon.

On July 4, Mike took a break from working on the script to attend a party at the beachside Malibu home of Jane Fonda and her soon-to-be husband, Roger Vadim. It was an unexpected convergence of Hollywood's old guard and its young bucks. Fonda's father, Henry, was there, celebrating his belated sixtieth birthday by roasting a pig on a spit for the guests, including William Wyler, Darryl Zanuck, Sam Spiegel, Gene Kelly, and Lauren Bacall among the firmly established elders. Representing the new generation were Peter Fonda—who had hired the Byrds to play—and his friends Jack Nicholson and Dennis Hopper. Others, like Warren Beatty, Tuesday Weld, and Natalie Wood, were on a course for the Hollywood mainstream. It was a memorable affair. Even Andy Warhol appeared with two of his self-appointed superstars in tow. The generational divide was obvious as each age group settled into distinct areas of the house or the beach, and each faction partook of its recreational substances of choice—alcohol for the establishment, marijuana for the counterculture. "In the middle of the party, and yet, as always, standing at a cocked eyebrow distance from it, was Mike Nichols," writes Mark Harris. It marked a generational shift that was about to occur in Hollywood along with the social upheavals of the 1960s, and Nichols—the only director there who had not yet made a movie, an arriviste who didn't know anyone very well and who felt somewhat alienated—stood in the midst of that cultural sea change, on the cusp of his own influence, about to stir things up.

On the day before the actors were due to report for rehearsal, Ernie and Mike once again worked together by the pool to further trim the script. The Albee play is such a bald, true depiction of human nature, and, on the darkening eve of production, Nichols questioned aloud his ability to make a film that would get it right. He had been gravely concerned about how to get the actors to inhabit their complicated roles, and in particular Elizabeth. Martha was a challenge and, Mike believed, the most important character to get right. "There is no such thing as a tough woman alone in a room," Mike observed to Ernie on that last evening before the Burtons arrived, implying that, despite Martha's hard-boiled demeanor and her vicious tongue, she was vulnerable, wounded, and lonely. Once again, he lamented the fact that Ernie had not cast Bette Davis instead. Asking Taylor to play Martha, Mike fretted to Lehman, was "like asking a chocolate milkshake to do the work of a double martini."

Chapter 7

The Most Famous Couple in the World

A good marriage doesn't make two people one; it makes two people two.

—EDWARD ALBEE, QUOTING JAMES THURBER

E xhilarating" is how Ernest Lehman described the first day of rehearsal on July 6, 1965. It began with the Burtons' chauffeur-driven, air-conditioned black Cadillac limousine pulling up to the Warner Brothers lot at ten A.M. Lehman—producer, diplomat, acting studio executive—was waiting there to greet them. Out of the back seat stepped Elizabeth Taylor, long black hair falling over her shoulders, wearing a printed silk dress and a finely woven straw sun hat, and then, Richard Burton in a white cardigan sweater. Elizabeth smiled and planted a polite kiss on Ernie's cheek; Richard was more effusive and, to Ernie's surprise, gave him a generous hug. As Lehman escorted them to their dressing rooms, Elizabeth mentioned that Natalie Wood had taken the trouble to call her the night before, thrilled to learn that Elizabeth would be occupying her former dressing room. To Lehman's relief, the Burtons were "delighted with their diggings." Elizabeth beamed at Lehman's gift of white lilies of the valley with white roses and the *three* bottles of Dom Perignon. "Somebody knows what I like," she said. After reading Ernie's card, she "came over and gave me a little kiss," he recorded in his journal, clearly besotted by the movie star's attention. The Burtons' entourage had preceded them and sat waiting in Richard's dressing room: their agents, Hugh French and his son, Robin French; the press agent, John Springer; their personal dressers, Bob and Sally Wilson; and the costume designer, Irene Sharaff.

Elizabeth and Richard did not dawdle, as it was already ten thirty A.M. and Mike Nichols was expecting them on Stage Two. On the way over, Burton told Lehman how excited he was about the script. "I like it so much that it frightens me a little," he confessed. "Before it's all over," Lehman later hammed to the Dictaphone, "Richard will get over both his liking it all that much and his fear too."

Nichols had spent the previous evening doing critical homework— listening to the entire Broadway cast album of *Who's Afraid of Virginia Woolf?*, attuning himself to the rhythm of the language and the emotional tenor of the stage actors' voices while parsing out the motivation of the characters scene by scene. Nichols, excited and trepidatious in equal measure, now stood there talking to George Segal, who had arrived from Europe late the night before and looked tired, if continental, in his olive gabardine suit. Sandy Dennis was standing with them, too, "in something pink." She had been in high spirits when Lehman called her the night before and welcomed her to Los Angeles. She was happy with the house the studio had rented for her and grateful for the flowers and the champagne that Ernie had sent over. Already into her second glass of bubbly when he called, she confessed on the phone that she had taken a tranquilizer for the cross-country flight and given one each to her two dogs and her cat, turning the long trip with her domestic menagerie into a pleasant magic carpet ride. She had been looking at the *Virginia Woolf* script and declared to Ernie that it was going to be "the picture of the decade."

There were warm welcomes all around on Stage Two. The close relationship between Nichols and the Burtons was evident immediately when Mike asked them how they liked their house present: upon arrival at their lavish, neo-Moorish lodgings on Carolwood Drive in Bel Air's Holmby Hills, a five-hundred-pound taxidermied moose head had awaited them at the door. "Oh, God," Burton groaned. "We'll have to build a whole new wall to hold him." This turned out to be a running joke between the two men that had begun a year before, when Burton opened in *Hamlet* on Broadway. Nichols had sent Burton a large moose head with a note reading "O for a *moose* of fire," a pun on "O for a muse of fire," the first line of Shakespeare's *Henry V.* Before Nichols arrived in Los Angeles, the Burtons sent him a life-size moose made entirely of flowers for the opening of *The Odd Couple*, his Broadway hit. When Mike got to Los Angeles and set up his office at Warner Brothers for *Virginia Woolf*, he requested a life-size stuffed moose from the props department, which took up half his office. "So, to go with his moose," Burton explained in his orotund voice, "we sent him a riding crop with a concealed dagger, a beret and megaphone, a corset, Prussian Junker boots, and jodhpurs."

Promptly, Nichols asked everyone to take a seat around the large table: the actors Elizabeth, Richard, George, and Sandy; Ernie, the producer; Buck Hall, the assistant director; Meta Rebner, the script supervisor; and Mike himself. Neatly laid out at every seat was a script, a pad, and pencils. Nichols greeted each actor by name, and then pointed to the two police officers stationed at both entrances, assuring the group that it was a closed set and there would be no interruptions from anyone who was not directly connected with the production—neither the snooping press, nor errant autograph seekers, nor fellow actors like Frank Sinatra or Marlene Dietrich dropping by to say hello.

"I realize we sound like an atom bomb project," Lehman later told a reporter for the *Saturday Evening Post*. "But, otherwise, it would be a circus—we're like the Beatles! This way we don't embarrass Mike or render anyone nervous." Burton, who was with Lehman at the time of the interview, chimed in, further explaining the rationale. "Edward Albee is well known, Mike Nichols is well known and wanted absolute protection, and Elizabeth and I are fairly well known—if we belch, they photograph it. So, we're all for the present policy."

Thus began the first read-through, with Taylor speaking Martha's opening line—*Jesus H. Christ*. For weeks, Lehman and Nichols had been fretting about the very phenomenon of Elizabeth Taylor, wondering if the imperatives of her fame would short-circuit her ability to mine the depths of her character. Until then, her talent had resided in her radiant beauty. Her beauty was her currency. Her preparation just to leave the house required the ritual construction of "Elizabeth Taylor" to present to the world—the splendor of her face, the mystique of her image, the myth that was larger than life—whether for the screen or for the public or just going about her daily life. She had become a performance, like Marilyn Monroe. She had come to expect the very aura of her beauty to elevate her above—and insulate her from—everyone else, despite her occasional wish to simply be her natural self among regular human beings. The studio had distributed an official list to all production personnel at Warner Brothers titled "How to Treat the Burtons." Number ten on the list instructed employees not to address the Burtons unless they initiated a greeting first. "I had never seen people treated like that," Segal later marveled about the level of reverence afforded them.

Yet all the world-famous glamour fell away that first morning of rehearsal as the four actors sat at the table on Stage Two reading their lines, each of them trying on their roles for the first time, fumbling around to establish their characters' relationships with each other, while Rebner interjected script directions as they went along. Lehman saw a more approachable Taylor seated there, closer to the woman Truman Capote depicted when he wrote about an encounter with her at an intimate luncheon in a socialite's apartment in New York: "Her legs are too short for the torso, the head too bulky for the figure in toto; but the *face*, with those lilac eyes, is a prisoner's dream, a secretary's self-fantasy: unreal, unattainable, at the same time shy, overly vulnerable, very human, with the flicker of suspicion constantly flaring behind the lilac eyes."

At one point, Mike and Ernie caught each other's eye and nodded in approval—or was it relief—as Elizabeth read her lines with a semblance of her character, Martha, coming through. Later, Taylor would tell Nichols that it was the first time in her movie career she had ever read the lines of a screenplay while seated at a table, all at one sitting. In fact, in twenty years and almost three dozen movies, she had never once been asked to rehearse. She always prepped her lines with the director before each specific scene.

At noon, someone poured Bloody Marys all around, and everyone sipped their drinks as they continued the read-through. It would be an hour before they broke for lunch, when Ernie sat together with Elizabeth and Sandy. The two women embarrassed him by comparing their bellies. Elizabeth claimed that her soft belly was the permanent result of three caesarean births; Sandy disparaged her own belly, which, she declared, made her look like "a woman who's been pregnant for twelve months." Elizabeth took the moment to confront Lehman about the edict he and Mike had issued her while still in Europe to gain as much weight as she could for the role of Martha. She had "positively forced" herself to put butter on her morning croissants and to eat elaborate French dishes with cream sauces and to indulge herself with chocolate mousse and crème brûlée. Now she was at least ten pounds too heavy and blamed Lehman with a kind of mock annoyance. "I told her that I think she looks just right for the role of Martha," Lehman wrote.

In the afternoon, the quartet picked up the script where they had left off. Burton had been uneven in the morning, but as the day progressed, he was able to calibrate the deep tenor of his voice to the milder demeanor of George, his character. Segal had been operating at a disadvantage when they first sat down, as he had not yet seen a copy of the script; while he read his lines with some initial confusion in the morning, he was a more surefooted Nick before the day was out. Dennis did not try to give a performance of any kind; she barely whispered her lines, to the point that the other actors could hardly even hear her. Lehman and Nichols assumed that she was just finding her way into the role of Honey. Intermittently, Mike would stop the proceedings to make a point about one character or another or to suggest a way of thinking about a particular moment in the story. Mostly, though, he just listened.

During one break, Elizabeth pulled Mike and Ernie aside to question the motivation of George, Burton's character. While she thought it was an effective " 'gun in the drawer' for him to say, 'just don't start in on the bit' " to Martha—about their imaginary child—she didn't think it tracked with the ending, when George claims to have killed off their child precisely because Martha broke the rule by "starting in on the bit." Lehman agreed with Elizabeth and acknowledged his own reservation about it while writing the screenplay. Afterward, Mike took Ernie aside and scolded him, telling him emphatically not to take sides with any member of the cast without talking to him first. Mike felt that the director and the producer had to be completely aligned in front of the actors. "I made what you might call a mistake," Lehman reported in his journal, conceding that Nichols was probably right. "But it certainly does inhibit any expression I might have."

The first day of rehearsal ended at four thirty, when Jack Warner arrived on the set to "ordain" the production. He greeted everyone and shook their hands. He "kissed Elizabeth about eight times, made her turn around as if she were a model, and told her she looked just great"—meaning that she was the right weight for Martha.

∾

The Burtons had barely arrived when they were obligated to attend the gala premiere of *The Sandpiper*. Elizabeth had to leave rehearsal early on the second day to prepare for an official appearance as the star of the film. Before she left the studio, she had a fitting with Sydney

Guilaroff for one of the gray "Martha" wigs. She came down to the set and asked what everyone thought. "The only trouble was that she looked ravishingly beautiful, even with the gray wig," Lehman said, which left them in a quandary about how to age Elizabeth by fifteen years.

The task of muting Taylor's glamour seemed impossible. At rehearsal the next day, Elizabeth was wearing a yellow linen dress, with a matching linen hat and matching high heels, her star power emanating whether she was even aware of it or not. Ernie, always sensitive to the way he was being treated, noted that Elizabeth waved to him once in the morning, but did not speak to him all day. "The only time she flashed me a look was when she was complaining to Mike Nichols that her contract stipulated that she did not have to report for work earlier than 10 AM." Mike politely countered that her contract specifically required her to be there at nine A.M., and she turned to glare at Lehman. "I'm beginning to think that when she looks at me, she not only sees me as a producer, but as all the producers she has ever had in her long career," he wrote.

By midweek, the good cheer was wearing off and the enormity of the work ahead loomed large for everyone. For Mike, who assumed the weight and the responsibility more than anyone else, it felt like a monumental undertaking. No better description of what Mike was trying to do exists than his own explanation during rehearsals to a young Mel Gussow, who was on assignment for *Newsweek*. "My job is not to say that Albee did such and such and I'm going to *fix* it, but, rather, to make [his play] as clear as possible, as real as possible," Nichols said. "Such a man [as Albee] when he writes knows exactly what he's doing. My job is to say: Let me see if I understand what he did. Let me see what happens. The material is the most exciting thing. I've taken a very improvisational approach, not to the words, but to events, to the things that happen as we are telling that story."

In 1965, the growing influence of Albee's voice was resonant in universities throughout the country. *The Sandbox, The Zoo Story*, and *The American Dream* were each presented in more productions that year than any individual Shakespeare play. His voice had struck a universal frequency that was picked up by theater critics, magazine editors, New York audiences, and college professors and students alike. *Virginia Woolf* had been such a success on Broadway that in 1963 *Newsweek*—then a national arbiter of cultural importance and viability—had put Albee on the cover. By 1965, he was a Great American Playwright.

Nichols believed that *Who's Afraid of Virginia Woolf?* was a large enough story to summon any number of interpretations. He recalled that Albee himself at one point said it was the story of the decline of the West. By staging an evening-long argument between an over-the-hill history professor and an ambitious young biology professor, Nichols thought, Albee was concluding that history is powerless. Mike cited another interpretation from an acquaintance, the economist John Kenneth Galbraith, who saw *Virginia Woolf* as a story of academic failure. "I know the man," Galbraith said, referring to George. "He's never been published." Nichols's own description was "a story of two people who are so locked together that each suffers what the other has not become," he said. He described a husband and wife who keep peeling away the illusions by mercilessly telling each other the truth, and when the final layer is peeled away, "they *love* each other. They're living the truth. They can take it." For Nichols, the responsibility of rendering the play on film with this integrity of emotional truth and all the blood and guts, while also giving it popular appeal, felt like a high-wire balancing act that left him reeling.

Lehman, who strived to maintain his equanimity at all costs, worried more about being the target of Nichols's displaced anxieties than he did about any other obstacle that might throw off the steady course of the production. When, on the morning of the fourth day, Mike said that he would prefer it if Ernie was not on set during rehearsal, Ernie didn't fight him in the moment. But he reasoned to himself that, in order to cut the script by another twenty minutes, he had to sit in on rehearsals to hear the actors reading the lines. After lunch he paid a visit to Jack

Warner, seeking his advice. "I don't want to upset Mike if my presence on the set is distracting to him," Ernie explained, "although I don't know exactly why he doesn't want me there." Warner considered it an insult to Lehman. He said that the producer-screenwriter has every right to be on the set, whether the director likes it or not. Lehman thanked Warner for the clarity and assured him that he would remedy the issue himself.

Meanwhile, Warner took the moment with Lehman to bring up another problem. After looking over the script, Warner noted the "many, many words" that would not pass the industry censors' tough decency bar. Warner had already been in touch with the Motion Picture Association of America, whose production code for obscene language and illicit behavior on-screen was strict and unforgiving. In response to the second *Virginia Woolf* screenplay Warner had sent to the MPAA, Geoffrey Shurlock, the director of the production code, wrote: "We note that it still contains a good deal of the profanity, the blunt sexual references, and the coarse and sometimes vulgar language which we noted in the original playscript when we first commented on it."

Joseph I. Breen, Shurlock's predecessor, and the original "censor," set the tone of the production code—known as the "Hays Code" in honor of politico Will Hays, who established the rating system. Breen could be so strict in enforcing the code that, sometimes, the replaced language completely obscured the meaning of a scene. In 1951, he cautioned George Stevens about the dialogue in *A Place in the Sun*. In the script, Alice, played by Shelley Winters, visits her doctor. Her line had been: "Doctor, you've got to help me." She was seeking an abortion, but the subject was so taboo that the line was changed to the more generic and anodyne "Somebody's got to help me."

The MPAA was not the only hurdle. The film had to pass the decency standards of the National Catholic Office for Motion Pictures (formerly the Legion of Decency), as well. Warner's goal was to receive an A-4 rating for the film from the Catholic office, meaning that the film was "morally unobjectionable for adults, with reservations." That would enable the film's distribution in movie theater chains throughout the country.

Lehman confessed to Warner that after having several discussions with Nichols about the off-color language, Mike was "reluctant to shoot any protection shots or loop any words which might be slipped in later if the censors made us cut out what we had." Nichols knew that the studio would err on the side of caution and opt for the protection coverage, but he refused to compromise the authenticity of the original play. "Why wouldn't we want to protect ourselves?" Warner asked rhetorically, calling his secretary in on the spot to set up an official meeting with Ernie, Mike, the studio attorney, and the head of publicity to avert this "inevitable disaster." Lehman left Warner's office feeling a bit saner, as his sense of reality was confirmed, but, equally, with gnawing guilt for ratting out his comrade-in-arms. He did not want to alienate Nichols, whose power over him was his own private tyranny to bear. Still, he was not one to tolerate Nichols's imperious demands for long.

The first week was not yet out when, after rehearsal, Mike found Ernie in his office, closed the door, and let down his guard. He was certain that Burton could play himself and seem very much like George; Dennis was splendid all day, and she could simply play herself and be right for Honey; and Segal could play himself and be an ideal Nick. But Elizabeth, he agonized, could not play herself and be anything remotely like Martha. He grumbled about the amount of work required to transform her into her character, and how carefully he had to tread around her. He knew it embarrassed Elizabeth to be told how to do her lines, yet he needed to convince her to keep lowering the pitch of her voice to make her a believable, willful, forty-eight-year-old Martha.

What compounded the problem was that Taylor was so enthusiastic about the process of rehearsing, perhaps because it was still a novelty for her. What Lehman missed that day, according to Nichols, were the cracks in the "Dick and Liz" patina that surfaced at the table during the reading. Burton, acting like a drama coach and, at times, assuming a directorial tone, didn't hesitate to upbraid Elizabeth as she read her lines. He admonished her about the pitch of her voice, or accused her of not understanding a transition, or berated her for misreading the emotion required to carry this or that line. "They had a real student-teacher relationship," Segal later said, citing Burton's penchant for being elegantly, if theatrically, pedantic. "He had her reciting e.e. cummings and Dylan Thomas."

It was sometimes hard for the others in the room, including Nichols, to tell if they were witnessing the actors getting into character or simply watching the husband-and-wife dynamics of the Burtons' real-life marriage. Burton could deride Taylor's performance in front of the others to the point that she would storm out in tears. "It was very cathartic," Elizabeth later said, philosophically. "We would get all our shouting and brawling out on the set and then go home and cuddle." That might have been true some of the time, but, in fact, they fought both on and off the set. "Richard loses his temper with true enjoyment. It's beautiful to watch," she said on another occasion. "Our fights are delightful screaming matches, and Richard is rather like a small atom bomb going off." This behavior predated *Virginia Woolf.* A friend remembered the couple returning to their hotel suite at the Regency in London a year or so after they met, "reverting to their favorite pastimes, fighting and having sex. Or having sex and fighting." This friend described Taylor's wrath as she stormed about "with smeared makeup, her voice loud and shrill.'" Still, while their marital brawls happened in real time, Nichols lived with the fear that he would not be able to extract pure gin, so to speak, from milk and cocoa.

By Friday of that first week, Elizabeth's good behavior finally erupted into rage. She let the full force of her inner Martha out everywhere but in the actual read-through. As Lehman would often write in his journal, "her eyes flared" in anger more than a few times that day. First, after the premiere of *The Sandpiper,* the Burtons were disheartened enough about the film to call it a "pile of crap." That Friday morning, reading one review that claimed Taylor had given the best performance of her career, she became livid and cursed the reviewer all day long, spewing his name and threatening to sue him for libel. At the same time, she lumped her agent, Hugh French, into her molten fury, threatening to fire him because he had failed to stipulate in her contract a ten A.M. starting time on the *Virginia Woolf* set.

After lunch, a new tantrum was brewing in anticipation of being fully "made up" as Martha for the first time. Elizabeth was scheduled for full hair and makeup before trying on the various dresses that Sharaff had assembled for Martha's wardrobe. Taylor started complaining about her exhaustion from the rehearsals; then she was tired of being forced to lower her voice and to project from the diaphragm. Then, her resistance to being made up took a gothic turn as she tried to renegotiate Martha's age. "Martha could just as easily be thirty-three years old," she insinuated. Clearly, she was insecure about playing such a daunting character after feeling so degraded by the praise about her performance as a free-spirited bohemian artist in *The Sandpiper*, which she found ludicrous.

Nichols's fears that her youth and celebrity would overshadow her ability to meet the challenge of playing Martha were coming true. She had never played someone as old, never mind someone so complex. She could not possibly know what Martha's *age* felt like, what it was like to be seen as past one's prime. Taylor did not have a clue about being anything less than otherworldly beautiful and could not imagine the day when her own beauty would fade. And yet she herself understood that her superstardom was a force at odds with her ambition to play a serious role like Martha.

It was the middle of the swinging 1960s, and a new female archetype was emerging in Hollywood. "Elizabeth Taylor's lush, glossy beauty and her increasingly voluptuous figure made her unsuited to play the newly emerging American woman," write Sam Kashner and Nancy Schoenberger. On the cusp of the sexual revolution, with guilt-free experimentation and an evolving androgyny, the spirit of the age was embodied by a new crop of leaner, younger actresses—Julie Christie, Vanessa Redgrave, and Jane Fonda. "Elizabeth may have helped usher in that seismic shift in the sexual landscape, but by the age of thirty-three, with five marriages, four children, thirty-one films, and world infamy behind her, she simply had too much history to play a new woman." Playing Martha was her ultimate gambit, although nobody at the time knew how brilliant a career choice it would turn out to be. Instead, she was suffering the growing pains of an overwhelmingly ambitious role and taking it out on everyone around her. According to Joseph Mankiewicz, who directed Elizabeth in both *Suddenly Last Summer* and *Cleopatra*, she engaged in "a kind of reverse method acting, in which she drew on her theatrical roles to provide direction and add luster to her real life. . . . she was the reverse of most other stars . . . for her living life was a kind of acting."

No one indulged her wild delusion about playing Martha as a thirty-three-year-old. Reluctantly, she proceeded to the makeup department. After an hour, she was escorted in full makeup to her dressing room, where Guilaroff and Sharaff were waiting. They began to assemble Martha—first the wig and then the charcoal suede dress. When Lehman showed up, he acknowledged that the effect was remarkable: Elizabeth looked every bit like a frustrated, middle-aged, unhappy woman. Lehman observed that she had really been drinking too much, which added to her irritable behavior. She got angry that Mike wasn't there yet; when he arrived, he saw her in the charcoal dress, then a black wool dress. At that moment, in full costume, cantankerous and disillusioned, she seemed to be channeling Martha herself, and Nichols and Lehman were delighted. Finally, one hurdle had been overcome. Still, Lehman ended his account of the day in his journal at a stoical remove. "Well, *Who's Afraid of Virginia Woolf?* is not exactly a happy picture," he wrote at the end of week one. "And, with almost two weeks of rehearsal to go, we have a rather discontented bunch, and I suppose that includes everyone."

~

During the second week, rehearsal moved from the table on Stage Two to the set of George and Martha's house on Stage Eight. Again, Lehman marveled at Richard Sylbert's perfectly constructed facsimile of the house they had chosen on the Smith College campus. "That old house contained a few faculty offices, including that of my senior thesis advisor," Gloria Steinem remembered, "so I knew its exterior would be perfect—including a swing hung from a tree in its yard." Elizabeth had never rehearsed with the script in her hand the way Richard, George, and Sandy, experienced stage actors, were used to rehearsing, and she was still tentative when speaking her lines. Every few minutes, Richard would reassure her, walking over, squeezing her shoulder, giving her a little kiss. Lehman reported that Nichols could be very impressive as a director, talking the actors through their lines and showing them how he wanted things done. He would step into the role himself and become the character to make a point. "Mike would play all four roles and, I must say, he plays each role much better than I have so far seen the roles played by the cast. He is particularly great as Honey."

While Burton knew Nichols quite well by then, he had never seen him in action as a director. "He had an intuitive grasp of the microsociology of personal interactions, as a director ought to have," Burton would later say of Nichols. "He picked up the cues almost before they had been delivered. Most people aren't that fast."

Mike moved the actors around the rooms of the set. In the first few scenes, he had Elizabeth and Richard speaking their lines from the very top as they walked through the front door. "Jesus H. Christ," Elizabeth said, and he encouraged her to spit out the line as if in an exasperated sneer, as she stumbled into the house. "Martha, *Shhh*, for Chrissake, it's 2 o'clock in the morning," Richard hissed back, closing the door behind them. "Oh, George, what a *cluck* you are," she said. Mike told her to say that line while reaching for the lamp and turning on the light. He thought she should shake off her coat and throw it on the couch. Then he assumed her role, surveying the casual disarray of the living room with his hands on his hips, and looking around before delivering

Mrs. Frankie Albee and six-year-old Edward walking in Palm Beach, Florida, 1934.

Top: Albee with William Flanagan, his lover and mentor in the 1950s.

Center: Albee with Terrence McNally during their romantic idyll on Fire Island while he was writing *Virginia Woolf.*

Bottom: At the 1963 Tony Awards, from left: Edward Albee, Richard Barr, Alan Schneider, Clinton Wilder, Uta Hagen, and Arthur Hill.

The first Broadway production of *Virginia Woolf* with, from left, George Grizzard, Arthur Hill, Melinda Dillon, and Uta Hagen.

A scene from the film with Elizabeth Taylor, George Segal, Richard Burton, and Sandy Dennis.

Willard Maas and Marie Menken, the couple Albee used as models for the characters George and Martha.

Taylor and Burton, who play the screen version of George and Martha, during the rehearsal phase of *Virginia Woolf* at Warner Brothers.

Top: Nichols setting up the kitchen scene with Taylor and Burton; Haskell Wexler kneeling.

Left: Scene from the film as Martha delivers the line "She's discontent."

Right: George looking in the fridge while Haskell Wexler does a lighting check.

Top: Taylor and Burton in their roles as George and Martha.

Left: The thirty-two-year-old Taylor before getting into costume as the forty-eight-year-old Martha.

Bottom: George and Martha posing for press pictures on the bedroom set.

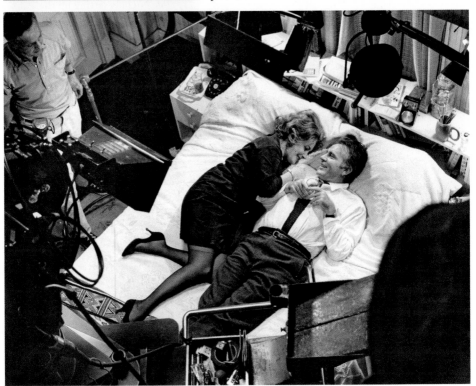

A moment of levity on the set with Ernest Lehman (left), Nichols, and Taylor.

Above: Nichols talking Taylor through a scene before shooting.

Right: Taylor getting into costume as Martha.

Top: The guests arrive: Sandy Dennis as Honey and George Segal as Nick.

Right: Martha has changed into something more seductive— her "Sunday chapel dress," as George observes.

Bottom: Honey senses that Nick has become Martha's prey for the evening.

Mike Nichols discussing a scene with George Segal as Nick.

Above: Nichols fretting, as he was known to do.

Right: Lehman and Nichols playing Anagrams, a favorite pastime while waiting for the Burtons to arrive on the set.

A tense moment between
Nichols, the director, and
Lehman, the producer.

Lehman, Segal, and Nichols on the chartered flight to Northampton, Massachusetts, described as a party in the sky.

Jack Warner, the studio head, in
a rare appearance on set, with
Nichols.

Sam O'Steen, the film editor, syncing film and sound reels under Nichols's watchful eye.

Nichols talking Burton through the parking lot scene at the Red Basket outside Northampton.

Nichols conferring with Wexler about a lighting issue on the living room set.

Top: Taylor and Burton hamming it up with Martha's wig.

Right: Taylor, the gorgeous young movie star, talks to a reporter at the fish fry she and Burton threw for the cast and crew in Northampton.

Bottom: Taylor with Gloria Dickson, her double as Martha, in the parking lot of the Red Basket outside Northampton.

Top: The facsimile of George and Martha's house constructed by Richard Sylbert on Stage Eight at Warner Brothers.

Left: George and Nick on location in Northampton, waiting to shoot the "bergin" speech.

Bottom: The Tyler Annex on the Smith College campus was used as George and Martha's house for the opening scene of the movie.

Top: Nichols demonstrating how George should choke Martha for a scene at the roadside tavern.

Right: The choking scene, where Nick pulls George off of Martha.

Bottom: The ensemble between scenes at the roadhouse tavern.

Left: Nichols suggesting to Taylor how to curtsy when George gives her the flowers.

Below left: The scene where Martha curtsies.

Bottom: The ensemble in the living room just before the final scenes.

George and Martha in the last scene of the film, shot by Haskell Wexler, foreground.

the opening salvo: "What a dump!" He wanted her to issue this sorry appraisal with her whole physicality. Then, a glimmer of amusement should animate her face as she swings around to George. "Hey," she blurts out, poking him, "What's that from?" She repeats the phrase with the exacting elocution of Bette Davis—"WhaT a DumP"—and looks at him expectantly. "How would I know?" George says, turning away with an air of impatience and hanging up his coat.

Nichols had them walk into the kitchen, and he showed them where he imagined Elizabeth to be standing, and where Richard should be seated. He acknowledged that his directions would change according to how everything looked through the camera during the actual shooting, but he felt that it was important for them to familiarize themselves with the lines in the context of the set and the scenes. He believed that the actors should have something to do while delivering their lines, to ground them in believable reality. At one point, while Mike was explaining to Elizabeth that Martha should look in the refrigerator for something to eat, Richard wandered into the living room and picked up a copy of the *New York Times Magazine*, which had been put there as one of the props on the coffee table. Ernie was standing there, and Richard showed him a photograph of the sculptor Alberto Giacometti. "I can't believe a man with a face as beautiful as that could have been the great artist he is," Richard said. Ernie wondered aloud why he would arrive at such a conclusion. "I believe all great art comes from people who are either ugly or have a terrible inferiority complex," Burton said. "I know of no one who is beautiful and produces art." He acknowledged that Laurence Olivier, for example, was a great artist and, also, beautiful, but then described the great Olivier's terrible inferiority complex: he never liked to play a role unless he could put on something that would modify his looks. Lehman wasn't sure what to make of the conversation, other than to think Burton was confessing his own insecurity, doubting his own greatness because of his rugged good looks. Or was he hinting that his wife was simply too beautiful ever to be Martha?

During that second week of rehearsal, the publicity department had arranged a morning photography session for the press, with the understanding that these were the only pictures that would be taken during the entire production. Outside the set, sixty press photographers from all over the world waited to be let in for one hour. Before they opened the doors, Elizabeth, in a lemon-yellow linen sheath, her dark hair long and straight, her jewelry twinkling, walked up to Lehman and batted her lilac eyes. "Listen, Ernie, you must be sure to tell them that you and Mike have ordered me to get fat for this picture." She didn't want them to think that she was overweight and sloppy simply because she didn't know any better. She wanted to make sure that Ernie and Mike would mention it whenever they talked to the press. "I want you to tell them I was ordered to stuff myself and drink malted milk shakes between meals—for the realism of the role."

As the photographers were let in, everyone started posing, and they fired away. The cast, slightly embarrassed by the whole thing as a group, started clowning around. Mike "staged" a scene in which Burton-as-George is lying on his back on the bed. At first Mike was going to have Elizabeth-as-Martha sit astride Burton, as she would do in the picture, but Lehman warned that it would look bad in the newspapers. Everyone would think they were making a "dirty" film, so she sat alongside him on the bed. It became one of the most widely published pictures of the production. After an hour, the photographers were chased off the stage, and the cast then proceeded with the rehearsal. Later, the publicity department at Warner Brothers gave each of them a bottle of liquor for their cooperation.

Later that week, Lehman and Nichols trudged off to Jack Warner's office for the dreaded meeting about the off-color language in the script. Warner had marked every problematic word, telling them what he thought would get past the Decency Code and what would not fly. "On practically every point Mike fought him effectively," Lehman wrote. "I would say that in the entire script, about all we gave up were two 'Jesus Christs' and one 'God damn.' They were about to leave when

Warner surprised them with an issue they thought had been resolved. Benny Kalmenson, the vice president of Warner Brothers, who lived in New York, had called Warner to explain that many exhibitors back East—that is, the movie theater chains—were asking for *Who's Afraid of Virginia Woolf?* on a "roadshow basis," or limited theater release. "Benny thinks that, under these circumstances, we should do the picture in color," Warner announced.

Lehman and Nichols were shocked. They thought they had won this battle a month ago. Worse yet, screen tests were beginning the next morning. Mike explained all over again that the entire picture takes place at night, and it would be very difficult to shoot it effectively in color. All the costumes had been designed for black and white; Elizabeth's gray wig and her special makeup would look phony in color. All the sharpness and bite and power of the drama would vanish if the picture were done in color. "I simply will not do the picture in color," Mike then asserted, emphatically. "We will be destroyed by the critics. The picture would seem sort of obscene in color."

In the silence that followed, Nichols and Lehman were visibly shaken. "Look," Warner said. "Forget about it. Don't worry about it. Shoot the test tomorrow in black and white and we've got enough ammunition to change Benny Kalmenson's mind. I'll take care of it." As they were leaving, Mike said, "Can I relax now? It is in black and white, isn't it?" And Warner, with all the assurance of a Hollywood studio head, said, "Yes sure, don't worry. We'll look at the results of the test on Friday and then we'll talk further."

Mike was so perturbed that he followed Ernie into his office and shut the door. He wanted to have a heart-to-heart talk. He expressed his exhaustion at having to defend their vision for this picture all on his own and told Ernie that he had to step up too—even if it meant wrangling with Mike if they didn't see eye to eye. "I agreed that I had stopped fighting a lot of battles," Lehman wrote, "but I pointed out that it was due, in part, to Mike's insistence on taking over himself, that he had taken away a good deal of my authority and that he was now paying the price for having done that." Mike acknowledged that to be true, claiming that he had felt like a child who was looking for Daddy; because Daddy was not there, he was trying to assume that paternal role himself. "From now on," Mike said, "I expect you to fight Elizabeth, fight Richard, fight Jack Warner, fight Harry Stradling, and fight *me*—Mike Nichols, if necessary, but, at any rate, just please fight."

Mike then turned the conversation to Stradling, the cinematographer. It was the eve of the first screen tests to shoot the actors in costume and to check the lighting on the set. The tensions between Nichols and Stradling had been escalating. It might have begun with the simple fact that Warner Brothers had hired him as the cinematographer for *Who's Afraid of Virginia Woolf?* before Mike was even attached to the movie. But the generational divide between them and the clash of personalities— never mind their conflicting sensibilities—did not help. Stradling had not done himself any favors by calling Fellini's *8½* "a piece of shit" after Mike screened it as an example of the kind of filmmaking he admired. And Stradling had lost Mike's trust altogether when he suggested that they shoot the film in color and print it in black and white, thus showing his hand in favor of Jack Warner at the expense of the film itself.

Nichols had major misgivings about Stradling. He could neither communicate with his own cinematographer nor trust him to do what he wanted. He was sure that Harry was more concerned about having Elizabeth look the way Jack Warner wanted her to look than the way Mike Nichols wanted her to look. "Oh, Ernie, isn't there some way you can make Harry Stradling like me?" Mike bemoaned. Lehman suggested that they wait to see the tests before passing any judgment on Stradling's loyalty. "Once again, I think it is a case of Mike being comfortable only with *his* kind of people," Lehman later concluded in the journal entry. "Harry is an old pro. Mike likes them young and hip."

The next day, they started shooting wardrobe and makeup tests. Mike was not happy with the tweed suits selected for Burton and sent Sharaff on a mission to find something with more of a rumpled professorial look. There was talk of bleaching Segal's hair and tinting it for a more blond look, but Segal got wind of the conversation and, literally, fell to the floor in a mock tantrum, refusing to allow it. Dennis, wearing no makeup at all, was given a squirrel coat to wear over her "mousy blue dress." Mike asked to have her eyes made up and to add a subtle bit of lipstick. Finally, Elizabeth appeared with her "middle-aged makeup" and graying hair. "Mike and I looked at each other in some dismay," Lehman said. "She's the greatest looking middle-aged lady we had ever seen." Mike asked Elizabeth to please allow them to put some rubber appliances underneath her eyes to give her the effect of bags and she absolutely refused. Every time they looked at her in front of the camera, she appeared too glamorous and too beautiful. Someone told Mike that Elizabeth didn't like Gordon Bau (the head of the makeup department at Warner Brothers, who had been doing her special makeup). Nichols was afraid that it meant they would have less control over the way she looked. After lunch, Mike was even more depressed: Elizabeth had been fooling around with her own makeup and still succeeded in looking nothing like Martha.

When they saw the tests the next day, Mike felt that Stradling had not given them the harsh black and white lighting he had asked for. On top of that, Elizabeth definitely did not look old enough. Mike suggested more makeup tests for her—one test in which she would make herself up exactly the way she wanted to look, and another test in which she let Bau make her up exactly the way *they* wanted her to look. In the tests, Richard looked much too strong in his scene. Segal's hair had to be lightened. And Dennis looked four months pregnant. In part, they blamed it on the dress that Sharaff designed for her, but the truth was that Dennis's stomach protruded. They asked her to wear a girdle, but she refused, promising to lose ten pounds in the few weeks before shooting began. The tests were disconcerting, as if Nichols were confronted all over again with the enormity of the mountain he needed to scale.

$\sim$

Lehman was worried about Dennis. A friend who had just had lunch with her told him Sandy felt that Nichols had never really wanted her to play the role of Honey and had as much as conveyed that to her. She claimed that it didn't bother her, though, because she intended to work hard and prove to him that anyone else in the role would have been wrong. Lehman asked Mike if he disliked Sandy, wondering aloud if that might be the reason that she was not giving a strong performance, and he balked. But then, not twenty minutes later, he became critical of her and her performance, and Ernie pointed out that maybe he was unaware of his effect on her. He suggested that Mike make a more concerted effort to bolster her confidence.

Soon after that, Lehman had lunch with Segal, who complained that Dennis's listless performance during rehearsal made it difficult for him to play his own role. He was being handicapped. Yet Segal acknowledged that when it came time to shoot the film, she would very likely give a performance that would steal the scene. Then he made Ernie promise not to say anything to Mike or to Sandy. A day or so later, Nichols told Lehman that he was thrilled with the rehearsals. When asked about Dennis, Mike said that he wasn't worried. "I guarantee you that when the time comes, I will make her give the performance."

After the first screen tests, Mike complained to Elizabeth that he was unhappy with Stradling's work. Unfortunately, Agnes Flanagan, the hairdresser, was in immediate earshot. She was married to Frank Flanagan, the head grip, who was a close friend of Stradling. Mike realized his indiscretion and recounted it to Ernie, then complained that he was sure Stradling didn't like him and would never provide the kind of photography he wanted. Once again, Mike claimed that Harry was in cahoots with Jack Warner, and avowed that he couldn't work in such hostile conditions. Would Lehman do something about it?

Lehman summoned Stradling to his office. The cinematographer was emphatic about his allegiance to Jack Warner, Elizabeth Taylor, and Warner Brothers, and disagreed with what Lehman and Nichols wanted as a photographic style for *Virginia Woolf*. When Lehman reiterated that they wanted a harsh, realistic black-and-white type of photography, Stradling countered, "Yes, but are you worried at all about what the public might want?" This confirmed what Nichols had been complaining about all along, and Lehman concluded that Stradling's lack of creative loyalty was detrimental to the picture. Later, Lehman conveyed the conversation to Mike, who was grateful for the clarity, but disheartened, nonetheless. Leaving Ernie's office, Mike saw Stradling huddled together with Frank Flanagan. When they saw Mike, they walked away.

Two days before shooting was to begin, after the final set of tests came back from the lab, the first major crisis of the production blew up. The scenes, shot with sound for the first time, were either badly lit or overlighted. Stradling was the first to see them and went immediately to the Burtons. If this was the kind of picture that Nichols wanted to shoot, he said, then he didn't want to have anything to do with it.

Lehman gathered Mike, Stradling, the production manager Hal Polaire, the assistant director Buck Hall, and the production designer Dick Sylbert into a screening room to watch the tests. It was obvious to everyone that they were badly lit. No one liked them less than Mike. But before the director could speak, Stradling got up belligerently and lashed into him. "If that's the kind of picture you want to make, if that's the kind of lighting you want, I don't want to have my name on the picture," he bellowed. "I have a reputation and I intend to keep it. I don't want to do a picture like that." Mike stood up and shouted back: "Harry, you haven't even asked me what I think of these tests. First, they were only experiments. . . . I hate these tests as much as you do, but you didn't even wait to find out what I think of them. You assumed that I liked these tests without even asking me. You went to the Burtons and told them that I would like these tests before you even found out how I feel about them."

Stradling backed down a little. "Look, I had a heart attack a few years ago," he said, as if to wave a white flag. "I don't need this kind of trouble. I don't think you and I are ever going to agree on how this picture should look and, frankly, I don't want to shoot this picture unless I can do it my way. I think I know enough about how to make pictures and I want you to let me shoot it the way I think it should be shot. But, if you don't want do it that way, then I'll just get off the picture."

Lehman, proving that he was willing to protect Nichols when it was called for, rose to the occasion and defended him. "Harry, it would be an untenable position for Mike as a director not to be able to tell his cameraman how he wanted things to look." Lehman suggested that a parting of the ways might be the best outcome. The meeting broke up, and Lehman called Warner, explaining that there was a crisis, and he and Mike needed to see him immediately. When they laid out the situation for Warner, he agreed that it was impossible to make a picture under these conditions. Warner knew that Stradling had been unhappy about things and agreed to let him quit. Lehman assured Nichols that he was right to take a stand and assume his authority over the photography of the picture. They should get somebody else. Years later, Nichols would remember Stradling's departure from the production differently, as an even more fractious event. Recounting the way Stradling had done Jack Warner's bidding by trying to convince him to shoot the film in color and print it in black and white, Nichols claimed to have said, "Oh, Harry, I'm so sorry. I have to fire you." Lehman's account, written in real time, would put Stradling's resignation several weeks after that, though, after rehearsal had begun.

Nichols had wanted Haskell Wexler all along. Now, when Walter McEwen, head of production at Warner Brothers, mentioned Wexler's name at the same moment Mike did, it only confirmed the choice for all involved. The only wrinkle was that Wexler was set to shoot *A Fine Madness*, with Irvin Kershner as director and Jerry Hellman as producer, also for Warner Brothers. It took some serious negotiating to convince them that extricating Wexler for *Who's Afraid of Virginia Woolf?* was a priority for the studio. "We have Wexler," Lehman was finally able to tell Nichols late, late the following evening. There was no time to waste. Shooting was to begin in three days, on Monday, July 23.

That Friday night at six P.M., Warner summoned Lehman and Nichols for another meeting. He wanted them to shoot color tests over the weekend, along with those in black and white. Mike and Ernie could hardly believe what they were hearing. The scene turned ugly. Mike insisted that there was no sense in shooting a test in color. He would not shoot the picture in color. At this point, Warner rose to his feet. "If I wanted to, I could simply order the picture in color, but I'm not that kind of fellow." In a moment of desperation, Mike invoked the Burtons. "They had come into this picture on the express understanding that it would be shot in black and white." Warner got nervous whenever the Burtons were mentioned, and this gave him pause. "I wonder if I can find Benny Kalmenson on the phone, because, after all, fellows, I'm on your side. You know I want this picture to be in black and white, and I have to find a way to convince Benny." Kalmenson, Jack Warner's right-hand man, was a strict numbers guy who spoke in pure, bottom-line terms. Warner reached him at home in New York. Initially, Warner couldn't budge him. He handed the phone to Nichols, but Nichols pointed to Lehman.

Lehman told Benny that there were many good reasons why they could not shoot the picture in color, but Benny stopped him. "You could talk for 4000 years and never change my mind," Benny countered. "Anybody who does the picture in black and white today is setting back the motion picture business 20 years." Lehman handed the phone back to Warner, who repeated Nichols's argument that the Burtons had agreed to do the picture with the understanding that it would be in black and white. "We could upset the whole applecart if we made a fuss over this," Warner said. The tide seemed to turn, and now Warner was assuring Benny it would be a great picture in black and white. The battle had been won by the Burtons in absentia.

Before hanging up, Kalmenson asked to speak to Lehman. He wanted to make sure there were no hard feelings. "I'm not mad at you," said Ernie. "I understand your point of view. I just hope you understand ours." Benny said, "Look, I don't even know the subject matter of your picture." What a revelation for Ernie! All along, Kalmenson had approached the issue from a business standpoint with no regard for the picture itself. "Benny, our picture is going to be in black and white but it's going to be like a rocket when you get it," Lehman said. "It will explode in your hands, so don't worry about the fact that it isn't in color," at which point Benny said, "OK, Ernie, just don't be mad at me."

After the call, Warner apologized for having caused all the trouble. "It wasn't my fault, it was Benny's," the head of Warner Brothers said. He hoped it had not upset Mike too much. Mike looked bewildered. "Wait a minute," he said. "What just happened here? Am I to understand now that we are going to do the picture in black and white, that I don't have to worry anymore about this color business?" Warner said, "Yes, the film will be in black and white." Lehman, with George Burns–like deadpan clarity, concluded in his journal: "What upset Mike the most was the realization that it wasn't his threat to quit the picture that turned the tide, but, rather, the invocation of the Burtons."

Chapter 8

The Art of Filmmaking

My father basically had two ways of judging anything—
whether something was poetic, or it wasn't.

—Bernardo Bertolucci

Mike Nichols may have given the impression of being an arriviste luxuriating as a Hollywood grandee. But the glare of his larger-than-life existence obscured the more subtle refinements of his native sensibility. He was an aesthete, wanting everything in his life to match the level of his *taste*. "He always lived like a prince," Candice Bergen observed. "I don't know where that came from. But he was more princely than anyone I ever knew." In fact, after he died, Annabel Davis-Goff, his third wife, marveled at the quality of his discernment: "Anything he did, he did well. There was his ludicrous preoccupation with Arab horses," which, she explained, he bought, raced, and bred over the years. "He knew the Polish stud book by heart, in Polish. . . . He did the same thing with paintings. I think he was really good at that, paintings that he bought and collected. He had some particularly nice Hockneys, a pretty good Lucien Freud, the Gericault above the fireplace, the Matisse and his Picassos." At Nichols's palatial Cole Porter estate, for instance,

Mr. and Mrs. André Previn would become regular dinner guests. Nichols might accompany the celebrated composer at the piano in a four-hand version of a Beethoven sonata. Then, sitting alone at the keys, Nichols would think nothing of tinkling out part of a Chopin nocturne or a Bach polonaise—"just enough to sound like someone who can play and then gives up because he's bored," he told a reporter. Nichols knew enough about music, but he was not a musician. Imagine, then, the cheeky thrill he got as an amateur performing a duet with the renowned Previn at his own dinner parties—and then getting to gloat about it to Ernest Lehman afterward.

Nichols liked to wield his self-importance (at times to obnoxious effect) partly because he felt perpetual disbelief at his ongoing good fortune. His introduction to that social stratosphere had begun only five years earlier with his best friend, Richard Avedon, who, Nichols acknowledged, had "taught him how to be a rich person." Avedon's tutorial introduced him to rare culinary delicacies, the restaurants that served them, and the correct way to order them. He showed Nichols how to dress and where to shop, where to vacation and how to travel there. Through Avedon, he accessed New York's inner sanctum of wealthy, famous, and accomplished people. If Mike felt intimidated by any of them, "just ask them about themselves and they don't stop talking," Avedon advised. Once, a friend invited Mike to come along to Leonard Bernstein's one Saturday night, and he balked. "*That* crowd?" he said in a panic. But then, Avedon remembered Mike "dominating the whole crowd. He became necessary to all of them. He was an outsider, and he became an insider."

The waters kept parting for Nichols because, as he went about garnering his own notoriety, others detected that he *knew* something. He could charm people with anecdotes that were wry and always apropos of the moment, and he could make them laugh at his mock self-deprecation. He was uniquely talented as a performer and, more recently, as a stage director. He worked hard, while often complaining that he didn't know what he was doing. In fact, he was exacting to the core. "Nichols, at really astounding speed, found his way as a movie director," Lehman told a reporter during the first few weeks of shooting. "I had some apprehension about Mike, for his sake. But he's cool. He knows what he's doing." Around the Warner Brothers studio and on the set, Nichols's determination to make a great film set the tone, his expectation so contagious that it kept everyone on the production at an almost impossible pitch of anxiety.

～

Nichols believed that *Who's Afraid of Virginia Woolf?* reflected not only the depths of his own experience but also larger truths about human nature. "My job is not to *fix* what Albee wrote, but to reveal it," he would say, which is why he was stealthily stripping Lehman's screenplay back to Albee's original script. After the film came out, Albee scoffed about Lehman's screenwriting credit. Aside from almost an hour of dialogue excised from the play for the sake of the movie's length, and two additional sequences—late-night dancing at a local roadhouse, and the scene at the swing under a tree out on the lawn—"every line in the film is my play fucking word for word," Albee declared to Mel Gussow, his biographer. Nichols's refusal to abandon the incendiary dialogue revealed as much about his regard for the original script as it did his épater les bourgeois tendencies. He became a custodian of the play's integrity. His dogged resistance to shooting the film in color also speaks to his fidelity to the material. Finally, Nichols understood that, while *Who's Afraid of Virginia Woolf?* is about *a* marriage, it is also about *marriage*—a structural foundation of nearly every society on earth. He was intent on seeing past the spectacle of George and Martha's drunken behavior to uncover the truths that resonate through every marriage—including his own.

At thirty-three, Nichols had been married—and divorced—twice. He met his first wife, Patricia Scot, in Chicago in 1956. She was a jazz club singer and host of a nightly TV show about cultural goings-on about town. She came to see Nichols and Elaine May one night at the

Compass Theater after their improvisational skits began attracting local attention. Pat was a former model, and it puzzled everyone at the Compass when Mike, a misfit by all accounts, started dating so glamorous a personality. Pat's picture appeared on billboards, and she lived in a fancy apartment—"wall-to-wall carpeting and an Eames chair"—while Nichols and his cohort lived in bohemian squalor. Mike and Pat soon got married, but their relationship was troubled from the start. "I was not in his league intellectually," she told Mark Harris, Nichols's biographer. "I was this little girl from Milwaukee, kind of from the sticks, who never went to college." Scot would later claim that Mike—the University of Chicago dropout who had attended the best private schools in New York—"was a snob, but a funny, brilliant snob."

Everyone assumed that Nichols's most significant relationship was the one he had with May, and it certainly felt that way to Pat. (She and May even bore an uncanny resemblance to each other.) Mike and Elaine worked together constantly, making each other laugh incessantly, and Pat felt like a third wheel "because of their twosome-ness," she said. "I was jealous. Elaine was incredibly beautiful, in that zaftig Jewish way. She was ripe. . . . If they had been having sex, which they weren't—maybe once but who cares—it would have been one thing, but they were so much closer than just sexual partners." When Nichols and May took their show to New York, Scot gave up her contract at the Chicago TV station, and she and Mike rented a duplex apartment on the Upper East Side. They bought some nice furniture, got a St. Bernard puppy, and tried to act like a married couple. But she acknowledged that she just couldn't keep up with him. He got bored. She got depressed. By 1960, they were divorced.

Several years later, he met the tall and stunning Margot Callas, who came with literary credentials: she had been the girlfriend of Robert Graves, the much older British poet, who called her his "muse," his "white goddess." Nichols was directing an out-of-town tryout of *Barefoot in the Park* at the time, and the entire company was dumbstruck when Margot first swept into their Bucks County rehearsal space. "Mike would bring people as presents for us to play with—interesting, fabulous people," said Elizabeth Ashley, who starred in the play, recalling on-set visitors such as Stephen Sondheim and Susan Sontag. "One of them was Margot. She was just earth-shatteringly beautiful. If I use the word 'trophy,' I don't intend it to be derisive. It was almost like a Scott Fitzgerald thing—the most beautiful woman and the smartest, most creative man." Callas and Nichols were married in 1963, but a year later, soon after Margot gave birth to their daughter, Daisy, she suddenly left him, taking the baby and moving to Europe permanently. Her departure was a mystery to all his friends. When Nichols was asked many years later how he knew that his marriage to Margot wasn't working, he answered, "when she pulled a knife on me." The claim may be apocryphal, but Nichols's sense of injury was real. The collapse of his first marriage had not embarrassed him, but to be twice divorced at thirty-two seemed like a profound defeat.

The initial intoxication of love and the electricity of sexual attraction that brings any couple together does not foretell the complexities of the marriage to follow, yet every long-married couple recognizes the entire tzimmes of "marriage" in the thumbnail glimpses of marital discord in others. In Sondheim's *Company*, one character is asked if he ever regrets getting married. "You're always sorry," he sings. "You're always grateful. You're always wondering what might have been. Then she walks in. And, still, you're sorry. And, still, you're grateful. And still you wonder. And still you doubt. And she goes out."

Nichols believed that what makes *Who's Afraid of Virginia Woolf?* so compelling is how the play volleys back and forth between George and Martha. Albee balanced the weight evenly between them, and as the focus shifts from one to the other, the audience is thrust into the role of a referee—or of a child witnessing a parental fight. Loyalty shifts: "I'm on her side. I'm on his side. I'm on her side," as Nichols once described it. He thought that the intensity of the volley depended on "who was playing the characters and how lovable each of the actors is," but also "on the power of the dialectic of the jokes." It did not escape

Nichols that fate had provided the most remarkable gift for him as a first-time director—his two stars, Elizabeth Taylor and Richard Burton, who were perfectly matched to each other in terms of charisma, and whose real-life marriage echoed that of George and Martha. If he could just extract performances from the core of their native attraction to each other, then, *then*, the crackling charge of their chemistry would add the kind of verisimilitude that could make the movie ignite the screen.

∼

The day that shooting finally began on *Virginia Woolf*—Monday, July 26, 1965—the occasion was marked with yet more gifts. Lehman sent two dozen white roses to Taylor's dressing room. Nichols gave her a bassinet for "the little bugger"—as the imaginary child is referred to in the play—filled with bottles of bourbon. The Burtons gave Mike a whip. And, as if everyone had read the same invisible book of protocol for Hollywood machers, Lehman received a bottle of champagne each from Freddy Fields, Dennis's agent, and Hugh French, the Burtons' agent.

The plan was to shoot as much of the movie in sequence as possible. Taylor and Burton arrived at ten A.M. on Stage Eight, where the facsimile of the house at Smith College had been built—the facade on one set, the interiors on another. Segal and Dennis did not need to be there, as their characters do not appear until fifteen minutes into the film. Elizabeth's hair-and-makeup transformation into Martha would take almost two hours—which was just as well, because there were delays on the set, first with lighting adjustments and then with the positioning of the cameras. Finally, Elizabeth's high heels clicked too loudly on the floor of the house, so rubber tips had to be found and fitted to her shoes to muffle the sound.

Cinematographer Haskell Wexler designed his own apparatus for shooting—a tall device in the manner of a wheelchair with two large bicycle wheels and a platform on which he could sit or stand at any height. There was only a half inch of clearance between the base of the platform and the floor so that he could step off the platform when it reached the limit of its mobility and continue to shoot while walking toward the subject with the camera. He used a 35 mm Eclair handheld camera equipped with a 24-to-240 mm Angénieux zoom lens.

~

Nichols did not start what would be his first "printed" take until after noon, beginning with a shot he had been imagining for months— George and Martha coming into the house through the front door. Wexler stood on the camera apparatus situated in the back of the foyer. "I want it to look like when you first come into your house from the dark and the light hurts your eyes," Nichols told Wexler. "I want it bright, bright, bright!" Wexler's instinct was to resist, because "I could just hear my fellow cinematographers saying: 'Aw—the so-and-so over-exposed it!' But I took the cue from Mike because I thought it was a good cue. I did overexpose the scene a full stop so that when they come in from the dark and throw the switch, the light really blasts."

Lehman and Nichols had dispensed with the play's first line, when Martha snarls "Jesus H. Christ" from behind the door as George tries to unlock it, one of the two "Jesus's-name-used-in-vain" that were sacrificed for the censors. In the film, the front door fills the frame side to side and then opens suddenly toward the audience. George and Martha appear in close-up, shoulder-length, their heads silhouetted by the porch light behind them, with moths circling about. Martha switches on the foyer light, and there they are, our main characters, their faces full-screen and straight-on, their features rendered with crisp optical clarity in luscious velvety tones of black, white, and gray. Martha: her salt-and-pepper hair in a loose, above-the-shoulder beauty-parlor coif, a lighted cigarette between her lips, her eyes squinting to adjust to the light, her cloisonné metalwork earrings dangling, a matching necklace around her neck, and a camel hair coat over her fashionable décolletage. George: dignified with his professorial glasses, hair longish at the top, short on the sides, his handsome features heavy with exhaustion, a

tweed jacket over white shirt and tie. They close the door behind them.
Martha walks toward the darkened living room, her back to the camera,
and turns on another light. She takes off her coat, throws it over the
back of a chair, and the audience sees it slip to the floor. Here, Taylor,
following Nichols's precise direction and utilizing all of her physicality,
inhabits Martha's disgust as she looks around the living room, hands
on hips, and shakes her head. Her face in profile, she exhales a puff of
smoke from the cigarette between her lips, captured as potent cinematic emphasis as she issues a sorry appraisal. "What a dump," she says.
George picks up her coat, hangs it up on the coatrack, and Martha's
face lights up. "Hey," she says, remembering something, reaching out
to him with wagging fingers. "What's that from?" Then, with her hand
circling the air, she repeats herself in a mock performance: "WhaT a
dumP." George sighs, lost in the haze of his inebriation, and mutters
"How should I know?" then walks away.

"We all found each other through rehearsals," Nichols later
concluded, believing that the three weeks of preparation had been
helpful, if only for the chance to understand some essential qualities
about his actors. "Elizabeth is very physical," he said, in an interview.
"It helps her to know where she'll be standing, what she'll be wearing . . .
the physical aspects of it, the business—the busy-ness." Taylor recalled
one way in which Nichols led her into an understanding of her character. In the kitchen, the first time she opened the refrigerator door,
she discovered "a complete portrait of the total disorder of Martha's
mind and Martha's life," she said. Nichols had designed everything in
the refrigerator: "He had an ear of corn, all chewed and put away. There
was a tangle of leftover spaghetti on a plate. A can of beans had been
opened and left completely full, with the lid folded back." None of this
is clearly visible in the film—Nichols arranged everything purely for
Taylor's benefit.

In the kitchen scene, Nichols gave Elizabeth the task of eating a cold
chicken leg as she describes the movie she wants George to remember
in which Bette Davis says "What a dump." Nichols made her do several

takes until he felt her voice achieved the right balance of excitement and petulance. Here, Martha takes the drumstick from the refrigerator, her face filling the screen as she bites into it with Rabelaisian savagery, signifying her bawdy appetite and unsatisfied hunger. "Taylor wanted to create her own Martha, as distinct from Uta Hagen," according to Richard Meryman, a *Life* magazine reporter who was writing a biography about her during the filming of *Virginia Woolf.* Elizabeth described Martha as "a desperate woman who has the softness of the underbelly of a baby turtle. She covers it up with the toughness of the shell, which she paints red. Her veneer is bawdy; it's sloppy, it's slouchy, it's gnarly." Meryman claims that Elizabeth was describing herself. "But there are moments when the facade cracks and you see the vulnerability, the infinite pain of this woman inside for whom, years ago, life almost died but is still flickering."

"Richard is about the sound," Nichols said. The goal was to strip Burton of his ferocity and make him seem somewhat defeated and resigned to his circumstances. "He would ask: 'How should I say it?' and I loved that," Nichols said. "Because he was such a lover of poetry and such a great reader of poetry, you tell him how to say it, and you've given him a thought." Burton later credited Nichols with a certain ruthlessness that proved to be helpful to him: "His behavior, his manner, is silky soft. He appears to defer to you, then in the end he gets exactly what he wants. He conspires with you, rather than directs you, to get your best. He'd make me throw away a line where I'd have hit it hard . . . and he was right every time."

George is now sitting at the kitchen table, grazing a crossword puzzle with a pencil in his hand. Martha is explaining that Davis comes home from the grocery store after a hard day, and George looks up. "She works in a grocery store?" he asks, feigning interest. Martha glares at him, exasperated. "She's a *housewife.* She *buys* things. She comes home with her groceries and walks into her *modest* living room of the *modest* cottage that *modest* Joseph Cotton set her up in," Martha says. "Are they married?" George asks. "*Yes,* they're married," Martha says, "to each *other*, you cluck." She describes Davis coming in, setting her groceries down, and looking around. Now, again, Martha's hands rise, as if for leverage, as she assumes Davis's signature hauteur, and repeats the line: "WhaT a DumP." She looks down at George while chewing the rest of her chicken. She expects him to clap—or at least to name the movie, but he just looks up at her, bewildered. She says in a voice flattened into wistful regret, "She's discontent."

The directorial choice here is intentional and distinctly cinematic— Martha devouring a drumstick and throwing it back into the fridge, George sitting at the table working on a crossword puzzle; evident, too, is the intuition of the actors—Taylor's Martha walking back and forth crazily while explaining a scene in a movie, Burton's George passively sitting still and actively ignoring her. This essential scene leads to the seminal moment when Taylor, using her seductive powers assertively, putting all her weight on one hip, her arm akimbo, and planting her other hand firmly on the table, looks down at her husband, the target of her character's blame, and utters the word "discontent," resignation muffling her contempt. This is Martha's gambit, enunciating her own unassailable disappointment in life—the first line-in-the-sand of the evening.

At the end of that first day, Mike complained to Ernie that he was going to have to break up Elizabeth's performance into very small bits, since she did not give him what he wanted in long takes. She was used to working scene by scene. Once, when Mike forgot to give the stars their cue, Elizabeth said, "I can't act until you say 'action.' "

Only one hiccup interrupted their progress that first day. Elizabeth and Richard asked if they were obligated to say their lines exactly as written. When Nichols told them, emphatically, yes, they did not take it well. Later in the afternoon, Lehman heard several approximations of the lines he (or, really, Albee) had written, both Elizabeth and Richard at times changing the words to accommodate the action or expression— or their memory lapses. Yet the variations were minor enough not to require a reshoot. By the end of the afternoon, they had gotten as far as the kitchen scene. It was six thirty P.M. "All in all, the first day was a very slow day, a total of a page and a quarter was shot, a total of 1 minute and 54 seconds of usable film," reported Lehman.

The following day they saw the rushes—a print of the raw footage—and Lehman reported that "after all the deep pessimism of last night, there was an overreaction in the other direction." Ultimately, everyone was relieved. Elizabeth and Richard sat in on a later viewing, and Burton, who was always self-conscious about how his pockmarked face might appear on film, said that it was the first time he had watched his own rushes since 1945. He alerted everyone that he might run screaming from the projection room after the first few seconds, but he stayed, conceding that he was pleasantly relieved.

"We were all awed by Elizabeth's knowledge of film acting," Nichols would much later reflect, long after the daily trials that were about to take their toll on everyone on the *Virginia Woolf* set. "I knew she was the world's most beautiful girl, but over time all four of us from the stage marveled at her ability to handle the verbal material and her knowledge of what the camera would do." He explained that she was one of the very few actresses who had that kind of unique relationship to the camera. "I would call it a day after Take 18, and we would see it the next day, and it was 50 percent better than I imagined it. There were all those things you couldn't see just standing six feet away, but they were there. Her essential nature informed so much of it."

The success of the kitchen scene is a small victory not only in terms of Nichols's direction but, equally, because of Taylor's desire to give a bravura performance. Whether Taylor was aware of it or not, there are several invisible layers of irony in the reference to the Davis film: It had been Albee's wish all along to see Davis play Martha on-screen. *Beyond the Forest*, directed by King Vidor in 1949, is the film to which Martha attributes the opening line, "What a dump," although the film is never identified in *Who's Afraid of Virginia Woolf?* Taylor's delivery of the line has taken on a life of its own over the years, repeated at dinner parties with a camp resonance that, perhaps, Albee had intended all along, particularly when he lamented the absence of humor in the film. Certainly, *Beyond the Forest* is the kind of film noir flop worthy of dinner party mockery. Bosley Crowther began his review of the film in the *New York Times* in this way: "Of all the no-good women that Bette Davis has portrayed in her numerous elaborate demonstrations of the deadliness of the female sex, she has never done any more unpleasant nor more grotesque than the creature she plays in Warner's *Beyond the Forest*. . . . she is so monstrous—so ghoulishly picturesque—that her representation often slips off into laughable caricature." This information makes Taylor's performance seem that much more knowing.

≈

By the end of the first week, they had gotten as far as the crucial bedroom scene, ten minutes into the final cut of the film. After Martha drops the news that "guests" are coming over for a drink, George looks at her, first incredulous, then exasperated, aware of his powerlessness to stop this late-hour train wreck of an idea. He follows Martha upstairs, indignant but resigned. "*Who's* coming over?" he demands to know. There are two separate shots of Martha—one as she walks up the stairs from the living room and tosses "whatstheirname" over her shoulder, and the other on the landing, as she walks toward the camera and heads into the bedroom. "You met them tonight," she adds. "They're new. He's in the math department." George claims not to remember meeting anybody in the math department at the party, and he asks her to be more specific. Martha walks into the bathroom and repeats through the closed door that "he's in the *math* department. He's *young* and he's *blond* . . ." It took Nichols a while to get Elizabeth to say those lines with the right singsong inflection, which he believed to be integral to the poetry of Albee's words. George opens the door a crack. "Good-looking, well built?" he asks. "Yes," Martha says. George closes the bathroom door, attached to which is a full-length mirror that Nichols had specifically requested. As the camera closes in, George appears in close-up, his face reflected in the mirror; he sighs to himself and mutters, "It figures." His distress is underscored by the close-up double view of him in the frame. Martha goes on to tell him that the wife is a mousy little thing without any hips. "Remember them now?"

George sits down on the bed and sips his drink. "I guess so," he says. But why, he wonders aloud, did she have to invite this couple over at *two A.M.*? She opens the bathroom door and says, "Because Daddy said to be nice to them, that's why." Nichols, with nose-thumbing impudence in his arsenal, delighted in coaching Elizabeth to repeat this line in self-mocking baby-talk, to signal Martha's own awareness of how absurdly childish it sounds: "Because *Daddy* said to be *nice* to them." George, protesting, says, "But, why now?" Martha, putting a piece of ice from her drink into her mouth and chewing on it, repeats emphatically, contemptuously, through her teeth, "Because Daddy said to be nice to them." Daddy, of course, is George's boss.

Martha straightens up the bedroom, picking up items of clothing thrown over the chair, on the dresser, and across the bed. She sits down at her vanity to touch up her makeup. "So, where are they?" George asks impatiently. "Did they go home and get some sleep first, or something?" He lies down on the bed and bemoans that she always springs things on him. She pats her hair in place in front of the mirror and says, more playfully now, "Poor Georgie-Porgie, put-upon pie." Then, turning around to see him lying down, curled up on his side, she walks over to the bed and crawls up alongside him. "Are you sulking?" she asks in a tender, more conciliatory voice. "Awwww," she says, petting him on his head and touching his cheek affectionately. "Never mind," he says, turning away from her to lie on his stomach. In her black cocktail dress, newly made up, earrings dangling, she climbs on top of him, straddles his back, and massages his shoulders.

"Hey," she erupts, suddenly remembering something else and banging him on the side. "Who's afraid of Virginia Woolf?" she sings to the tune of "Here We Go Round the Mulberry Bush." In her excitement, she drums her hands against his back, laughs, and starts to tickle him. He tells her to stop. "Didn't you think that was *funny*?" she says.

"I thought it was a *scream*." He mumbles something into his pillow, and Martha reacts to his indifference like an insult. "Well, *you* laughed your head off when you heard it at the party," she says, as if to accuse him now of not getting into the spirit of the witticism, or the swing of her mood. He corrects her. "I smiled. I did not laugh my head off." She insists, her voice now sharpened to a fine contempt. "You laughed your *goddamned* head off!" Martha is picking a fight and adds childishly, as if out of nowhere, "You make me puke." He looks up at her over his shoulder. "That isn't a very nice thing to say, Martha," he tells her in a calm, paternal voice. "Oh, I *like* your anger," she says sarcastically, getting up, calling him "a simp," and staring down at him. "You don't even have the . . . the . . . the . . . *what*?" she says, gesturing for him to come up with the word. "Guts?" he suggests, which brings just a hint of a smile to her face. "*Phrase*maker," she says, almost admiringly, and they both burst out laughing. She climbs back into bed and lies down next to him, messing up his hair affectionately and reaching over him for her drink on the night table. "Why don't you ever put ice cubes in my drink, George?" He counters that, indeed, he does, but "you just chew all your ice, like a cocker spaniel."

They lie together and banter tenderly, making each other laugh, now like two puppies pawing each other, giggling together, their intimacy gentle and honest and believable. And then, George turns to Martha, looking directly into her eyes, and says, finally, touchingly, knowingly, softly, "Hello, honey." At that moment, it is as if Richard, the actor, stepped outside the character of George and said "Hi, honey" to Elizabeth, his wife, instead of Martha. It is one of the truest moments in the film, this affectionate, isolated glimpse of simple recognition, when they briefly locate each other and surrender, as if sighing to one another in utter relief. Martha takes it as an invitation. "Give Mamma a big, wet, sloppy kiss," she says to George, who shuts down immediately. "I don't want to kiss you right now, Martha," he says quietly, with certainty, moving her hand away. "Where are these people, anyway—this good-looking, well-built young man, and his slim-hipped wife?" He gets up and walks out of the room. We see Martha deflate, devastation all over her face as she lies there on her side, all dressed up, alone in the middle of an ocean of rejection. "Why didn't you want to kiss me?" she asks, to no one, looking over her shoulder toward the empty doorway and then, saying in a voice desperate and frantic, *"George?"*

We are left to wonder whether Martha has roused George's jealousy by flaunting her attraction to a young, handsome rival, or merely spurred his indignation with her barrage of mercurial insults. Either way, clearly his refusal to kiss her has cut deep, not only injuring her pride, but also stoking her hunger for affection and exposing her emotional fragility. Despite her evident disappointment in him, Martha loves George, and he knows it. But he can tolerate only so much abuse. Now, his brusque rejection is the true opening salvo precipitating the domestic World War III that follows, the source of the tempestuous fury and psychological retaliation that Martha will brandish at her husband and the soon-to-arrive guests in their long, emotionally unwieldy journey to sunrise.

~

"There is a slight air of dissatisfaction among quite a few people, and it seems to stem largely from their feeling that the Director does not pay too much attention to them," Lehman concluded about the morale of the crew during the first week of shooting *Who's Afraid of Virginia Woolf?* Nichols never intended to hurt anyone's feelings. But his laser focus on Elizabeth's and Richard's individual performances—wringing out the unique temperament of their characters, prompting Elizabeth to deepen her voice before every take, counseling Richard to soften his demeanor, attuning them both to the emotional undercurrents in George and Martha's casual banter—were tasks that required total vigilance. At every turn, the obstacles seemed to Nichols overwhelming and insurmountable.

He knew what the stakes were. He kept hearing about the murmurs of doubt circulating among the "important people" in New York, a consensus that would be given public voice in a *Life* magazine cover story on the eve of the movie's premiere the following June. "Everybody seemed to be going about things the wrong way when they set out to make the movie," the article begins, citing the Albee play as "too earthy in both theme and dialogue for a Hollywood film. Elizabeth Taylor was too young, too beautiful, and not skillful enough to play a drunken, sluggish woman in her 40s. Richard Burton was too British, too authoritative to be a henpecked American college professor. Mike Nichols was a superb director of light Broadway comedy—but wasn't he presumptuous making a film debut with violent drama?"

Nichols's single-mindedness would serve the film well, but he alienated those around him who rightly considered themselves necessary to the production and who might have made his life just that much easier. "I find that very few people on the picture, and that includes me, feel like forcing themselves upon Mike Nichols, if they sense that he would rather be by himself and would rather pick and choose whomever he wants to consult at any given time," Lehman wrote. "This is bound to cause hurt feelings, but apparently, that is the name of the game. It's called 'movie making.'"

It is possible that, because Nichols had been a stage director, he envisioned the entire film as a series of long takes in which the action is continuous, just as in live theater. If that was an impossible goal, it was still an ideal he aspired to. The transitions from one scene to another had to appear seamless and nonstop. Doane Harrison, the production advisor on *Virginia Woolf*, had for years worked directly with Billy Wilder, initially as a film editor but, increasingly, as a hands-on consultant who understood better than anyone what was needed for the continuity of a film. It was Wilder who urged Nichols to hire him, assuring the novice director that Harrison would be his most reliable secret weapon on the set. Harrison knew what was required for additional coverage of a scene—different setups and angles—to be able to make smooth transitions, such as those Nichols envisioned, from one cut to another in the editing room.

"I think he wants to leave the picture," Lehman's secretary whispered one morning as Ernie arrived at work, explaining that Harrison had been waiting in his office for an hour. Ernie greeted Doane and closed the door. Harrison wasted no time asserting that he had had enough of Nichols and was resigning. Lehman tried to appease him, acknowledging that there were wounded feelings all around, and asking what, specifically, prompted this sudden turn of events. Harrison claimed that Nichols and Wexler ignored all his suggestions the day before about how to shoot George and Martha walking into the bedroom. "Mike is directing himself into an impossible corner and he will never get out," Harrison said. "So, what's the point of my being here if he won't listen to me?" Lehman tried to make him understand what a terrible loss it would be for picture if he left, but Harrison, seventy years old, was adamant, saying that Mike would put him in an early grave.

Lehman was saved by a phone call. The day's rushes were ready, and he convinced Harrison to come with him to the projection room. The rushes showed George and Martha on the stairs, on the landing, and then walking through the bedroom door. Before they could even discuss the footage, the phone in the projection room rang. Mike, perhaps with a sixth sense, had tracked them down. With panic in his voice, he asked why Doane had walked off the set. Doane did not mince words. Mike claimed it was all a misunderstanding. He didn't realize that the way they shot the entrance to the bedroom was not as Doane had intended. "Come over here right away. Please. I need you," Mike said, before getting in a little dig at Lehman's expense. "There is no sense in you sitting there with Ernie, because that's not going to help the picture." Doane hung up and looked rather grave. "At least you know who your friends are," he said to Ernie. He repeated his intention to quit. This was where Lehman, always the adult in the room, served the picture at the expense of his own feelings. "Mike needs you, Doane. I think you better go over there and help him." Lehman drove Harrison over to the set and watched as he started reframing the scene with Nichols.

Later, though, Ernie had it out with Mike in his office. "I'm sick and tired of you getting angry at me every time I open my mouth—if I dare to make the slightest criticism," Lehman said. Nichols accused Lehman of being a *noodge*, complaining that Ernie picked on little things and didn't let them go, "like for example, criticizing the *sound*." Ernie stood up for himself, fighting back, fighting Mike, as Mike himself had asked him to do. "If I don't like the sound, I'm going to say something about it," Lehman reminded Nichols. "Overlook my *noodge* qualities and listen to what I'm saying."

As long as he was on the subject, Lehman called Nichols on his behavior on the set. "I told him he doesn't pay enough attention to how he is offending the people he's working with," Ernie wrote in his journal. "That angered Mike, and he kept demanding that I tell him who had been offended." Harrison, for one, Lehman pointed out, then added, "And you know that I am offended." Nichols kept pushing Lehman to name just one other person, as if it were a game, as if he were restaging one of his skits with Elaine May, in which Nichols played a patient who badgers his psychiatrist (May) into naming, one by one, her other patients who are also in love with her.

What Mike wanted was for Ernie to stop making him feel guilty all the time. "If you mean unjustifiably guilty, I'm sorry if I do that," Ernie said, "but if you feel justifiably guilty, there's nothing I can do about that." Mike then launched into a litany of production problems that created enormous pressure for him. "You don't know what I'm going through," he said. "I have to worry about the actors; I have to wheedle a performance out of Elizabeth; I have to worry about keeping her happy. She doesn't worry about *my* feelings." Again, Nichols seemed to be improvising from one of his stand-up dialogues, turning the tables of classic Jewish guilt back on Lehman: "You must love me. You must dissemble and make believe you like me. You must not make me feel that I have to worry about *your* feelings. You've got to worry about *my* feelings, or I'll just collapse and be unable to direct this picture."

Lehman was annoyed that Mike made such egregious, one-sided demands of him, but he kept it to himself. Despite the progress made that first week, the mood on set felt fragile. Lehman was present one morning when Elizabeth was delivering lines that did not match the script. Mike asked her to please stick to the dialogue, and she stormed off the set. Richard followed her. Ernie asked Mike and Meta Rebner, the script supervisor, what the policy was on improvising, but Mike—frustrated, and worried about having offended Elizabeth—turned on Ernie with the same mercurial rage that Martha turns so suddenly at George. "You speak to her," Mike said, dropping the responsibility on Ernie and ordering him not to bring up such matters again. Lehman countered, "Don't get so angry at me with such little cause so quickly."

It was well before lunchtime. Mike, Ernie, Haskell, Doane, and other members of the crew stood there for a long while in a state of exasperated suspension, expecting Elizabeth and Richard to return so that they could continue shooting. They finally concluded that "George" and "Martha" were not coming back until after lunch. It was almost four o'clock when they returned, in the best of spirits, chatting gaily, and laughing together with another couple in tow. Elizabeth then introduced Nichols to the Duke and Duchess of Windsor, with whom she and Richard had just had lunch. It seemed to put the entire matter of who was in charge in stark relief.

∽

Aside from the power struggles between the producer and his director, and the kid-glove diplomacy required to manage his famous stars, two leitmotifs were persistent through the strains of Lehman's anxiety—the shooting schedule and the production budget. Between the Burtons' fluid sense of time—their four-hour lunches and Elizabeth's recovery period after her outbursts on the set—and the additional production costs anticipated by the location shooting in Northampton, even the glamour of meeting the duke and duchess couldn't deter Ernie from adhering to the old saw "Time is money." While tensions simmered on the set, another delay in shooting was somewhat more compatible with Lehman's interests. A second day had been set aside for members of the press to meet with the stars on the set, and reporters were now swarming about the production. Lehman and Nichols, competitive with each other and equally strategic, hand-chose the ones they granted selective access to, particularly when it served their own interests. The feature that Lehman had orchestrated about himself for *Cosmopolitan* magazine was proceeding; working directly with Helen Gurley Brown, the editor in chief, he had been given the choice of writer and, even more remarkably, permission to edit the story himself before publication. Meanwhile, Nichols was talking to a reporter for his own cover story in the *Saturday Evening Post*. "I hate publicity," Lehman told the reporter for *Cosmopolitan*. "I suppose it's necessary but there's something wrong with it. It's like a doctor advertising." The reporter asked him if he had his own public relations people. "Yes," he said, "but I hate it because the worst side of me has, temporarily, gotten the upper hand." (Ironically, he may have edited that disavowal into the piece after the fact.) Both features would appear in October 1965, before shooting for *Virginia Woolf* was even completed.

Revisiting media artifacts a half century later provides a sidelong view of history. The discrepancy between the public narrative and the subtext of actual events tells its own story about how mythology evolves. The *Saturday Evening Post* cover story, titled "All for the Love of Mike," is crafted to foreground the best qualities of an increasingly public figure, yet the description of the production of *Virginia Woolf*, while not exactly untruthful, is as airy as the meringue on a fine key lime pie. "The parking spaces outside Stage 8 at Warner Brothers Studio in Burbank, Calif., are filled with Rolls-Royces, Bentleys, Ferraris, Lincoln Continentals and Cadillac limousines," the piece begins. "CLOSED SET— ABSOLUTELY NO VISITORS, say the huge signs outside." Already, the reader feels privileged to be gaining such exclusive access to the inner world of Mike Nichols. Here, though, Nichols puts on a show for the public, describing Taylor and Burton as consummate professionals who have mastered their roles effortlessly. "Their flexibility and talent and cooperativeness and lovingness is overwhelming," Nichols is quoted as saying. "I've had more trouble with little people you've never heard of—temper tantrums, upstaging, girls' sobbing—than with the so-called legendary Burtons. They are on time, they know their lines, and if I make suggestions, Elizabeth can keep in her mind fourteen dialogue changes, twelve floor marks and ten pauses."

The profile of Nichols goes on to describe his effect on the set, where, according to the journalist, he "inspires both love and lunacy." Nichols and Burton would often play word games between takes as they waited for the camera to be moved and the lighting to be adjusted, sometimes with sizable bets on which of them could define the most obscure words, such as "porbeagle" (a kind of mackerel) or "pleach" (a trellis or arbor). Or they would recite lines from a novel or a play for the other to guess the source, whether James Joyce or Henry Miller or Molière.

"Mike's a very disturbing man," says Burton. "You cannot charm him—he sees right through you. He's among the most intelligent men I've ever known, and I've known most of them. I dislike him intensely— he's cleverer than I am. But, alas," he says with an affectionate wink, "I tolerate him." Elizabeth speaks well of her director, too, saying nothing unexpected to the reporter, following studio protocol: "I adore Mike, and I could talk about him for hours."

The magazine profile goes on to describe the long hours on the set, the one-hundred-degree summer temperatures, and the grueling and tedious complexities of making a movie. All true enough. But then, Mike is quoted about the tone he tries to set for the actors and the crew on Stage Eight. "It should be happy; we're all doing it for pleasure. We want people to like it, but we have to like it along the way. I don't want any long faces. I want everyone to have fun." Certainly a worthy aspiration for the director of any film, but the anodyne comment is self-serving at best. If the day-to-day chronicle in Lehman's real-life journal is any guide, the *Virginia Woolf* set was anything but a happy one, and Nichols himself was responsible for the consternation and low morale of most of his crew.

Chapter 9

Those Damned Guests

Don't talk to me about hatred if you haven't been married.

—Jonathan Franzen, *Purity*

Fifteen minutes into the movie, several fundamental conditions have been established. We know by now that George and Martha are an educated, sophisticated middle-aged couple who are settled into the tattered comfort of a respectable—if turbulent—marriage. We can see that the balance of power between them tips in Martha's direction because of her father, who is George's boss, yet it shifts back to George when he withholds his affection. She is starved for love; he has been defeated—emasculated—by failed ambition. She is mercurial. He is sardonic. They are both alcoholics. It is painful for the audience to watch them tear into each other, at least until the guests arrive.

The sequence in *Virginia Woolf* that leads up to the guests' arrival is an uninterrupted fifty-second take, followed by one of thirty seconds. The two takes were cut together seamlessly to appear as a single, uninterrupted squabble between George and Martha, a complicated scene for any actors to play. Nichols has George standing at the bar in the living room and pouring himself another drink. We hear Martha's voice calling out his name, but we see her only when George turns around to reveal her behind him leaning against the jamb in the living room doorway. "Why didn't you want to kiss me?" she asks, quite sincerely, gobbling her words with vulnerability. The potent question demands George's honesty, and delicacy, too, if not also, perhaps, some quick-thinking deflection, given the impending social obligation that hovers over the moment. Burton affects just the right amount of playful sarcasm to carry off the line with amusement in his voice. "Well, dear, if I kissed you, I'd get all excited and beside myself," George explains. "Then I'd have to take you by force right here on the living room rug, and our guests would walk in, and, well, what would your father have to say about *that*?" Martha chuckles as she tidies up the coffee table, emptying one ashtray into another, clearing a few glasses, and tells him to fix her another drink.

The Burtons could certainly play a believable married couple, but the challenge was for them to play their specific characters—George and Martha—instead of themselves, and their success was a feat of artistic virtuosity that did not come easily. In the previous scene upstairs, George's refusal to kiss Martha had been a rejection that cut deep to the core. In this scene, Elizabeth plays Martha more exposed, fragile, defenseless. "God, you can swill it down, can't you?" George says while pouring her another drink, a comment leveled with equal parts admiration and disapproval. Playfully, in a little-girl voice, she replies, "Well, I'm thirsty," now sidling up to him, twisting his tie in her hand, angling for a hug or an intimate squeeze, clearly in need of some reassurance, a little affection. "Oh, Jesus," George says, irritation in his voice, pushing her hand away. This unmistakable rebuff slices even deeper than his refusal to kiss her, and, in a flash, she turns into a shrew spewing venom and bile at her husband.

Nichols was deliberate about shooting in sequence as much as possible for the reward, as he said, of seeing the emotional notes deepen throughout the movie. He had all the actors working their way to that goal. "We were at it so long and we spent so many days," Nichols reflected. "As an actor you are so grateful for having such amazing things to say. There is such joy in that, in those lines. I felt I owed it to the actors to let them feel that. Or find their way to the meaning in each line. Albee had given everybody such a gift." Nichols's ambition for this scene to work as a single long cut required the timing of the lines to be consistent with the actors' physical tasks. Martha launches into a litany of vituperations as she straightens up the living room, shoving an article of clothing under a couch cushion, throwing cigarette butts from a large ashtray into the fireplace, gathering sections of the newspaper strewn about and stacking them on the desk. "I swear, if you existed, I'd divorce you," she snarls at George through gritted teeth. George stands there, impervious, his voice rising above hers as he slices back with his own insult: "And try to keep your clothes on. There aren't any more sickening sights in the world than you with a couple of drinks in you . . ." Martha's voice, now piercing through George's recriminations, screeches with repulsion as she calls George "a *big* zero." Nichols was intent on having the two of them talk over each other, a cinema verité technique, true to the way people speak to one another in social situations—and even more so the drunker they get.

The doorbell rings, and Martha orders George to go answer it. He refuses. She barks the command again. The audience is aware that their raised voices can be heard by the guests on the front porch. Martha barks at George yet again: "Go answer that door." These echoes are not incidental. Early readers such as Ned Rorem and Terrence McNally had commented on the musical structure of the dialogue in *Who's Afraid of Virginia Woolf?*, noting how Albee wrote like a composer. One such motif is the repetition of certain phrases three times, as with "What a dump." Nichols coached Taylor, in particular, to tease out these repetitions, finding different line readings and varying the emphasis on particular words. In the bedroom scene, the words "Because Daddy said to be nice to them" recur three times; as Martha, Elizabeth says the line first as an explanation, then in self-mockery, and, finally, in anger. The three door chimes, and Martha's orders, become yet another triplet.

George pauses at first, then assumes a feigned deference before nodding his head and conceding. But, walking to the door, he turns to her with an ominous warning: "Just don't start in on the *bit*"—meaning their (imaginary) son. As she kneels to shove a box under a table near the door, George turns to her and emphasizes that she stands "*fore-warned.*" She screams up at him with unbridled hatred: "GODDAMN YOU."

By this point in her career, Elizabeth instinctively understood how the camera would render her. Her awareness of the camera frame and where to place herself within it was second nature. While she was still struggling to match her voice with the experience of the forty-eight-year-old character she was playing, it was her idea to kneel and scream "Goddamn you" up at the camera, letting the lower angle magnify the intensity of her rage. "Some performers greatly aid the cameraman if they understand their craft," said Haskell Wexler, the cinematographer. "One of the best-schooled actresses is Elizabeth Taylor, who is keenly sensitive to nuances of lighting and camera angles."

Martha curses George as he opens the front door, and the scene jumps to a close-up of Nick and Honey standing in the threshold with stunned faces. The abrupt cut from the seething Martha to the young, attractive midwestern couple is catch-your-breath comical, with Nichols's signature timing written all over it. Their eyes veer in the direction of their hostess, Martha, kneeling on the floor and looking up at them, her obscenity having missed its target, landing on the unwitting guests instead. We watch Martha recalibrate from embarrassment to strained affability, standing, greeting the guests, and inviting them in.

Nick and Honey sense the charge in the atmosphere as they enter the living room with visible trepidation. They sit down on the couch, fidgeting, like lost children. A moment of deafening silence fills the room, followed by a round of predictable and innocuous small talk.

"Who did the . . . *painting*?" Nick asks randomly, grasping for something to hinge a friendly social exchange on. George seizes upon his benign—if desperate—question as an opportunity to brandish his contempt for the young man, as well as his displeasure about these *damned* guests at so ridiculously late an hour. George is sarcastic. Nick is politely displeased. Honey's manic laughter bubbles out. Finally, George makes a witty, if disparaging, remark, and everyone laughs, including Martha. The ice is broken, for the moment.

"Fix the kids a drink, George," Martha says, now with folksy good humor. Nick hesitates before asking Honey what she would like. "Oh, I don't know," she says. "A little brandy. Never mix, never worry." George nods and turns to Nick. "What about you, *uh . . . uh . . . uh*," snapping his fingers, rudely suggesting he's forgotten Nick's name. "Bourbon on the rocks, if you don't mind," Nick says, very politely, refusing to react to George's provocation. "Mind, *mind*?" George says, snidely. "I don't mind. I don't *think* I mind. Martha, rubbing alcohol for you?" Martha, something of the residual party girl still alive in her, lets out a bawdy cackle. "Sure," she says. "Never mix, never worry."

~

"If there's a phony premise, the lines couldn't matter less," Nichols said. "The premise, of course, must come from the playwright. There's no such thing as a brilliant production of a nonexistent play." The language in *Who's Afraid of Virginia Woolf?* is rigorous, and it is brought to life and given anchor in Burton's meticulous diction, as if he were etching every word with his elocution, further animating its meaning with his keen actorly intelligence. Every word is given its precise emotional chord and storytelling intention with his performance. "We understood the power of this material and what was demanded of Albee's writing, which contained aggressive and provocative dialogue and controversial subject matter," Segal said, remembering that, from the outset, during rehearsals and throughout the production, Burton was at the top of the pyramid. "He set the tone for the rest of us. His incredible capacity as an actor raised our game because he came in at such a high level!"

"Sandy [Dennis] does a lot with her voice, but did she understand what she was telegraphing? Or was she more intuitive?" Nichols asked rhetorically. "She did both. She could handle it all technically, very easily, but she could also go with the impulse of the moment. She could summon up an emotion or stumble into it when it happened."

Despite his coldness to her on set, Nichols considered Dennis to be a very skilled actor. She was by no means Hollywood pretty, though as a blonde she was a natural fit for the role of Honey. Her milky-smooth complexion, along with her rounded lips and toothy smile, gave her face an eccentric innocence that made her believable as the character, the midwestern daughter of a wealthy evangelist. Her voice was deeper and more resonant than what might be expected from her wispy demeanor, adding depth and complexity to her performance. "The thing about Sandy, a non-drinker getting drunker and drunker, was that she was brilliant at extreme states of all kinds," Nichols observed. "She always found some strange new way of coming at it that no one had yet done or thought of. Nothing she did was ever conventional, and for Honey it was perfect."

There was mutual respect among the actors on the set, and they all worked together well. Segal, for example, marveled at Dennis's ability to play Honey. "There is never a false moment with Sandy," he said about his costar. "I don't know where that comes from. It's different from acting, what she does. Elizabeth, Richard, and I were acting. She's like a natural, Sandy. She was doing stuff that no one else does, completely unexpected stuff, and it was fresh every single time."

"Honey has to be annoying," Mike said. "If you don't go there you've taken two teeth out of the piece. She's annoying but also you feel bad for her when she is taken advantage of. The main thing about Honey is you have to get a comedienne. . . . The glory about Sandy Dennis was that whatever she was playing she was funny, at least part of the time. She was in every way an unusual person. Because of Elaine May, I used to define great acting as someone being inside the role and outside the role at the same time . . . the knife edge between showing someone and being someone. Sandy did that."

Regarding Elizabeth's performance, Nichols described redoing scenes a dozen times while missing what she was doing so successfully in front of the camera, yet "when I was editing and scoring, she even left some room for the score. She counted on all that in some semi-conscious way. It was a great surprise for everyone, her ability to handle the verbal material." Elizabeth turned out to be a revelation for everyone. "Oh, Martha, she's frightening to play, but I understand her," Elizabeth Taylor told the theater critic of the *Boston Globe* during the production. "Richard and I have talked about Martha and George so long we sometimes feel we've become them."

"Elizabeth had a mouth on her that was really funny, all unprintable stuff," Segal said. "She was down and dirty. Everybody was raw in that thing. Everybody was defenseless, and that's Mike, too. He's right there. He was present. Everybody on that picture—the cameraman, everybody—they were *present*. It was a gift, the whole radical project." Yet, despite the camaraderie among the actors and the collegial teamwork during the sequential scenes, Taylor and Burton were still the most famous couple in the world, and their stardom created unusual frustrations during the production. It was in their contracts that they could not work past six o'clock. "When they were called back to the set after lunch, they often wouldn't come down from their dressing room, sometimes not until 5 o'clock," said Bobbie O'Steen, the wife of Sam O'Steen, the film's editor. "Mike would walk around, exasperated: 'Cocksuckers, I hate their fuckin' guts,' he would rage to Sam, complaining that they were costing him time, and the production money." Late in the day, the Burtons would saunter onto the set in a jocular fashion as if nothing were wrong. "Mike, old buddy, sorry we're late," Richard would say. "Let's shoot." Once they were shooting, Mike would forget his rage, but the production was falling further and further behind schedule, and costs were mounting higher and higher.

"At the end of the day—5:00 or 6:00 PM—no matter where we were in the shooting, if Mike had one more shot to make, it didn't matter—a guy came in with two Bloody Marys, one for Elizabeth and one for Richard," said Segal. "That was the end of the shooting day. And Elizabeth didn't come in until 10 AM. . . . The good old days. Never heard that happen before or since."

~

Honey and Nick are a typically conventional couple, and Dennis plays the obsequious wife with bewildered virtue. Honey tries to be cheerful in the context of the psychological minefield she and Nick have stepped into, soldiering forward despite the signs of adversity in George and Martha's living room. She is the epitome of innocence and purity, in contrast to the taint of world-weariness that Martha brings to the party. Soon after arriving at George and Martha's, Honey, fulfilling her role as a new faculty wife, blithely compliments the house and speaks well of Martha's father—their host earlier in the evening—gushing over his party for new faculty members, which made them feel welcome as a new couple on campus. She describes the difficulty they had in getting to know people at the last school where Nick had taught. "You won't believe it, but we had to make our own way all by ourselves," Honey says. "Isn't that right, dear? I would have to go up to the wives in the library, or the supermarket, and say 'Hello, I'm new here. You must be Mrs. So-and-So, Doctor So-and-So's wife.' It really wasn't very nice at all." Martha looks at Honey as if she were barely a speck of dust, and then proceeds with her own agenda, putting her hand on Nick's knee and squeezing it as she acknowledges, meaningfully, that "Daddy"—her father—"knows how to run things."

Segal was movie-star handsome, and *Who's Afraid of Virginia Woolf?* would launch his career as a big-screen leading man. When Segal initially auditioned for *The Knack*, off-Broadway, Nichols cast him, but with reservation. "I saw a kind of arrogance I didn't want," Nichols recalled about Segal at that audition, yet he added that he was glad he took the risk. "I learned he is not the tough guy he seems to be. What you get with George is masculinity and sensitivity, plus a brain. His conflicting quality—half rough and half gentle and the mind to control it—gives an element of surprise to whatever he does." While Nichols's first choice for the role of Nick had been Robert Redford, he went to Segal immediately when Redford turned the role down. "George was close enough to the young god he needed to be for Elizabeth and witty enough and funny enough to deal with all that humiliation," Nichols explained.

Nichols succeeded in having Segal's dark hair dyed blond for the role of Nick, accentuating the wholesome midwestern aspect of his all-American good looks. He plays Nick, a recent recruit to the college faculty, with a tight, cock-of-the-walk arrogance that is thinly disguised under his polite, boy-next-door manners. We will soon learn that he had been an award-winning college athlete, as well, which proves to be of lascivious interest to Martha. Burton, thought to be too strong a countenance for the role of George, contrasts Nick's *aw, shucks* sense of entitlement with seething circumspection. George is threatened by Nick's virility in the presence of Martha—his embarrassingly preda-tory wife—and he will goad Nick relentlessly, refusing to give him the natural courtesy of a faculty elder to a younger colleague. We watch Nick struggling to maintain his equanimity, aware that he is in the home of the college president's daughter and that he must tread carefully to avoid any false move that might undermine his career ambitions.

When Honey sees Martha's hand on George's knee, she bolts up from the couch and says, "I'm going to be sick," and asks to use the . . . the . . . "Euphemism?" offers George, a clever reference to the bathroom (the movie popularized the usage of "euphemism" as an ironic way to refer to a bathroom—at least among urban cognoscenti). When Martha takes Honey upstairs, George and Nick are left to contend with each other. The banter between them is not unlike a ping-pong game in which the host keeps serving the ball with a spin on it across the net, and the guest keeps refusing to hit it. "So, Martha said you're in the math department," George begins, pouring them both another drink. "No," Nick says. "No." George walks up to him and hands him a drink, the question of Nick's department still on his face, but Nick just stares back at him, deliberately withholding the information. "What made you become a teacher?" George asks Nick, a serious question, a reasonable one. "Well, the same things that motivated you, I imagine," Nick says, throwing the question back at George, refusing to give an inch. "And what were they? What were the things that motivated *me*?" George snaps back. Nick, caught off guard, responds that he doesn't really know. George, now provoked by Nick's insolence, doesn't let up. "But you said what motivated you to be a teacher were the same things that motivated me."

Nick understands he is being challenged, although he is not aware that his tight-fisted refusal to reveal anything about himself is a provocation of its own. He does his best to turn the other cheek, now looking up at the stairs for Honey to materialize so they can escape. Resigned to waiting, he sits down again, sips his drink, and takes an anxious stab at conversation. "You've been here for quite a long time, haven't you?" Nick asks George. The camera closes in on George, a daring and telling close-up that lingers on his face for a few tense seconds as he does nothing but stare out, blankly, lost in some internal reverie. The camera allows us to scrutinize his inebriated condition before he realizes he is expected to answer the question. "Oh, yes, ever since I married what's-her-name. *Martha*," he says, snapping out of it. "Even before that. *Forever.* Dashed hopes and good intentions. Good. Better. Best. *Bested*," he says, turning to Nick. "How did you like that for a declension, young man?" Nick gets up, annoyed, disgusted, finished with this interaction, but George repeats that he asked Nick a question. "I really don't know what to say," Nick responds with strained civility. "Don't you condescend to me," George fires back at him. "I asked you how you liked that declension." This brings Nick to a boiling point, and, finally, the young man erupts. "All right, what do you want me to say? Do you want me to say it's funny so you can contradict me and say that it's sad? Or do you want me to say that it's sad so you can turn around and say it's funny? I can play that damn little game any way you want to." George nods, as if Nick has passed a test, and compliments him, but Nick declares that they're leaving as soon as his wife comes back downstairs. Nonsense, George says and offers him another drink. The following conversation is central to understanding the competition between George and Nick that will play out in various stages throughout the rest of the film.

"Listen," Nick says. "You and your wife seem to be having some sort of a . . ." George shakes his head. "Martha and I are having nothing," he says. "We're merely *exercising*. We're merely walking what's left of our wits. Don't pay any attention . . ." Nick is now visibly distressed. "It's just that I don't like getting involved in other people's affairs," he says. George hands him another drink, chuckles, and sits down. "Oh, you'll get over that. Small college and all. Musical beds is the faculty sport around here." This is the gauntlet George lays down before Nick—exposing Nick's own inchoate agenda with Martha before he realizes it himself, as well as daring him to risk it. Nick is taken aback, and George uses the opportunity to ask again which department Nick is teaching in. "I'm a biologist," he finally allows. "Oh, *you're* the one," George says, suddenly, going off on a drunken rant about scientists threatening humanity by rearranging our chromosomes. "I'm very mistrustful," George adds, suggesting that it's because he knows too much about history. "Martha tells me often that I am *in* the history department, as opposed to *being* the history department, in the sense of *running* the history department." Magnanimously, and somewhat drunkenly, too, Nick offers solace by saying, "Well, I don't run the biology department." George, now amused, says, "Well, you're twenty-one." Nick corrects him: "Twenty-eight." George suggests that when Nick is his age, he may be running the history department. "Biology," Nick again corrects him. George continues his meditation on the fear that science is creating a single, superior race that will do away with the necessity for music, art, and literature. "Then we will have a race of sublime young men, very much like yourself," George says. Nick shakes his head no. "You don't know very much about science," he says. George counters with a wise and whimsical chuckle. "I know something about *history*," George says. "I know when I'm being *threatened*."

Several themes play out in this antagonistic volley of wits, words, and will. The first is George's characterization of the snarling tension between him and Martha. From his perspective, it does not signal trouble in paradise so much as it reflects the course of things in all mature marriages. "Exercising" is how George portrays their sharp bickering, as if it were merely salon banter, hardly worth mentioning. The second theme is of a more oedipal nature. George—the established elder—is threatened by Nick, a younger, more vital adversary. Albee's flair for dramatic construction shines through in establishing Nick as a biologist—the study of life standing in for virility—while casting George, a historian, as something of an impotent relic. George will later refer to Nick as a "historical inevitability," spermatozoically speaking, who is about to be indoctrinated in the faculty strategy of garnering tenure, as George describes it, by "plowing pertinent wives."

In the following scene, while Nick is in "the euphemism," George says to Honey, "Your husband was just telling us all about the chromosomes." "What?" Martha drunkenly interjects. George explains that Nick is in the biology department. "Math," she counters. They argue until Honey confirms that he's in the biology department. Nick walks back into the room, and Martha concedes. "So, he's a biologist," she says, sitting on the couch. "Good for him. Biology is even better." As Nick approaches the couch, Martha, stopping him with her hand on his leg, free-associates, "You're right at the meat of things." In a provocative directorial choice, Nichols frames the next shot to show Martha's gaze level with Nick's crotch. Liking what she finds there, she pats Nick on the leg and, sloshing her words, offers the studly young professor a bit of sexual encouragement: "You stay right at the meat of things."

Chapter 10

The Producer's Other Cheek

Extinction is the rule. Survival is the exception.

—CARL SAGAN

At the end of the fourth week of shooting, with about twenty minutes of solid footage in the can, the production of *Who's Afraid of Virginia Woolf?* was only two days behind schedule. In keeping with Mike Nichols's plan, they had shot every scene so far in consecutive order. They were up to the moment when Martha comes back downstairs after changing into something more comfortable—a blouse with a low, cleavage-defining neckline over skintight toreador pants. The camera closes in on Nick, the virile young guest, who eyes Martha with pleasure and utters appreciatively, "Well, now." George, reading the dare in Martha's sartorial provocation, gibes: "Oh, your Sunday chapel dress."

The consecutive shooting schedule would now be interrupted by an excursion to Smith College, where the filming of all the exterior location scenes had to be completed before the students returned for the fall semester in mid-September. In the weeks before the trip, several incidents erupted on and off Stage Eight at Warner Brothers that distracted

Ernie Lehman from the elaborate planning required for the cast and crew to fly to Northampton, Massachusetts. The first-time producer was learning all too well how the gravitational force of a major movie star could yank a studio production out of orbit.

One afternoon, Ernie paid a social visit to Elizabeth in her dressing room. "Richard was there, too, and a Pekingese dog, and we spent a very pleasant hour of conversation over a vodka and tonic," Lehman reported in his journal. "It was one of the nicest times that we have had, at least that I have had with Richard on this picture. . . . Perhaps the vodka helped." Elizabeth was wearing a double rope of large pearls around her neck and made a point of explaining that Marty Ransohoff, her producer on *The Sandpiper*, had given her the necklace at lunch earlier in the day, a way to thank her again for starring in the film. "The wonderful thing about Elizabeth is that she loves jewels so much that she makes even a stingy man like me want to buy her jewelry, just to watch the thrill on her face," Richard said. It was a natural segue for them both to point out, in effect, that Ernie had yet to pay homage to Elizabeth with a gift of jewels, even though they had been shooting now for several weeks.

The Burtons told Ernie that they had never met anyone quite like him in Hollywood. "We think you're so different from other Hollywood producers," Elizabeth said. "You're so Brooks Brothers." When he told her he got his clothes at Dick Carroll's, she said, "No, not your clothes, Ernie. You've got a sort of Brooks Brothers mind and intelligence." While suggesting he was a cut above the other Hollywood moguls, it was a backhanded compliment. Brooks Brothers, the epitome of Ivy League convention, was considered nothing if not "square." Ernie had a way of ending these entries in his journal with clever comebacks, raising the question about whether he actually delivered his punch line at the moment, or the screenwriter in him just wished he had. Here, he reported that as he left, he turned to Richard and deadpanned: "You can tell Elizabeth to give the string of pearls back to the props department now that she has made her point." Richard merely smiled.

Only days later, Nichols pulled Lehman aside in the strictest confidence to say that Elizabeth was in tears in her dressing room. Richard had called her "a sour puss" for being difficult on the set that afternoon. Worse, he chastised her in front of others for giving a lousy performance. Mike told Ernie he could make things better if he finally gave Elizabeth that gift of jewelry she had been angling for. "You can spend $1,500, Ernie," Mike told him (the equivalent of $13,000 in 2022). "After all, it's deductible." This presumption on Mike's part—in fact his bald manipulation on Elizabeth's behalf—unnerved Ernie. "I have no intention of spending my own money on an actress who is receiving $1,000,000 for the performance," he told Mike, adding that he had already asked Jack Warner once to authorize a piece of jewelry for Elizabeth to charge to the picture. Warner had said no.

Over the following week, it became clear to Ernie that he and the film were caught in dangerous crosswinds between Elizabeth and Mike, forcing the producer to navigate the whims of the star and the calculations of the director—or vice versa—with chessboard caution. In each case, Lehman was compelled to take the sword for Nichols. First, soon after Ernie's very pleasant visit with the Burtons in their dressing room, Elizabeth called him to ask a favor: She knew that it was strictly taboo to show footage to any outsider until Jack Warner signed off on the rough cut—a rule clearly stipulated in Lehman's contract—but could they make an exception and let Ransohoff see what they had shot so far? (What a coincidence that the rival producer had just gifted Elizabeth that double rope of pearls!) Ernie told Elizabeth he would be right over. "Well, I don't see why you need to come over," said the most famous woman in the world. "Can't you just say yes?"

On the way to her portable dressing room on Stage Eight, Ernie asked Mike what he thought about Elizabeth's request, and Mike said he had already rejected the idea. Ernie arrived at Elizabeth's dressing room to find Ransohoff sitting there with her. She denied having been told no by Mike. Now Ernie found himself in a trap, a "he said–she said" contretemps with the star. When he looked for clarity from Mike, the preoccupied director suddenly remembered it differently, saying that he told Elizabeth he'd rather not show Marty any footage but that it was Ernie's call. Mike, either afraid to say no to Elizabeth or in cahoots with her, refused to own up to his participation in the misunderstanding and left Ernie holding the ball.

The following evening, Ransohoff called Ernie at home to say that Mike showed him the footage that morning and to apologize for causing such a rift. Mike had satisfied Elizabeth's wishes while defying—even further vilifying—Ernie. "The worst thing that could happen on a picture is for a star like Elizabeth to be angry with the director," said Ransohoff, speaking as a producer who had worked with Taylor directly. He offered advice on how to handle the million-dollar movie star. Ransohoff suggested that Lehman take the blame, do a lot of "aw-shucksing" in front of Elizabeth, and apologize for having goofed. "Of course, the only goof I made was in not braving her wrath by telling her absolutely no in the first place," Ernie wrote in his journal.

Lehman not only had to swallow his pride on more than a few occasions, but he found himself at that moment juggling logistical arrangements well beyond the set. Hal Polaire, his assistant producer, had flown out to Northampton ahead of the production to size up accommodations for the stars, the director, and the producer. Ernie was not prepared for Polaire's call reporting the dearth of houses that were lavish enough to fit the Burtons' requirements, never mind Nichols's expectations, or, for that matter, his own standards. Just as he was absorbing this unanticipated new wrinkle, Segal appeared in Lehman's office to express dismay at being relegated to a Motor Lodge room without a kitchen. Segal, who was bringing his wife and daughter to Northampton, demanded to be given a house, as well. Not only was Lehman obligated to manage his stars' happiness, but, equally, he feared that his own comfort level and reflected status was jeopardized by the limited choice in accommodations. This added to his headaches about the schedule— would it delay the shooting on location, and expand the budget? And how much more would they need to spend for housing? Around this time, he started relying on tranquilizers and amphetamines to bury the humiliations and to endure the daily frustrations. "I must say that 7 1/2 milligrams of Desbutal goes a long way," he wrote, referring to a popular upper at the time. "Even though I had only six hours of sleep last night, after I took one half of one of those 15 milligram tablets, I really got a lift . . ."

The other "major emergency," as Lehman characterized it, began with Elizabeth's impromptu campaign to get rid of Buck Hall, the assistant director. One afternoon after shooting had ended, Elizabeth sidled up to Ernie to say that she and Richard could not stand Hall, adding that practically every member of the crew found him difficult to work with. She even alleged that he was undermining Nichols: "Mike was saying to an unnamed person, 'I would be a swine if I did a thing like that,' and Elizabeth claims that she overheard Hall, who was sitting nearby, mutter to himself, 'What makes you think you're not?'"

Ernie described the Burtons' displeasure with Hall to Mike. "I think you ought to know that George Segal cannot stand Buck either," Mike said. He acknowledged his own misgivings about Buck, too, but made it clear that he considered it a personnel problem for the producer to solve. Au contraire, Ernie told Mike. They would be sharing the decision like two adults. Mike suggested that they mull the issue overnight.

Back in his office, Ernie called Elizabeth to say that he and Mike would sleep on it. She ignored him, instead bringing up the name Hank Moonjean, an assistant director on several of her recent pictures at MGM, who might be available to replace Hall. Hank was about to start on another picture at MGM, and Elizabeth had just asked Dick Hanley, her secretary, to call Moonjean to see if he still had time to leave that picture and come on board for *Virginia Woolf*. Lehman was emphatic that Hanley's call to Moonjean would have to be strictly exploratory.

At eleven P.M., Mike called Ernie at home to say that it would be very dangerous to fire Hall just now. "Who would know except Buck about all the shots I am going to take in New England?" He told Mike that Elizabeth's secretary had already put the ball in motion with Moonjean, but Mike thought it was a bad idea to change horses midstream. "We should try to get the Burtons to make some sort of peace with Buck Hall," Mike told Ernie. Ernie then called Hanley, told him of his conversation with Mike, and asked him to withdraw the inquiry to Moonjean before he embarrassed himself the next morning at MGM.

Around midnight, Ernie's phone rang. It was Elizabeth. "What a shitty thing to do," she said, accusing Ernie of changing his mind with no consideration for her and for Hank. In fact, Hank was there at her house at that very moment, having expressed his enthusiasm about the job to Hanley. "It isn't a matter of changing my mind," Ernie told her. "It is a case of your director exercising his prerogative to reevaluate a position he had taken at 6:00 PM in the afternoon and later coming to a decision."

It was clear to Ernie that Elizabeth was solidifying her alliances, conspiring to replace the assistant director with a friend and previous colleague. She had jumped the gun, and now her agenda was being thwarted. Elizabeth launched into a diatribe worthy of Martha, blaming Ernie, her producer, for putting her in this awkward position. (Ernie did not point out that she had put herself in the awkward position.) At that moment, Richard returned after an evening of drinking, and Elizabeth put him on the phone. "We seem to be making an awful lot of fuss about what is really a minuscule subject," Richard told Ernie. "It's rather like talking about changing one's housekeeper, isn't it?" (Moonjean was in earshot.) Richard, slurring his words, became increasingly ill-tempered: "The facts of the matter are that this picture is really going to be a flop anyway. It's badly written. It's badly acted. It's badly directed. And it's really not worth our bother, at all. So, I am just going to go play billiards." He handed the phone back to Elizabeth, who said to Ernie: "I'm not getting through to you at all." He countered: "No, it's just the opposite. I don't think I'm getting through to you. Nothing has happened other than Mike and I wanted to wait until the morning before we put Hank in the embarrassing position of talking to MGM." At that, Ernie said goodnight.

The following day, Lehman and Nichols met with Charlie Greenlaw, production manager at Warner Brothers, and they decided to keep Hall for now. Later in the afternoon, Ernie ran into Burton on the set and asked him how his billiards game went. He smiled and told Ernie he had been angry at practically everyone the day before, which Ernie took as a half-hearted apology. "I was being George and Elizabeth certainly was being Martha," Burton said. Lehman rued the fact that, while Nichols had a screenplay to refer to when directing the Burtons, it fell to the producer to improvise his way through real-life scenes with "George" and "Martha." "In the first few months of filming of *Virginia Woolf*, Elizabeth had occasionally found it difficult to shake off the iron grip of Martha," write Sam Kashner and Nancy Schoenberger. At times, "Martha completely took me over," Elizabeth admitted. "Richard and I would be out with friends, and I'd hear myself saying to him, 'for Chrissake, shut up. I'm not finished talking.' And then the next morning I would think, 'that wasn't me, it was Martha,'" Richard, too, experienced a merging with his character and observed his arguments with Elizabeth intertwining with those between George and Martha. "We will often pitch a battle purely for the exercise," he said. "I will accuse her of being ugly, she will accuse me of being a son of a bitch, and this sort of frightens people . . . I love arguing with Elizabeth, except when she is in the nude . . ."

At the end of that humiliating week—in which Lehman was caught between Taylor's hegemony and Nichols's invincibility—he asked Mike how things were going. "On the surface everything is wonderful, but way down deep underneath there are unhealable wounds," Mike lamented, as if putting his finger on Ernie's precise predicament. Ernie snickered: "Give me a few days and I'll bring what is way down deep up to the surface where it can really cause trouble."

As they both probably realized, Mike had turned Ernie into something of a father figure. Ernie—sincere, straightforward, competent, practical, and levelheaded—was fifteen years older than Mike. He represented the corporation and provided the boundaries that Mike, the emotionally rambunctious auteur, needed to push against to sharpen his rebellious nature, which, in turn, brought him back to his own gravitational center. Mike was psychologically astute, emotionally sensitive, and uniquely talented, but he was also self-serving, laughably manipulative, and, ultimately, a brat. As someone who knew him at the University of Chicago said, "He was a guy who would go into a White Castle and send back the hamburger."

~

Ernie wasn't taking the emotional turmoil on and off Stage Eight sitting down. While he tried to keep a scrupulous eye on the production schedule and a tight grip on the allotted budget, and to manage the ego-based eruptions of unpredictable personalities, he was also pursuing an extracurricular agenda of mogul-like proportion. When production of *Virginia Woolf* had commenced, everyone seemed to sense that it was going to be an important film. The agent Irving "Swifty" Lazar, who became known as "king of the deal" in Hollywood, smelled big money. Swifty chipped away at Lehman, eventually weaning him from his longtime agent, Abe Lastfogel, by dangling in front of him the prospect of a four-picture deal with one of the major studios. A studio courtship began that filled Ernie's weekly calendar with Dodgers games in the private box of Twentieth Century–Fox with Richard Zanuck and David Brown; dinners at Chasen's with David Picker of United Artists; and relevant premieres and receptions where he could wheel and deal and wine and dine in preparation for his next conquest. Lehman felt like a highly regarded asset in the film industry at large—just not on the set of his own picture.

On Friday afternoon, as the production was packing up for two weeks in Massachusetts, Mike, in a disarmingly magnanimous gesture, walked up to Ernie and "gave me a little kiss on the cheek," the ego-bruised producer noted. Then, as if trying out his best borscht belt material, he added: "After all, it was the cheek that I had used so many times during the making of this picture—the *other* cheek."

∾

On Saturday, August 21, 1965, the cast of *Who's Afraid of Virginia Woolf?* and a crew of more than fifty people boarded a chartered United Airlines Boeing 727 flight to Hartford, Connecticut. The Burtons, who hated to fly, took seats over the wing, and ordered double vodka and tonics before the ten thirty A.M. departure. They were told that the plane had to make a refueling stop in Chicago, which upset them, as they feared takeoffs and landings the most. But weather conditions were in their favor, and the flight proceeded to Hartford nonstop. Everyone was drinking and laughing and in great spirits throughout the flight, and at one point Mike said, "I could stay on this plane forever."

Limousines were waiting at Bradley Airport in Hartford to drive the Burtons, Nichols, Lehman, and the Segals to their respective residences in Northampton. Polaire had organized the first-class transportation for the VIPs and buses for everyone else. He had methodically final-ized the accommodations after scouting houses for a week and sending meticulous documentation of the options. The Burtons got first pick, then Nichols, then Lehman. When Nichols arrived at his residence—a rambling New England house with five bedrooms, a billiard table, a ping-pong table, and a separate guest cottage on magnificent grounds that included a trout stream—he called Lehman immediately to gush and to gloat. It would be perfect for his houseguests while shooting in Northampton—Stephen Sondheim and Mrs. Leonard Bernstein among them.

Lehman, too, was very happy with his house and its magnificent view over 150 acres. Since George Segal's contract stated that he had to pay for his own accommodations, Lehman had authorized the production to cover adjoining rooms for him and his wife and daughter at the Town House Motor Lodge, where most of the fifty or so crew members and staff were being put up. The Segals hated the motel the minute they arrived and had already complained to Nichols, who invited them to come stay in his guest cottage instead.

Polaire followed the Burtons from the airport to make sure everything was to their liking. They loved their lakeside house, Polaire reported to Lehman, but hordes of locals were visible on the street out front trying to get a glimpse of the famous couple. The lack of privacy made it impossible for the Burtons to remain there. Lehman offered them his rental instead and, within half an hour, the motorcade showed up at Ernie's house—the Burtons, their young daughter Liza, Polaire, the publicist John Springer, and four security men. Ernie popped the champagne that Polaire had stocked in each of the houses, and the Burtons looked around the lovely grounds, Elizabeth walking barefoot on the rain-dampened grass. But while they liked the house, it, too, was not private enough for their safety. In the end, the Burtons switched houses with Nichols. They were so contrite at putting everyone else out because of the encumbrances of their fame that they even offered to let the Segals remain in the cottage, but Mike insisted that George and Marion come stay with him in his new house. ("Musical houses is the faculty sport around here," Lehman quipped.) The following day, Sandy Dennis arrived from New York with her boyfriend and settled in comfortably at her assigned house.

On Sunday afternoon, Thomas Mendenhall, president of Smith College, threw a cocktail party at the campus art museum to welcome the cast and select crew members of *Who's Afraid of Virginia Woolf?* The paintings were beautiful. The faculty members were charming. The pink champagne was to everyone's liking. "Mr. Mendenhall is a very witty and vibrant man and we all, particularly the Burtons, enjoyed the party much more than we thought we would," Ernie said. Perhaps he had imagined Mendenhall in the vein of Martha's father, the president of a college not unlike Smith, and the cocktail party not unlike the one George and Martha would be leaving in the opening scene the following night.

Before the reception, Nichols, Lehman, and their assistants gathered in front of the building designated to be "Daddy's house" to choose about twenty members of the Smith faculty to appear as extras (guests) leaving the party along with George and Martha for the late-night opening shot of the film. After the selection was completed, a young man from the Smith public relations office approached Lehman to express a "philosophical bone of contention" about the extent to which the production team had distressed the Tyler Annex—a house on campus normally used for college offices—to be shot as "George and Martha's house." He claimed that the daughter of the college president would not live in a house that looked like something out of *Tobacco Road*. Lehman agreed that it looked ratty to the untrained eye, but the art director had it "distressed" for the sake of the camera, and the lighting setup at night would counterbalance the tattered aspect of the house in daylight.

The following day, the call time was six thirty P.M., two hours before nightfall. Almost one hundred local police officers and private security guards stood in a line along the police barricades around the perimeter of Seelye Lawn, the quadrangle in the center of campus. Hundreds of onlookers lined Green Street, a public thoroughfare, to watch the Burtons' arrival in a blue Cadillac at Hubbard Hall, the production's designated "VIP house." Days later, an article in the *Boston Herald* described the level of security around the Northampton campus, claiming that "it's easier to obtain an audience with President Johnson than it is to break through the security protecting the Burtons in this normally quiet city."

Elizabeth decided that she didn't need the face makeup for Martha, since, in the film's opening scene, they would be walking in the dark, at a distance from the camera. But Nichols insisted, explaining that it was the character's first appearance in the film, and calling over Haskell Wexler, who told Taylor that she would be walking close enough to the camera for her face to be seen. While Elizabeth was being made up,

Wexler proceeded with the elaborate lighting, which could only be tested for its effect after nightfall. Shooting exteriors after dark was trickier in 1965, an exercise of a thousand approximations. How far does the light extend to illuminate the shooting area? What to do about the changing shadows? How to cope with insects and birds flitting into the camera frame across the beams of light? In Northampton that August, the fixed light stands shook in the sudden gusts of wind. And, in the coming days and weeks, the rain on the pavement caused reflections that competed with the shapes of the characters on the lawn and, later, in the parking lot of the roadside tavern.

Meanwhile, the extras had arrived at six P.M., and chairs had to be gathered for them to sit down and wait. They were offered drinks until shooting began at nine P.M., when Nichols finally called out "Action!" George and Martha leave the party at "Daddy's house" and walk across the quadrangle. The single long shot of one minute and fifty-one seconds begins with the camera descending from the treetops and falling on the stalwart campus library in dramatic moonlight, slowly swooping past the massive trunk of an ancient tree and steadying itself at eye level across the leafy lawn. In the distance, a door opens on a lighted porch, perfectly framed by the graceful branches of an old maple tree. Light spills out from the doorway as a dozen people emerge and bid one another good night. One couple—George and Martha—begins to walk in our direction, toward the camera. Elizabeth had to practice the drunken walk with her weight falling from side to side. "Martha walks stumpy," Elizabeth told the journalist Mel Gussow. "Somewhere between a strut and a waddle."

As the shot continues, George and Martha veer around the building to the right. Nichols did half a dozen takes with various numbers of guests spilling out the front door, ending the shoot at eleven thirty P.M. After seeing the rushes the following day, Mike and Ernie concluded that the lighting was too bright in front of the house; there were too many people pouring out the front door; and too many bicycles were inadvertently scattered in the foreground. They had to reshoot the entire scene the following night.

~

Given the cheeky content of *Virginia Woolf*, the gravitas of its playwright, the scandal-tainted radiance and the untouchable glamour of its world-famous stars, and the New York cachet and cultural audacity of its first-time film director, the entire package was already a magnet for journalists. Shooting on location at Smith College only enhanced the production's visibility with New York media, many of whom hailed from the constellation of Ivy League and Seven Sisters schools. Reporters clamored for access, but Warner Brothers was obligated by the agreement with Smith College to turn the press away.

Lehman should have known that trouble was ahead when Springer appeared among the Burtons' entourage that first night of musical houses upon their arrival in Northampton. On August 23, the first day of shooting, Springer, the personal publicist for both the Burtons and Nichols—and the person Warner Brothers had contracted to help promote *Virginia Woolf*—began to pressure Ernie to lift the ban on the press. The contradictions and conflicts of interest are notable: On the one hand, Springer's first allegiances were to the Burtons and to Nichols, in that order. The movie they were making—on which Springer was temporarily employed—was simply a lucky vehicle for him to garner first-class press attention for his clients. The studio executives Carl Coombs (the unit publicist) and Mort Lichter (the studio publicist)—to whom Springer reported on matters related to the movie—were there on location as watchdogs to keep the press away while overseeing still-photography coverage of the production for future media use at the time of the film's release. Lehman motioned Coombs and Lichter over to ward Springer off.

There were legitimate reasons why the ban on the press was in place. "Mike and I thought it unwise to have photographers and journalists reporting what we felt were some of the secrets of the picture," Lehman later told one reporter. "We wanted to withhold any revelation of how Elizabeth looked as Martha and Richard as George until sometime in 1966, closer to the release date. And I think the director, his cast and everyone else felt very much more relaxed, much freer to devote themselves to the difficult task of making this picture, knowing that the press was not looking on." Yet this mandate had not stopped Lehman himself from orchestrating his own *Cosmopolitan* magazine profile, which would run soon after the Northampton shoot. Nor did it prevent him from being interviewed for a story on Nichols—with a cover photo featuring Nichols with the Burtons—that would run at the same time in the *Saturday Evening Post*, a wide-circulation national magazine that competed with *Life*.

"Remember, we had an agreement with the college," Coombs told one journalist, explaining that Warner Brothers was legally bound to honor Smith College's demand to protect the school's privacy and keep the press away. "We couldn't let anybody outside the unit on campus; We could not publicize the film as being shot at Smith College."

At three thirty A.M. of that first long evening, on a break in the middle of shooting the rest of George and Martha's walk home, Nichols stood there with Springer, their breath visible in the cold air. The temperature in Northampton had dropped significantly—at times to forty degrees that August—auguring further weather-related delays to the shooting schedule. Nichols called Lehman over and, with Springer in tow, confronted him about obstructing the press and spurning so much available good publicity. "My mind is made up, Mike," Ernie said, explaining that, aside from their obligation to the terms of Smith College, there was enough trouble shooting the film itself with all the temperamental personalities. "I don't feel this picture needs that kind of circus-y publicity right now. We will lose a certain amount of dignity in the publicity. I can tell from the coverage in the local papers that everyone seems interested in digging up scandal." When Nichols was called back to the set, Springer apologized to Lehman, claiming that Nichols was the one who put him up to raising the subject again.

Soon after this conversation, Lehman was proved right when a three-part series about the *Virginia Woolf* production at Smith College appeared in the *Boston Globe*, casting doubt on Taylor's ability to pull off the role of Martha: "To many it seemed like asking Debbie Reynolds to play Clytemnestra. Martha is a blowsy, boisterous, soul sick woman who might have been written by Strindberg. She is a *tour de force* for any actress but for total conviction the role requires extraordinary talent. Miss Taylor's films have made millions, but so far, her skills have remained poverty stricken. She has shown intermittent flashes of something like brilliance, but flashes only."

The partisan lines between the producer and director were now clearly defined. Mike, while profoundly committed to making a great film and angsting over every detail for all the right reasons, was also doing the Burtons' bidding at every turn—whether showing Ransohoff (an industry mole) the footage against studio policy; convincing Ernie to buy Elizabeth expensive jewels with his own money; or now, bullying him into allowing press access to the Burtons—despite the legal terms of the contract with Smith College. Certainly, Nichols wanted to keep the "talent" happy at all costs. But allying with the Burtons clearly had other advantages for Mike—both professionally (because their power over the production protected him) and personally (because their reflected glamour upped the wattage of his own celebrity). Nichols sided with the Burtons consistently over Lehman, who had an allegiance to the studio. Nichols derided him, but Lehman was a man of genuine integrity who was equally passionate—despite his cool-as-a-cucumber demeanor—about the quality of the film. Of course, he, too, had his own former-press-agent's eye on securing his legacy—in particular, through his potentially lucrative four-film courtship with several rival studios.

One night at the end of that first week in Northampton, Coombs informed Lehman that Tommy Thompson, *Life* magazine culture editor, and his colleague Ann Guerin were heading to see the Burtons in the "VIP House," along with Howard Thompson (no relation) of the *New York Times*. Ernie arrived at the Burtons' dressing room to await these members of the national press, unsure how to handle the situation. Yet, instead of policing these harbingers of "good publicity," Ernie greeted them in Elizabeth's presence with unexpected bonhomie. A few minutes later, as they all waited downstairs for Nichols to begin shooting an important scene outside "George and Martha's house," Polaire rushed up to Ernie with a genuine crisis: Herbert Heston, head of public relations at Smith College, flew into a rage when he saw the journalists and claimed that the production was violating its "no press" agreement with the school. "If you don't do something about this immediately," Heston threatened, "we will stop you from shooting on campus altogether."

Lehman called Springer over to gather the journalists immediately and bring them to his office at the VIP House. Upstairs, Lehman closed the door, poured everyone scotches, and explained the situation. Just then, Polaire bounded into his office to say that Heston was threatening to shut the entire production down, since the journalists still had not cleared out. "If those three people are not off the campus in ten minutes," Heston declared, "I will call the police. What's more, we would consider it an irrevocable breach of contract with the college."

Lehman drove the three journalists to the Northampton Inn, where they all downed several more scotches. After buying them dinner, Lehman confessed that, despite having agreed to the college's terms, he found it laughable that Smith College had thrown *Life* and the *New York Times* off the campus. "After an hour of drinking and talking, we got to be such good friends," Lehman recorded. He even hosted Thompson and Guerin at his house the following day, where he served them a champagne lunch and a cold buffet prepared by his cook and his housekeeper (among the crew paid for by the studio). Lehman, the author of *Sweet Smell of Success*, couldn't help himself from nabbing the attention of these journalists, despite his resolve to keep the press away. He understood the significance of *Life* magazine's interest in the film and its public reach. And he was fully cognizant of the calling-card effect of good publicity on his own "four-picture-deal" ambitions in Hollywood. So much for his conviction.

That weekend the journalists were present at a fish fry the Burtons held for the entire cast and crew at their commodious lakeside house. Police officers surrounded the property to keep the local celebrity stalkers away. The lake had been stocked with trout, and people were fishing, taking walks on the grounds, drinking on the patio, and playing ping-pong and billiards in the basement. Four of the Burtons' kids were visiting. Elizabeth was flipping burgers on the grill before the fish had been caught and fried. Perhaps the Burtons threw the party in the spirit of noblesse oblige, as a gesture to keep up production morale, or for the benefit of the press. But, in situations like this, Elizabeth, whose straight, shoulder-length black hair and casual summer wear gave her the look of a beautiful girl next door, was relieved that she didn't have to be "Elizabeth Taylor." Everyone was having a great time. "There was no way not to love Elizabeth because she was so simple with everybody," Mike said about her in this relaxed state. "She didn't change tone when saying people's names. She didn't grade them. They were just people."

Before the party, Bob Willoughby, the Warner Brothers photographer, showed Lehman the dozens of pictures that he had taken during the Northampton shoot so far. There were almost no pictures of Ernie, and he ordered Willoughby to include him in more of the coverage—in other words, to keep him written into the story. So, at the party, Willoughby asked Ernie to pose with Richard Burton. Burton put his arm around Ernie, but the producer wriggled away from the actor's affectionate gesture, not wanting to be documented in so intimate a manner. The Burtons were not wrong when they called him "so Brooks Brothers": Lehman could be very uptight.

⁓

In the film's second act, as George and Nick drink whiskey by themselves in the cool night air, George discloses a story from his past. As

Mel Gussow, Albee's biographer, revealed, the resulting monologue—a high point of the entire play—describes an actual event in the playwright's youth:

> Home on vacation, he and his friends from Choate would occasionally meet in New York for an evening of underage drinking at a receptive bar. One excursion left a particularly deep impression on Albee. When he was sixteen, they went to "Nick's," a popular jazz club on 7th Ave and 10th St, featuring such jazz stars as Muggsy Spanier and Pee Wee Russell. One of the teenagers in the Choate group had apparently accidentally killed both his mother and father. When the boys ordered drinks, the young man fumblingly asked for "bergin" instead of "bourbon." "I'll have bergin," he said, "give me some bergin, please . . . bergin and water." Albee and his friends laughed at the mistake, and the laughter soon spread. Almost everyone in Nick's started to laugh. The laughter would die down, then someone would say "bergin," and it would begin again. With its shared camaraderie and euphoria, Albee said he remembered the incident as "the grandest day of my youth." Eighteen years later in his first Broadway play, *Who's Afraid of Virginia Woolf?* Albee replayed that scene, transposing it to the 1930s during prohibition and making it a childhood memory of George.

The "bergin" speech was the second scene to be shot on location in Northampton, on the lawn beside George and Martha's house. Crew members had hung a thick-roped swing from the sturdy branch of an old elm tree. Klieg lights pinpointed Burton and Segal in a single beam against the leafy darkness. A technician wafted smoke toward the two actors to thicken the night fog. This is what Howard Thompson from the *New York Times* managed to observe in the few minutes he had on the set before being thrown off the campus that night with his *Life* magazine colleagues: "Beneath the towering elm sat the two faculty husbands, glasses in hand and a bottle at their feet. The younger man stared in glazed fascination as his host rested his head against the tree trunk and slowly began a long, sad soliloquy. As Richard Burton spoke and George Segal listened, a cricket symphony rhythmically ignored the Hollywood visitors filming."

While shooting that scene, Nichols got a point-of-view long shot of George sitting on the swing as seen by Nick from the side porch of the house. It would have to be reshot, as it turned out in the rushes to be completely out of focus. Nichols next attempted a very long and difficult take, in which Nick walks toward the swing, and then, as he leans against the tree, the two men start talking about their wives. Nick tells George about the circumstances that drove him to marry Honey. She was pregnant. They had to get married. "But you said you didn't have children," George counters. Nick describes it as a "hysterical pregnancy." In the continuing scene that Wexler shot in a single cut of five minutes and thirty seconds, George reaches for the bottle in Nick's hand, pours himself a little bourbon, takes a sip from his glass, and coughs—an unexpected accident that Burton incorporated seamlessly into his acting; he stands up with his back to the camera, walks to the tree and then turns to sit down at its base. George then proceeds to deliver the four-minute-long "bergin" speech, the steady camera slowly closing in on his face.

"It's *the* great speech in the play and it's the very essence of Albee," Nichols later reflected. On location, he described his directorial decision to Thompson, the *Life* magazine reporter. "We're letting the camera itself tell the story," Nichols said. "I'm remembering something that Hitchcock is supposed to have said once: 'every camera shot should convey an emotion.' I really believe we're hitting it." During this soliloquy, the camera focuses on George's face, closing in slowly and holding it as he speaks. "Richard was not so great at remembering long things and he was terrified," Nichols recalled. "And I didn't let on that I was terrified that he would never get through the single cut. I knew I could cut to Nick, but I wanted to make that decision depending on what was happening. And then this thing happened that you pray for. He did this very beautiful and moving version. He just did it perfectly. We were thrilled and I kissed him."

The following day, though, when they looked at the rushes, the exposure was completely off by at least eight stops. Everyone was heartbroken. "It looked like high noon," as Nichols remembered it. "We're never going to get this speech as good again," he told Wexler at the time. "You have to just dupe it and dupe it and dupe it until we get it right," he insisted, meaning that they had to print the film darker and darker and darker. But the following day, Nichols looked at the footage that editor Sam O'Steen had cut together of the scene. The lighting was completely mismatched between the long shots of Nick walking toward the swing from the house and the "bergin" speech. Lehman felt the gnaw of panic. Jack Warner was already accusing them of budget overages. Now add to that the delays caused by the weather conditions and by Wexler's interminably long lighting setups. The last thing Lehman needed was more reshooting due to what he perceived as inexperience.

∼

The third location in the Northampton shoot was a parking lot outside the Red Basket in nearby Southampton, a white clapboard roadside tavern for which Warner Brothers created a flashing neon sign, the words alternating between RED BASKET and DANCING. The parking lot was filled with multiple klieg lights, a ninety-thousand-dollar camera boom on a wooden rack, electrical equipment, a sound booth, a coffee canteen, and a crew of fifty or so milling about amid the trucks. In the gravel driveway stood George and Martha's car—a 1964 Ford station wagon with a drop cloth to protect it from the evening dew, and beside it, a row of black director's chairs with a name on the back of each one: Ernest Lehman, Doane Harrison, Mike Nichols, Elizabeth Taylor, and Richard Burton. At ten P.M., it looked to the drivers on Route 10 as if there had been a roadside accident, with dozens of police officers waving their flashlights to keep the traffic moving along.

All of this was in preparation for a hideous argument between George and Martha that takes place in the parking lot, after a barroom scene in which Martha seduces Nick on the dance floor and then sadistically humiliates George—a scene to be shot later, in sequence, back on Stage Eight. The roadhouse location does not exist in the play and was added to the screenplay, although every word of the dialogue is Albee's and was drawn directly from the play. Nichols told interviewer Steven Soderbergh that it was an intentional cinematic choice to stage scenes beyond George and Martha's living room. "When people say that it spoils the claustrophobia, well, in the theater claustrophobia is one thing; in a room that holds 1,000 people, a very large room, there are intermissions. Nobody is cooped up at all. But to subject [movie audiences] to the rhythmic similarity and the visual similarity of just staying in one room, it's not necessary."

~

Elizabeth and Richard were across the highway in a roadside house where they were being made up for the scene. As everyone waited for their arrival on the set, Nichols walked through the tangle of wires and cords, dropping casual jokes to members of the crew as he chewed steadily on a piece of gum. Tensions were high, as Richard was being temperamental. "I am moody, vicious, and dangerous tonight," he told Lehman before shooting began. Nichols knew Burton well enough to understand what he was going through. "Sometimes, when he couldn't perform, or refused to, it was Burton's old fear of inadequacy cropping up, his *hiraeth* (a Welsh word for longing)—his sense of alienation, his longing to feel at home," Nichols said. At other times, "it took the form of being abusive to Elizabeth, which was horribly upsetting to us. It was infrequent, but what happens is, when such a day occurs, everyone is constantly afraid another is coming." Nichols insisted that he was not afraid of Richard, claiming he would stand up to him and call him a "schmuck" when he took it out on Elizabeth. "But not that night in Northampton, because I saw it as despair and inability. How can you tell him he's a 'schmuck' when he's telling you he is so untalented and hopeless?"

They managed to get through part of the shoot. The scene begins with George and Martha bickering as they leave the tavern. Ugly things have just transpired inside: After Martha throws herself at Nick on the dance floor—a mating ritual, essentially—Martha further humiliates George by suggesting that the "bergin" boy was George himself, claiming the story appears in his unpublished novel. To get even, George embarks on a round of a game he calls "Get the Guests." He narrates a (phantom) *second* unpublished novel, about a couple from the "middle West" who had to marry because of the wife's hysterical pregnancy. Nick realizes George has betrayed his confidence; Honey recognizes the story and flees the tavern. Nick warns George that he will get even and runs after Honey. Now, while leaving the tavern, Martha accuses George of screwing up badly, and George reacts: "You! You can go around . . . slashing at everything in sight, scarring up half the world if you want, but let somebody else try it, oh no . . ." They are walking to the car, and Martha shakes her head. "You really screwed up, George," she says. "You really have."

It was now midnight—dinnertime for this nocturnal cast and crew. The back room at the Red Basket had been converted into a VIP dining room—the meal catered and the bar open—while the rest of the crew dined on portable canteen fare in the parking lot. Lehman had invited one of the journalists to join them for dinner. As Lehman walked with him through the tangle of equipment toward the tavern, a burly police officer stopped them: "Hey, you two guys got passes?" Lehman explained that he was the producer. "Hold on there, you gotta have passes," the officer insisted. "I'm the *producer*," Lehman said again, now losing patience. "I don't care if you wrote the damn thing; you gotta have passes." Lehman smiled, signaled for help, and he and the journalist were ushered through.

After dinner, at close to three A.M., shooting recommenced. Now Elizabeth and Richard were in sour moods, worsened by the intermittent spritzing of rain that interrupted their rehearsal before each take. The Burtons were annoyed with Mike, too, claiming that he was staging the scene improperly, and then with Wexler, for dragging out the lighting for every single take. Richard was so irritated at the late night / early morning hour that he was vocal about wanting to stop. Still, aware that this parking lot scene needed to be shot at night, and all the equipment was in place, and all the people involved in putting the shot together were not only watching but counting on his cooperation, he rose to the occasion. Burton, with his raw talent and consummate professionalism, inhabited George like a spectral force. And Action! Now standing at the driver's side of the car—embattled, humiliated, bitter, *exhausted*, he seethes at Martha: "You can sit around, the gin running out of your mouth, you can humiliate me. You can tear me to pieces all night. That's perfectly OK, that's all right . . ." His thought trails off as he opens the car door. "You can stand it," Martha barks at him. "I *cannot* stand it," George snaps back. Then the camera closes in on Martha's face, contorted into fulminating accusation. "You *can* stand it," she screams. "You *married* me for it."

George slams the door and stands there, staring out beyond the roof of the car, now despondent. "That's a desperately sick lie," he says quietly, with somber dignity. This scene, this moment, finally drained the life out of Burton. He stopped, turned on his heel, and walked away. He crossed the highway, went into the roadside house, and shut the door. That was the end of the shoot for the night. Nichols prayed that they had gotten enough footage to complete the arc of the scene. For the close-up scene of Elizabeth bellowing at George, "I had two cameras almost side by side with different lenses," Nichols later said, describing another revelation about filmmaking he learned that night. "One take was deadly dull and the other one really exciting, surely no more than three feet between the two of them. A huge lesson for me about the camera—that these subtle differences in detail can make a huge difference."

Ultimately, these moments of actorly pique were not the greatest obstacle to the production's progress. It rained off and on that night. In fact, the weather prevented them from shooting for days at a time. That, along with Wexler's slow pace in setting up the elaborate lighting for the evening scenes outdoors, plus the intermittent insecurities of the actors that ate up hours at a time, set the production back by two weeks and hundreds of thousands of dollars. This was exactly the outcome Lehman had hoped to avoid.

The entire cast and crew finally returned to Los Angeles on September 21, 1965, after almost a full month of shooting on location in Northampton. Years later, Nichols would reflect on the decision to shoot the exteriors of *Virginia Woolf* at Smith College. "It was a symptom of how green I was and how little I knew," Nichols told Soderbergh. "And how very bossy. If everyone weren't so scared to tell me, it all could have been shot on the back lot with no compromise whatsoever. There was no artistic superiority in going to Smith College. But I didn't know that. I thought it had to be in a real place. . . . The 'bergin' speech could have been done on any stage in the world. But I was dumb. And I mistrusted all the Hollywood stuff and I wanted to be sure it was real."

Chapter 11

Getting to the Marrow

I disgust me.

—MARTHA, IN *WHO'S AFRAID OF VIRGINIA WOOLF?*

In 1965, Mike Nichols was more famous than Andy Warhol. Unbeknownst to Nichols, Lehman, or anyone else at Warner Brothers, in the spring of that year, when the production of *Who's Afraid of Virginia Woolf?* was just gearing up in Hollywood, Warhol set out to make his own unscripted film version of the Edward Albee play. Warhol personally knew the experimental filmmaker Marie Menken and her poet husband, Willard Maas, who had been Albee's colleagues at Wagner College—and the likely primary inspiration for his characters George and Martha. Warhol intended to make a film of Willard and Marie fighting. "Menken and Maas were notorious bickerers and heavy drinkers whose weekend salons at their rooftop apartment in Brooklyn Heights were typically marked by the pair's rambunctious and theatrical sparring," according to Sheldon Renan, the film historian, who was part of Warhol's crew that day, along with Factory stalwarts John Hawkins, Gerard Malanga, Edie Sedgwick, Ronald Tavel, and Chuck Wein.

The resulting sixty-seven-minute film, called *Bitch*, was shot in the Menken-Maas living room in Warhol's signature home-movie documentary style. Willard and Marie, drunk on a Sunday afternoon, sit amid an eclectic array of Victorian-style furniture trading insults and barbs. "You don't seem to be able to finish your sentences," Willard says to Marie, making tongue-in-cheek mockery of her drunkenness. "We usually have a monologue of a hundred thousand hours about anything. You could be one of the great bores of all time." She nods off for a minute, then picks up the thread. "I happen to be your wife, and that's a big job," Marie says, waving her arm toward him. Willard sips his drink and responds in a kind of taunting singsong. "*You* are not so easy to live with," he says. "You think *I'm* so hard to live with? *You* are the problem." Marie ponders this and holds out her glass for another drink. "You don't know what it's like to be married," she says, as if to herself. "He gives me hell all the time." Before the hour is up, John Hawkins, Gerard Malanga, and Edie Sedgwick enter the frame, respectively, sitting down and draping themselves around each other as Willard and Marie each embrace one or the other of "the guests," who are there to keep the conversation going. Because Willard and Marie were so drunk, Warhol did not get the vérité hyperbole he was hoping for on camera. Still, the film remains in the Warhol archive as a notable example of his early filmmaking—and a telling document. You can glean the way Albee absorbed the tenor of Willard and Marie's conversational style— their unfiltered honesty and barbed affection—to create the characters of George and Martha.

Malanga, the poet—Warhol's studio assistant and a ubiquitous presence at the Factory throughout the 1960s—studied with Maas at Wagner College and considered Willard and Marie to be something akin to surrogate parents. "Willard and Marie introduced me to the poetry of Ezra Pound and W. H. Auden; the essays of Herbert Read; the novels of Carl Van Vechten, whose photography I'd become enchanted with, as well," Malanga wrote in his unpublished memoir.

"Poetry was my life commitment and Marie picked up on that. She may have even seen in me the son who died of pneumonia within a week of birth. Willard and Marie never talked about it; but Marie may have alluded to it once (or was it Willard?)."

Marie, a big-boned woman over six feet tall with close-cropped hair, "looked just like Broderick Crawford in drag," Warhol quipped, referring to the Hollywood heavy who starred in *All the King's Men*. She towered over Willard, who was about five foot six, with silver hair, a gravelly voice, and the stance of a bulldog. Willard was bisexual, and Marie made a sport of toying with his boyfriends. "They were an odd couple, and genuinely in love with each other," Malanga said. "But they had their harmless weekender harangues, like who could shout the loudest." Despite their eccentric demeanor and intemperate social behavior, Menken and Maas were undeniably accomplished, traveling in an avant-garde circle of artists, writers, and poets whose influence would reverberate through the legacy of arts and letters in America. As a professor of literature at Wagner College, Maas used his enduring friendships with the New York poets to organize public readings and symposia. As faculty advisor to the *Wagner Literary Magazine*, Maas regularly published their poems, and those of e. e. cummings, Marianne Moore, and William Carlos Williams.

Menken exhibited her paintings, first at the Betty Parsons gallery and then at Tibor de Nagy, two of the best contemporary galleries in New York in the 1950s. She went on to work with film and inspired a younger generation of filmmakers with her hand-held camerawork. Warhol, too, acknowledged her influence on his early films. He made "screen tests" of both Menken and Maas before Menken appeared in several of his films. All of this is to say that George and Martha, despite their slovenly drinking and unsavory psychological cruelty, were conceived as characters with substantial cultural gravitas. They sprang from the imagination of Albee within the avant-garde gestalt of Menken and Maas, whose free-thinking artistic circle placed them at the embryonic core of the 1960s zeitgeist. Nascent were the Theatre of the Absurd (of which Albee became a prime exemplar); pop art (which Warhol helped initiate); and the New York School of poets.

Willard and Marie's storied weekend soirees in their penthouse on Montague Street in Brooklyn Heights included regular guests such as Albee; Arthur Miller, who lived in the same building; Anaïs Nin; Charles Henri Ford; Daisy Aldan; Larry Rivers; Leroi Jones; Joan Mitchell; Barney Rosset; Warhol; and a rotating who's who of Beat poets. Kenneth Anger, the filmmaker, who shared their apartment for a time, was witness to some of the weekends with Willard and Marie that inspired Albee to write *Who's Afraid of Virginia Woolf?* "They had what you'd call a symbiotic relationship," Anger said, explaining that Willard and Marie would drink unrelentingly all weekend and end up arguing with each other for most of it. "Edward Albee experienced some of these sessions," Anger said. "Stan Brackhage did, too, and I certainly did while I was living there. I think they wanted an audience. It was their kind of psychodrama."

If Menken and Maas caught the attention of Albee and Warhol— eventual reigning avatars of that era—then the couple personified the cultural DNA of their period, and George and Martha carry the burden, as well as the glory, of symbolizing the dawn of a new age. It is no coincidence, then, that *Who's Afraid of Virginia Woolf?*—the play and the movie, alike—would challenge the hypocrisies of mainstream America, herald the sexual revolution, and register an entirely new psychological dimension to the public discourse.

Whether Nichols knew it consciously or not at the time, a similar set of intellectual challenges to the status quo were motivating his own large ambitions as the director of the film. Six years earlier, when Nichols was twenty-eight years old, he and Elaine May performed a unique—if mischievous and even subversive—skit at the 1959 Primetime Emmy Awards ceremony before a one-thousand-seat audience, which was broadcast live on national television. May was introduced as an award presenter and came out onstage in an elegant black cocktail dress. At the dais, she explained that the Academy had selected her to present a *special* award, the first of its kind in any category, so unusual that it wasn't even listed in the program. "There will be a lot said tonight about excellence, and the creative, the artistic, and the skillful will all be recognized and rewarded," she announced. "But what of the others in this industry? Seriously, there are men who go on in this industry year in and year out quietly and unassumingly producing *garbage*." She then presented the special award of "Most Total Mediocrity" in the industry to Lyle Glass (played by Mike Nichols).

Nichols jumped up from his seat in the middle of the glittering black-tie audience at the Moulin Rouge supper club theater in Hollywood to wild applause and made his way to the stage to receive this award manqué. "This is the proudest moment of my life," he said at the dais, smiling goofily. "My cup runneth over, I can tell you." He went on to say that he was often encouraged by his colleagues to create shows of substance, but he resisted. "I am very proud that you have shown your faith in me by sticking to my one ideal—*money*. I'd like to say briefly how I did it. Firstly, no matter what suggestions the sponsor makes, I *take* them. Secondly, I disregard talent in order to hire swell guys. And lastly, most important of all, I have tried to offend no one anywhere on earth."

Nichols brought his iconoclastic sensibility—plus an impish contempt for the banality of conventional society—to the making of *Virginia Woolf*. He wanted to shake up the traditions in Hollywood that fostered the kind of mediocrity he had accused the young television industry of slipping into. The Emmy Award winners that year constituted a menu of anodyne entertainment: *The Jack Benny Show*, *The Dinah Shore Chevy Show*, *Alcoa-Goodyear Theatre*, *Maverick*, *What's My Line?*, and *An Evening with Fred Astaire*. In 1959, 85 percent of American homes had television sets. Throughout the second half of the twentieth century, television was the most widely relied-on platform for a single common cultural dialogue in the United States—before the internet would balkanize information and diffuse the flow of common knowledge and experience into multitudinous universes. In twentieth-century America,

movies and sports were the other unifying vehicles that established
reference points for a predominantly common cultural dialogue that
no longer exists. As far as Nichols was concerned, the quality of that
common cultural dialogue was below-average intelligence, which, from
his plateau of intellectual refinement, he considered a shame.

When the production of *Who's Afraid of Virginia Woolf?* returned to
Stage Eight after its monthlong sojourn in Northampton, Nichols
became increasingly despondent. At the end of the first week back, he
called Lehman at home one night to kvetch. After listening to the
Broadway cast album recording of *Virginia Woolf* again, he claimed to
be hopelessly depressed. "They're all so great and the play absolutely
soars, and we *don't*," he told Ernie. "Here's what I think is going to
happen. Sandy Dennis is going to be fine. George Segal is going to be
fine. Richard is absolutely going to walk away with the picture, and
everyone is going to say there never was a George like Richard Burton.
But I just don't think Elizabeth is going to make it."

Nichols was comparing Taylor to Uta Hagen, who had embodied
the very essence of Martha on Broadway. Hagen was so much closer to
the character's temperament, sensibility, and maturity. She was even
pedigreed in the cultural ethos of Marie Menken's world—which so
thoroughly overlapped with Hagen's own—and the entire bohemian
impulse Albee was trying to put forward about "an examined life worth
living." By contrast, Taylor had been a Hollywood construction from
the time she was twelve years old, whose beauty eclipsed her talent;
whose extreme wealth catapulted her well beyond the common rituals
of daily existence; and whose professional expertise resided in an
acquired understanding of how the camera would read every nuance of
emotion in her facial expression.

When the twelve-year-old Elizabeth played Velvet Brown, James
Agee reviewed *National Velvet* in the *Nation*, weighing in on the very
young actress with his gimlet eye: "I wouldn't say she is particularly
gifted as an actress. She seems, rather, to turn things off and on, much
as she is told, with perhaps a fair amount of natural grace and a natural

bored female's sleepwalking sort of smile, but without much, if any, of an artist's intuition, perception, or resource." It isn't fair to apply this conclusion about her talent at the age of twelve to her wildly successful—if not exactly substantive—career as a movie star, although Agee would prove himself to be an astute film critic, and he wasn't wrong in predicting the kind of actress she would become. Clearly, Nichols had similar worries about Taylor before he started working with her, evident in his comment to Lehman on the eve of rehearsal for *Virginia Woolf* in which he doubted that Taylor's chocolate milkshake–like sweetness could be distilled into Martha's demon gin–caliber venom.

Elizabeth approached the character of Martha from the outside in. Nichols, while cognizant of her cinematic intelligence, had to reverse engineer her approach to Martha, bridging her emotional connection to the narrative motivation at each stage of the story. Even her age had to be reverse engineered. How could the thirty-three-year-old actor who had been married four times understand the existential discontent of Martha—a premenopausal, middle-class woman who had been married to the same man for twenty years? Not only did Nichols have to keep reminding her to deepen her voice to simulate the age of her character, he had to walk her through almost every scene, anatomizing the psychology of Martha's reactions virtually line for line, and enacting the gestures that reflected the emotional underpinnings of her words.

Ernie advised Mike not to compare Taylor with Hagen and then offered an example of how Elizabeth *was* comparable. "When Elizabeth as Martha cries 'I'm not a monster! I am *not!*' she is truly heartbreaking," Lehman pointed out to Nichols. "You believe she is not a monster. When some of the actresses who play it on the stage utter those lines, it is hard to feel that they are not monstrous." Lehman was right. There are moments of striking ferocity, as well as vulnerability, in Elizabeth's performance, in her voice, that cannot be denied. But Nichols was not yet convinced.

At the end of that first week back on the set, Mike was continually agitated. He managed to get through three quarters of a page of the script that Friday—less than a minute of usable footage. "Haskell Wexler fiddles around," he whined during his regular Friday afternoon lament to Ernie. "The camera crew isn't talking to me because I snap at them. Richard doesn't want to be called until we are ready, so we call him when we're ready, and then Haskell fiddles around for another 30 minutes. Elizabeth takes longer than other people to get her makeup ready, and we all have to sit around and wait for *her*. Then Charlie Greenlaw [the production manager for Warner Brothers] came to the set three times today. He was very nice about everything, but it's *pressure*. I can't stand it. I think I'm going to have a nervous breakdown."

While the mechanics of production were getting in the way of the actual filming, Lehman compared Mike's pleas for sympathy to "the boy who cried wolf." It didn't stop Mike: "I don't think anybody realizes how difficult it is to cope with the Burtons and Haskell Wexler, and this tiny set, and the difficulties in making this picture, and the fact that I have to give up certain shots that I want merely because I know we're behind schedule."

These were the run-of-the-mill frustrations of any director, but Nichols was a first-timer feeling overwhelmed. Still, Lehman thought he was being histrionic, exaggerating the pressure for effect. He told Mike that he had it easy compared with the travails of other productions and the demands of other studio heads, reminding him, perhaps with avuncular irritation, that, despite Jack Warner's occasional kvetching about the production deadline, they should be grateful for his hands-off approach.

Lehman knew what pressure felt like, but he wasn't one to complain about it. The production had spilled two weeks over schedule in Northampton; Taylor was due to be paid one hundred thousand dollars per week for any work beyond the contracted shooting dates, and Burton, fifty thousand dollars per week. Knowing this, Jack Warner had ordered Lehman to ask the Burtons for two additional free weeks—in effect, to give up three hundred thousand dollars—precisely to save the production money; this, in turn, would relieve some of the time crunch on Nichols. Lehman made an appointment with Burton in his dressing room, asked him the difficult question about sacrificing additional pay for two more weeks, and Richard agreed on the spot. When Lehman apprised Nichols of this coup, Nichols said, "Oh, they did it as a gift to *me*"—in effect, diminishing Lehman's small but valuable accomplishment. Lehman then had to go through the protocol of informing the Burtons' "people"—the agents, who all consented, and their lawyer, who did not. "Over my dead body," he said. So, once again, three hundred thousand dollars' worth of pressure was on Lehman's shoulders.

Over the years, many things have been said about Mike Nichols the genius; Mike Nichols the public figure; and Mike Nichols the shit. His level of discernment, however, could be in service of the highest artistic ideal. Mike Haley, who worked with Nichols as an assistant director on several later films, spoke of Nichols's taste and rigor with admiration, describing a moment in Nichols's office one day as they discussed the look of a particular scene in a film. Nichols tried to explain his idea of the color palette and then, in a lightbulb moment, asked his office assistant to bring in a painting from the other room. "Somebody brings in a small *Matisse*," Haley said—the real thing—and Nichols goes, "You *see*?"

~

David Hare, the playwright, recounted a conversation with Nichols later in his life that speaks to the more insufferable aspect of his sense of entitlement. There was a period when Nichols was on medication for depression, and he thought he was going broke. "So, I did this incredible thing," he told Hare. "I started traveling coach in airplanes . . . the state of the toilets, it's *disgusting*." He asked Hare if he had ever traveled coach class and experienced the same outrage. "Actually Mike, I travel coach all the time," Hare told him. "Most of the human race travels coach class." Nichols looked at him, bewildered. "You can do that, can you?" he asked, as if he were Burton imagining himself driving a Toyota Camry instead of a Rolls-Royce. "Well, yeah, Mike. I'm not very rich," Hare said.

In Nichols's state of anxiety, he had no compunction about blaming schedule delays on Wexler, despite the fact that Nichols himself expected the luxury of taking his own time to get scenes right. Wexler was by no means incompetent. He made mistakes because he was experimenting. "It is to the advantage of studios and directors to encourage the cinematographer to take these chances," Wexler said in his own defense. "If they don't, his work will be professional—true—but it can never be inspired."

Despite Nichols's frustrations with Wexler's pace, in the end his camera work is masterful—photographically immediate, visually articulate, and striking—a tour de force of black and white cinematic intelligence. Like Nichols, Wexler was a perfectionist. The amount of time it took to get the angles right and the lighting in place was, for him, simply the amount of time it took, regardless of the pressure on him from Mike, or the actors, or the studio. Nichols was blind to the mirror-image dilemma Haskell was presenting—two geniuses at work racing against the clock, at times against each other, canceling each other out. "The surprising thing about Mike Nichols is that every day during shooting he learned more about filmmaking than the average person would learn in years, because he has a fantastic mind and is an 'addicted' filmgoer," Wexler said. "It's essential for the cinematographer not to get his feelings hurt to the point where he stops giving. The important thing is to care. A good director can bring the best out of a cameraman and I feel that cameramen have a responsibility to help the director do his best, too."

∾

Throughout *Virginia Woolf*, the subject of George and Martha's son is a poignant leitmotif fraught with mystery and layered with tension. Early on, George warns Martha not to mention "the little bugger" to their guests. Later, when Nick asks George if he and Martha have

children, George responds, "That's for me to know and you to find out."
And then, when Honey comes downstairs after using the "euphemism,"
gushing that Martha just told her about their son, George gets furious.

Why is their son such a taboo subject? The mystery about the absent
son hovers over the evening until the emotional climax of the play. This
pendulum of ambiguity was constructed by Albee not only as a riddle
with a source in his own existence as an adopted child but, more important, in terms of the predominating symbol of the play: The imaginary child is the metaphorical heartbeat of George and Martha's
love for each other that resides so deeply hidden and protected—
inoculated—at the tender core of their marriage. Intrigue about the
existence of the imaginary child goes back to the very conception, as it
were, of Albee's play. Did Marie Menken have a miscarriage, as she said,
claiming to be the source of inspiration for Albee's play? Gerard
Malanga recounted a story about Menken and Maas's infant son who
died of pneumonia, but he couldn't remember which of them told him.
Willard also had a son from a previous marriage—an absent child in
Willard and Marie's household. While Albee was writing *Virginia Woolf*,
he described the play's subject to a friend in Berlin. "She has a son and
she and her husband are talking about that son, and she hasn't a son,"
he told her. When his friend asked him if he was being intentionally
enigmatic—either she has a son or she doesn't have a son—he smiled.
"You'll see."

Of course, the question about whether George and Martha's son
exists is one about the playwright himself. Albee was adopted. Was he
wanted, or wasn't he? He was an unexpected visitor in his mother's
womb, and she gave him away. He was an imaginary child to Frankie
and Reed Albee before they adopted him, and once they did, they
barely noticed him. He was the vacant child because there was no
emotional expression in the Albee home. He was the absent child
because he was sent to boarding school. Could it be that he felt more
like an idea than a living, breathing individual? It's not a stretch to
imagine that *Who's Afraid of Virginia Woolf?* was born out of Albee's

wish to be "the idea" that would spark love between Frankie and Reed, who would then be capable of loving him and making him feel, finally, like the genuine flesh-and-blood son of actual parents.

After the first round of unpleasant exchanges between George and Martha in front of their guests; following the sparring between George and Nick while the wives are upstairs; and, finally, after Honey drinks too much brandy and throws up, George and Nick have a bonding moment outside on the swing when George delivers the "bergin" speech. Nick confesses that he was forced to marry Honey because he had gotten her pregnant. Yet, once they were married, the baby disappeared, evaporated. "Poof," he says. Honey had had what was commonly called in that era a "hysterical pregnancy." "Pseudocyesis," the proper term for it, is rare. "Those who suffer from the disorder present a constellation of symptoms that mystify even seasoned practitioners," wrote the *New York Times* in 2006. The symptoms are real: menstruation stops; there is nausea and vomiting; the abdomen enlarges, along with the breasts; there are even odd food cravings. And yet, there is no embryo or placenta or heartbeat, no sign of conception, no baby.

Bertha Pappenheim, a well-to-do Austrian woman in the late nineteenth century, was a patient of Josef Breuer, Sigmund Freud's mentor. Breuer's sessions with Bertha led to the development of "the talking cure" at the foundation of Freudian psychoanalysis. During Bertha's treatment for a variety of neuroses with physical symptoms, she claimed that she was pregnant with Breuer's child—a false pregnancy. Breuer and Freud both wrote about it in a case study they called "Anna O." While Freud would later debunk his own conclusions about the sources of hysteria, and scholars in the field of psychoanalysis would volley back and forth over the years about Freud's ideas, "Anna O" was a prototypical example of the enigma of a "hysterical pregnancy."

In late September, when the production of *Virginia Woolf* returned from Northampton to Los Angeles, Dennis, who plays Honey, told Nichols she was pregnant. When Lehman learned of her condition, he wondered if she had succumbed to the actor's curse of taking on the behavior and circumstances of her character in real life, not unlike the way Richard and Elizabeth acknowledged George and Martha seeping into their conversations and affecting their behavior. It was hard for Lehman to believe that Sandy was really pregnant given that she was unmarried. How, he wondered, could she have a baby out of wedlock? (For all his sophistication, it was in conclusions like this that Lehman's 1965 "squareness" revealed itself.) Then he remembered that she had been sick and throwing up in Northampton and had taken a day off to go see her family doctor in New York.

The term "hysterical" might apply to Sandy's pregnancy only through the behind-the-scenes havoc it created on the set. Rumors were afoot that she was really four and half months pregnant. Lehman worried about scandal surrounding the production, as pregnancy out of wedlock in 1965 was considered a moral disgrace—the "scarlet letter" for any woman before the sexual revolution of the late 1960s recalibrated social mores. Nichols worried about how it might affect the shoot. Mike called a meeting with Ernie and Charlie Greenlaw, the production manager, to rework the schedule so they could finish her scenes as quickly as possible before she started showing. But then Mike couldn't bear shooting the picture out of sequence because he felt it would ruin the performances. Meanwhile, Lehman reported that "Sandy is eating too heavily and has gained about 20 pounds. There is no doubt," he wrote, "that her pregnancy is going to be a continuing headache."

In late October, Sandy's agent called Lehman and assured him that her baby was not due until May. Lehman asked that she go to an obstetrician in Los Angeles who could provide the studio with an official due date. Then, *Time* magazine reported that Dennis had gotten married secretly to Jerry Mulligan, her boyfriend, in Connecticut, back in June. Whether the studio planted the story, or reporters discovered her pregnancy on their own, Lehman felt relieved, if only to have averted scandal on the set.

Throughout the movie, Sandy's character, Honey—childlike in her innocence, fragile in her vulnerability, and increasingly drunk beyond her tolerance—will intermittently throw up, "dance like the wind," fall asleep, slur her words, and function both as a cipher and as an echo. After the roadhouse scenes—in which she watches her husband in erotic thrall to Martha and then flees from the barroom when George divulges to the group that he knows about her hysterical pregnancy—the two couples return to the house. Inevitably, Martha and Nick end up in bed together, which George discovers as he stands outside the house and watches their silhouettes in the bedroom window upstairs. George tries to shake Honey awake on the front steps to tell her what her husband is doing with his wife, but she pushes him away. "You don't know what's going on, do you?" George snarls at her. Honey is in some half-asleep dream state, and she says, "I don't want to know." He grabs her and pulls her to the lawn, bellowing "*Look* at them," pointing up at the window. "Leave me alone," she cries, falling on the grass and shaking her head. "I don't want any children," Honey screams, as if George might be assaulting her sexually or, perhaps, triggering a memory of abuse. "Please, I don't want any children," she beseeches him. George, rather cruelly, kneels beside her and says, "I should have known." He points to the window above. "Does *he* know that?" George growls, referring to her husband in bed with his wife. "Does that *stud* you married know that?"

Then, out on the lawn with Honey, George gets the idea for one final game. When all four characters are soon assembled in the living room, George sits next to Honey on the couch. "Our son," George announces. "Martha's and my little joy." Honey looks at him, bewildered. "*Who?* You have a child?" George's laugh is sinister as he turns to Martha. "Oh, yes, indeed, do we ever? Martha, you want to talk about him, or shall I?" Martha looks visibly frightened and beseeches him not to, but he launches into a brief description of their son's surprisingly pleasant demeanor, "in spite of his home life," George explains. "I mean, most kids would grow up neurotic, what with Martha here carrying on the way she does, sleeping till four in the P.M., climbing all over the poor bastard, trying to break down the bathroom door to wash him in the tub when he's sixteen." Martha objects, before deciding that she is going to talk about their son after all and launches into a lachrymose recitation. "Our son was born on a September night, a night not unlike tonight. Tomorrow. Sixteen years ago. It was an easy birth," she says, but George contradicts her, reminding her of how she labored. "It was an *easy* birth," she insists, "once it had been accepted, relaxed into. I was young, and he was healthy, a red bawling child with slippery strong limbs and a full head of fine, fine black hair which only later, later, became blond as the sun. Our son. And I had wanted a child. . . . And I had my child." "Our child," George corrects her. "I want a child," Honey blurts out, and repeats it again as she starts crying. "I want a child. I want a bay-bee." Honey's outburst occurs over Martha's heart-wrenching soliloquy, and we can hear Martha's voice, as if in refrain, in the background . . . "the sewer of our marriage, sick nights and pathetic stupid days," she says, disparaging their life. "The one light in all this hopeless darkness—our son."

A week before the end of production, when the last scenes were being completed, Elizabeth had a baby shower for Sandy in her luxurious dressing room. About twenty women had been invited, including the script editor, the makeup crew, and various secretaries. It was catered and there was champagne. Elizabeth gave Sandy a bassinet that was shipped back to Sandy's apartment in New York. But, one week after the film's last scenes were completed, on December 20, Lehman reported in his journal: "Terrible news in the paper today: Sandy Dennis has had a miscarriage. She has lost her baby. What a sad ending to the whole story of Sandy's pregnancy—an ending that came less than two weeks after she played the scene in which she cries 'I want a child . . . I want a baby!' "

Years later, in a 1989 interview with *People* magazine, Dennis discussed her miscarriage after just completing *Who's Afraid of Virginia Woolf?* "If I'd been a mother, I would have loved the child, but I just didn't have any connection with it when I was pregnant," she said. "I never, ever wanted children. It would have been like having an elephant."

~

A month before filming was completed, in November 1965, Nichols and Burton celebrated their birthdays under the sign of Scorpio, four days apart. Nichols's moods had been swinging wildly under the pressure he was navigating, on top of the glare of his increasing fame in association with the production. He went out and bought himself an extravagant birthday present: a brand-new Rolls-Royce Silver Cloud III Continental convertible. Nichols was always full of surprises—astute, confident, and charming one day, full of doubt, suspicion, and despair the next. Sometimes, though, his grandiosity knew no bounds. It's true that he garnered genuine respect from the cast for his original ideas, his ability to articulate the psychological motivation of each character, and the clarity with which he could pinpoint the action that would draw out the emotion required of each scene. Equally, though, he could leave the cast and crew exasperated because of his exacting standards and irritated at his imperious demands. When Lehman saw the car parked outside Stage Eight, he congratulated Mike on his taste. "You really have guts buying a car like that," Ernie said. "I mean, that's really saying I have a big penis and I want everybody to know it." Mike laughed, and deflected Ernie's judgment with his self-deprecating wit: "Yeah, and some people buy a Rolls Royce because they don't have a penis at all." Just before he bought the car, Nichols posted a (not so) self-mocking slogan on the side of the main camera on the *Virginia Woolf* set, which states: "When you're as great as I am it is difficult to be humble."

On Nichols's birthday, November 6—a Saturday night—he threw himself a thirty-fourth birthday party at his Cole Porter estate. The Burtons were there. Julie Andrews was there. The champagne and brandy flowed. Andrews inadvertently revealed to Lehman that she had seen an hour of the footage (Nichols bending the rules again) and told him how wonderful she thought the film was so far. During this period, Lehman was being offered stage-to-screen projects from the various studios courting him for his four-picture-deal—plays like *How to Succeed in Business Without Really Trying* and *Hello, Dolly*—to turn into film scripts. He was considering *Hello, Dolly* with the idea of casting Elizabeth Taylor in the role of Dolly Levi. He had asked her unofficially if she would be interested. She told him she would have to ask Richard, who commented, disparagingly, "Well, you're overweight enough and you're Jewish." (Taylor had converted to Judaism when she married Mike Todd, taking Elisheba Rachel as her Hebrew name.) Ernie sat next to Elizabeth at Mike's birthday table, and she asked him, as if in code: "So, any word on *Hello, Schwartz?*" (Lehman eventually wrote the screenplay and produced the film version of *Hello, Dolly*, starring Barbra Streisand.) As a birthday present to Nichols, Lehman gave him a framed Picasso print with a card that said: "In this town it's the picture that counts."

Four days later, on Burton's thirty-ninth birthday, he and Elizabeth walked out the door of Stage Eight to go to lunch, and, there, parked right in front, was a 1966 white Oldsmobile Toronado wrapped in a large red ribbon with a bow at the top. "Happy Birthday, darling," Elizabeth said to him. Of course, the Burtons already had a forest green Rolls-Royce convertible in the garage of their house in Gstaad, Switzerland. And they had a chauffeur-driven Cadillac to take them back and forth to the studio from Bel Air. The Toronado was a full-size muscle car wrapped in sleek, modern, rocket-style luxury—the perfect birthday toy for "the man who has everything." Burton was speechless with delight, and because he had no scenes after lunch, he spent the afternoon driving the car around the lot. There was a birthday party for him on the set at the end of the day with the cast, the crew, and a few studio executives, with a full bar, canapés, and a big birthday cake. Lehman's gift to him was impressive and well-considered, a 330-year-old edition of Francis Bacon's essays, for which Richard was so grateful that he kissed Ernie on the cheek.

While Mike had been gloating about how happy he was driving his new Rolls-Royce on the freeways, it didn't stop him from complaining about everything else. He was upset about the graininess of the film on the dailies. Wexler blamed the lab. The lab blamed the film Wexler had chosen to use, which was known for its grain. In the end, the film was not grainy at all.

$\sim$

In the final month of production, the encumbrances were enough to frustrate anyone. Elizabeth didn't show up on the set for several days because of an abscessed tooth, which had caused her pain and left her cheek swollen. They had to shoot around her scenes. Additionally, her contract allowed several days off a month during her period, as she was known to suffer severe cramps. Another day was interrupted because the Burtons had to appear in court in the matter of the custody lawsuit Eddie Fisher had brought against Elizabeth regarding their adopted daughter. And then, a full day was taken up waiting for grass to be laid out in front of the house on the set of Stage Eight for an added outdoor scene, a tedious process of matching the lawn in the footage from Northampton.

Finally, after Mike had spent a good part of a day directing Elizabeth in a crucial scene—one all-important soliloquy about her love for George—he was faced with a dilemma. After seeing the dailies, everyone agreed that her performance was virtuosic. "It was the kind of acting that might have won Elizabeth an Academy Award just for today's dailies alone," Lehman said. Yet Mike felt that she was so tearful in the scene and had broken down so completely that she would have nowhere to go after that emotionally. He wanted to save the emotional crescendo for Martha's final collapse near the end of the film. She had just given the performance of a lifetime, which took a great deal out of her, and now Mike was asking her to do it again and tone down the emotional intensity. Of course, she was livid. Richard agreed that, as an isolated sequence it was an amazing performance, but he sided with Mike, saying that they had to consider the overall emotional pattern of the picture. After a tearful spell off camera, Elizabeth finally agreed. Tight-lipped, she proceeded to do it all over again. "The Burtons are great to work with," Wexler said. "They're intelligent and completely professional. What I like most about Elizabeth is that she is so considerate of everybody down to the supposedly least important member of the crew. She's a real trouper who goes right on working even when she is actually ill. She is really a very, very fine woman."

It was the scene right after Martha calls Nick "a flop in some departments"—meaning sexually—and he accuses her of thinking everyone is a flop. She agrees (in something of a prefeminist call to arms): "I am the earth mother, and you are all flops." Then she begins her soliloquy: "You know, there's only been one man who has ever made me happy. You know that? *One.*" Facetiously, Nick asks her if it was a gym instructor or something. "No, no, no," she says. "*George.*" She turns around and looks at Nick. "My *husband*?" she reminds him. "You're kidding," Nick says. "*George,*" Martha repeats, now staring through the screened door out into the darkness, the camera outside closing in on her. "*George,* who is out there somewhere in the dark. Who is good to me, who I revile. Who can keep learning the games we play as quickly as I can change them. Who can make me happy—and I do not wish to be happy. Yes, I *do* wish to be happy. George and Martha, sad, sad, sad. Whom I will not forgive for having come to rest, having *seen* me, and having said, *yes,* this will do. Who has made the hideous, the hurting, the insulting mistake of *loving* me, and must be punished for it. George and Martha, sad, sad, sad . . ."

Over the years, Elizabeth Taylor said more than once that her best roles were Velvet Brown in *National Velvet,* and Martha. During the production, Elizabeth was surrounded by stage actors, all of whom performed their roles from the inside out, each one inordinately talented in their own singular way. She rose to the role of Martha under the tutelage of her husband and costar, Richard Burton, one of the most gifted Shakespearean actors of the stage, and aided by the psychological incisiveness of Mike Nichols, who, as a director, coaxed out of her a performance—such as this soliloquy—that would surprise everyone, and no one more than herself. Elizabeth pulled her performance up from the depths of her being—and perhaps out of her love for her husband, Richard, rather than his character, George— alongside her native understanding of what the camera records. "Elizabeth didn't mind looking puffy and haggard, nor did she want to resemble the fat lady in the circus," Wexler said. "Extremely conscious of her screen appearance, she constantly reminded me that she wasn't supposed to look good. Then she'd whisper, 'Well, I'm not supposed to look awful, either.'"

Nichols acknowledged moments like her soliloquy performance throughout his career, describing it as "that thrilling thing that I've only seen in actors like Dustin Hoffman and Elizabeth Taylor." It was an indescribable quality that snuck up on him, "that secret, where they do something while you're shooting, and you think it's OK, and then you see it on screen and it's five times better than when you shot it. That's what a great movie actor does. They don't know how they do it, and I don't know how they do it, but the difference is unimaginable, shocking. This feeling that they have such a connection with the camera that they can do what they want because they own the audience. Elizabeth had it, and by God, so did Dustin."

In the final crescendo moments of the film, George declares that the imaginary child has died in a car accident. To play the scene, Taylor had to handle several layers of simulacra at once, locating the genuine emotion for something twice removed from reality, registering grief about her character's imaginary son's death in front of strangers. She is heartbreakingly believable as Martha reacting to George's last stand. At the end of her soliloquy about their son, Martha says, "So beautiful, so wise. But, of course, his perfection could not last, not with *George* around. . . . a drowning man takes down those nearest to him." As she speaks, George is reciting from the Latin text of the Requiem Mass, and Honey finally screams, "Stop it." George asks her why. "Is this game over?" Nick asks with peremptory irritation. "Oh, no," George says, gleefully. "Not by a long shot."

The camera angles up at George, who towers over Martha seated in the chair. "Sweetheart, I'm afraid I've got some bad news for you," he says to her in prelude and then proceeds to explain that their son is not coming home. While she and Nick were upstairs—*in bed together*, he emphasizes, he received a telegram announcing that their son had been in a car accident. "Our son is . . . *dead*," he proclaims. "He was killed late in the afternoon on a country road with his learner's permit in his pocket. He swerved the car to avoid a porcupine and drove straight into a . . ." If this sounds familiar, it's the same story George told Nick about the "bergin," the boy who killed his father in a car accident when he hit a tree to avoid a porcupine. "NO," Martha screams, darting up in protest. "You cannot do that. You can't decide these things for yourself."

She lunges at George, and Nick tries to pull her off him. "Our son is dead," George now repeats with increasing vituperation in his voice. "*Poof.* Now, how do you like it?" Her wailing cry "No" comes from the depths of her disbelief, searing with pain as she drops to the couch in horror—as wailing a cry as any mother who just learned that her son had been killed. "You can't do that," she repeats, as if in a delusional state. "You can't let him die." Nick tries to console her, but George speaks over him: "There was a telegram, Martha." She looks up at him, beseechingly and enraged. "Show me that telegram." Then, in his most sinister voice, George chillingly mouths out: "I ate it." "What did you say to me?" she says, razors in her voice. "I.ate.it.," he says with sadistic glee. She spits in his face.

Suddenly, Nick sees the truth. "Oh my god," Nick says with disbelief. "I think I understand this." He repeats it three times. He realizes that the son is imaginary, that the death is not real, and that Martha's tears are about something else. It is all an illusion, a game, and he and Honey have been subject to a perverse and grotesque manipulation all night long.

George has killed their son—that is, the very idea that represents the love between them—out of revenge, out of disgust, out of desperation. After all, how many lines had Martha crossed throughout the evening, how many last straws had she thrown his way to taunt him, to test his love? Aside from breaking their rule about discussing the "little bugger," Martha divulged and disparaged the autobiographical story of his novel—emphasizing her father's demeaning repudiation that prevented its publication—just to further assassinate George's character before their guests. Then, the ultimate slap in the face of their marriage, she slept with Nick right under George's nose—at once betraying him and humiliating him. Of course, George had rejected her affections earlier in the evening—*twice*, a minor infraction compared with her disappointment over his larger failure as a husband, as a man, as an equal over the course of their marriage, the major factor in "the problem," as Betty Friedan defined the condition of the mid-twentieth-century married woman, "that has no name."

"Why?" Martha is asking George, now, whimperingly, beseeching him. "Why?"

"You broke our rule, Martha," he says. "You mentioned him."

It is dawn. The party is over. George tells Nick and Honey it's late. As they get ready to leave, Nick asks George tenderly, honestly, "You couldn't have a child?"

"*We* couldn't," George says.

"*We* couldn't," Martha agrees.

Now, the two of them alone in the tranquil, early Sunday morning light, a calmer Martha, still moistened from her tears, sits on the window seat. George walks up to her, puts his hand on her shoulder, and sings softly, "Who's afraid of Virginia Woolf?"

"I am, George," Martha says.

"Who's afraid of Virginia Woolf?" George says again, almost in a whisper.

"I am George, I am."

George's hand is resting tenderly on Martha's shoulder, and she raises her hand to his. The camera closes in on their hands entwined and then fades out to the silhouette of a tree in the window behind them, into the sunrise.

On Monday, December 13, Ernest Lehman declared the production over—finally. "At 9:00 o'clock tonight George stood with his hand in Martha's and sang softly, 'Who's Afraid of Virginia Woolf?' for the very last time. Never again will Elizabeth Taylor be Martha. Never again will Richard Burton be George. It all came to an end after a very hectic day."

～

The final scene was being completed as the wrap party was taking place on Stage Eight, five months after the first day of rehearsal on July 7. Presents were being given all around. "Elizabeth was absolutely thrilled with her 175-year-old turquoise and gold pendant with the pearl and platinum chain," Ernie said, after succumbing and buying her jewels, after all. Mike gave Ernie a sterling silver frame from Tiffany's with a picture of Ernie standing with Mike and Elizabeth, and inscribed, "Hello, forever. Love, Nichols." It seemed to be a beautiful apology for all the tsuris he had put Ernie through. But then, "he could be incredibly cruel," Annabel Davis-Goff, his third wife, said about Nichols years after his death. "I don't envy Ernie Lehman's experiences with him." To wit, his gift to Hal Polaire, the assistant producer, was a rectal thermometer in a sterling silver case, proving that Mike could still be the spiteful little shit.

Chapter 12

Labor Pains

I never understood why they had to shoot [the film] in black and white.
I wrote the play in color.

—Edward Albee

With the *Who's Afraid of Virginia Woolf?* shoot wrapped, Mike Nichols left a string of personnel casualties in his wake. Early on, Harry Stradling, the original cinematographer, left the production because of Mike, and eventually, Mike fired Buck Hall, the assistant director, while the production was still in Northampton. Doane Harrison, the "old Hollywood" legend, finally walked out in exasperation with Nichols weeks before the final scenes were shot. Harrison's departure was an embarrassment for the production, only further tarnishing Nichols's reputation at Warner Brothers. In fact, tensions had been mounting for months: While Jack Warner chafed at Nichols's imperious demands and audacious challenges, the goodwill of the studio's head of production, Walter McEwen, toward the first-time director eroded altogether as the movie was almost two months behind schedule, and, even worse, almost $2 million over budget. The total cost was $7.5 million (over $70 million in 2022 dollars), which, at the time, made it the most expensive black and white living-room drama to come out of any Hollywood studio.

Soon after shooting concluded in mid-December, a rough cut was screened for Jack Warner and the senior studio executives. They acknowledged the power of the film, but there was grumbling about the strong language, and no voice was louder than Warner's own. "We've got a $7.5 million dirty movie on our hands," he said. The immediate question, of course, was "Where can we cut?"—not for length but to excise the incendiary language. But, since Nichols had refused to provide coverage with alternative softer language, the studio had no hedge against the Production Code censors—the impending obstacle to a wide national distribution.

Nichols had already begun editing with Sam O'Steen, who had been at his side while shooting almost every scene, advising on the necessary B camera footage that would enable smoother cutting. Harrison had quit because of Nichols's reliance on the editor. O'Steen and Nichols, who shared a birthday as well as a vision for the film, worked very well together. When Nichols expressed his intent to have the characters talking over one another—the way people naturally talk— O'Steen created a method of overlapping the dialogue. While that can be done easily with audio-mixing technology today, in 1965 the audio had to be mechanically synchronized. O'Steen came up with a way to sync several separate soundtracks to match the film roll's code numbers. "So, say George is speaking Latin and Martha is wailing away, and they're talking between them," O'Steen explained, "well, when I started cutting first to her, then to him, it didn't matter if they overlapped, they would always be in sync. I could cut anyplace I wanted to." Using this same technique, Nichols could have had the sound reels shot with softer language as voice-over backup, but he refused to make that option possible—despite the flak he anticipated from Jack Warner. As far as Mike was concerned, he had already made several concessions in the script, giving up a "Jesus H. Christ" for "my God," and exchanging Martha's "Fuck you" for "Goddamn you" as George opens the door to greet Nick and Honey for the first time. Still, the crude language was not the hand that Nichols overplayed.

On January 5, 1966, Jack Warner sent a memo to Lehman and Nichols detailing a rush-rush schedule to ship the final cut of the picture out of the state by March 1—to beat the tax deadline. The memo also said that Alex North, the composer—who had not yet begun his score for the film—had agreed to this schedule, but when Lehman called North, it was the first he had heard of it. "It's unfair to expect me to write a score for such an important movie in so short a time," North said, balking. He had not seen any footage, nor had he even met with Nichols and Lehman to discuss what they expected for the music.

Nichols went into a rage about the deadline, pitching a fit in Warner's office, and convincing him to abandon the March 1 shipping date. Still on a rampage, he stormed into Lehman's office to complain. Lehman asked him how he convinced Warner to change the deadline. "I told him that if he tried to force me to do the film this way or took it away from me," Nichols replied, "I would simply go back to New York and give out interviews in the newspapers telling them exactly what had happened." Nichols then turned his rage on Lehman, resurrecting his old gripe about always having to fight the battles with Warner Brothers alone. Mike went even further and unleashed a litany of Ernie's short-comings, which Lehman sarcastically enumerated in his journal as if making a confession: "In which Mike claimed that first, I think only about my own feelings, not about the picture; Two, I am interested only in getting publicity for myself and not concerned about the picture; Three, all I ever do is complain about not being included in everything, but actually, I ought to be making sure that I am included even though there are those trying to exclude me [like Nichols]; Four, the better Mike works and the more effective his work on the picture, the more guilty I make him feel about me; and Five, he and I usually achieve the same end result in our dealings with people—he yells and screams without giving a damn what other people think and I do it by making other people feel guilty. The latter technique, according to Mike, is sneaky and dishonest . . ."

It is uncanny how psychological projection operates between individuals who work so closely together. Every one of Nichols's accusations about Lehman could have been said about himself. At the end of the recriminations, Mike walked over to Ernie's desk and shook his hand, as if clearing the air following his verbal slap down. He left as if they were friends again. Lehman maintained his equanimity, but the indignity was filed away.

The following day, North came in to watch three reels of the film with Lehman, Nichols, and O'Steen. After a healthy conversation, they all agreed to avoid a full orchestra treatment; instead, the music would be intimate but modern, consisting of very few instruments. Mike proposed that the music should be as minimal as a single instrument.

For the next month, Nichols and O'Steen toiled daily in the cutting room, periodically showing North specific scenes that called for musical treatment and discussing the thematic nuances of the score. Their meetings were fraught with conflict. North was a Hollywood stalwart. He had composed the music for a wide range of cinematic genres, from historical epics like *Spartacus* and *Cleopatra* to the film versions of serious plays such as *A Streetcar Named Desire* and *Death of a Salesman*. By 1966, he had received nine Academy Award nominations for Best Musical Score and won one Grammy. But despite North's accomplishments, Mike insisted on hearing Alex play the various musical themes he had in mind for *Virginia Woolf* on the piano before he composed the score, which left Alex indignant. North was adamant about maintaining his artistic freedom, and hostility between them grew worse.

On February 8, Jack Warner notified Lehman and Nichols that the editing had to be completed by February 15 for North to meet his scoring and recording date the first week in March. Believing that he was being rushed to accommodate the composer's schedule, Nichols unilaterally fired North without consulting Lehman. Then—behind

Lehman's back—he tried to convince McEwen to hire André Previn. When Previn turned out to be unavailable, Nichols suggested Leonard Bernstein, one of his closest friends.

This is the way O'Steen remembered the following sequence of events: "Ernie had signed Alex North as the composer. He was considered tops in Hollywood, but Mike didn't want him; he wanted Andre Previn. I said, 'Mike, they already signed him [North] and that's money, don't fight with Warner, don't push him into a corner.' But Mike didn't give a shit; he wanted Andre Previn. That's what finally did it. That was just before Warner threw him off the lot."

When Warner, who was in New York, learned what Nichols had done, he ordered McEwen to fire Nichols. When McEwen summoned Nichols to his office and gave him the news, Mike was quick on his feet, offering an ingenious—and, ultimately, helpful—quid pro quo: If Warner gave him until the end of the week to edit the last reels, he would invite his friend Jacqueline Kennedy to the all-important Catholic Legion screening. By then, Warner was aware of Nichols's friendship with the former first lady, as paparazzi shots had been published of the two of them dancing together at Arthur, the popular nightclub on the former site of El Morocco in midtown Manhattan opened by Sybil Burton (Richard's ex-wife). Nichols knew that Mrs. Kennedy loved Albee's play. As a Catholic, as a universally sympathetic figure after the assassination of her husband, and as the other most famous woman in the world, her opinion would likely hold sway with the monsignor. Warner was persuaded enough to grant Mike this final wish, and indignant enough to order Lehman to rehire North immediately.

Editing is an intricate puzzle, and Nichols had complete faith in O'Steen, one of the few people on the production he trusted. O'Steen's rule of thumb was to stick to the way the story was being told: "Movie first, scene second, moment third." *Virginia Woolf* was filmed consecutively, for the most part. There were complex master scenes—that is, single-shot overview scenes covering large segments of the action. The more intimate shots, including close-ups, were shot later; these were available to be cut into the master scenes, either for storytelling purposes or to edit around moments that did not work. Nichols believed O'Steen had great instincts as an editor. "Sam was listening to the currents that flow underneath human events," Nichols later told O'Steen's wife, Bobbie, a film historian. "He was a master at making manifest the thousands of small, nonverbal clues to a person's nature, to a relationship, to a story."

O'Steen described that grueling race to the end, working those last three days nonstop in the editing room from five A.M. until midnight. Nichols's last day at Warner Brothers was Friday, February 11, 1966. After that, he would no longer be allowed on the lot, not even to mix the picture—the process of combining music, sound effects, and dialogue into a single soundtrack. "I mixed the picture," O'Steen said, explaining that at the end of every day, he would make a stealth phone call to Mike, who had gone back to New York—long-distance calls were prohibitively expensive then—and hold the phone up so Mike could listen. "He would make comments like, 'Can you bring the music down there, I don't think we need that sound.' We did that every day for about a month."

∼

From the perspective of Hollywood, it seemed that Mike Nichols had wildly overstepped his boundaries. He had badgered Jack Warner without fear. He had walked all over Ernest Lehman without remorse. He fired Buck Hall and tried to fire Alex North—two film industry veterans—with no regret. And, without apology or shame, he finished the movie more than a month late and shockingly over budget. To make matters even worse, he flaunted his good fortune and fine taste, as if the birthright of his intelligence, talent, and selectively dispensed charm granted him the privilege of having a better time than everyone else.

And yet—and this is where his integrity remains intact—he was doing it all for the sake of the picture. (Well, maybe not the Rolls-Royce.) He fretted constantly. He made himself sick with anxiety, literally—intestinal problems, inability to sleep—over the unrelenting torment of his perfectionist standards. He genuinely, profoundly believed in the film. More than that, he believed in "film." He was passionate about *Who's Afraid of Virginia Woolf?*, the play, and wanted to translate it to the screen while maintaining complete fidelity to Albee's inspired language and to the play's harrowing emotional content. He believed that Albee's insight into marriage revealed something of the anatomy of human nature. Nichols wanted to install *Virginia Woolf* in the legacy of filmmaking that had spoken to him in his own life—*A Streetcar Named Desire*, *A Place in the Sun*, *8½*—films that reflected something about his experience of the world, some truth about all of us.

"There's only one question the audience asks: Why are you telling me this? There has to be a good strong reason," Nichols said about what motivated him as a director. "The more clearly and specifically you answer this question, the more you've done your job. . . . The aim is always, in a way, to imitate life believably, to make the people in the audience say, me too, I know that." He was aiming for an unreachable verisimilitude, and if that took breaking some rules, ruffling some feathers, and alienating everyone around him, well, his priorities were inviolate. He was making art at all costs.

Nichols saw himself as a David facing down the Goliath that was Warner Brothers—a money-wasting industry giant that squandered its responsibility to the public by producing often embarrassing, mindless, and soulless entertainment. On top of that, the inevitable tension between Nichols and Warner Brothers was also a culture clash between New York and Hollywood. New York looked down its nose at the film industry. Perhaps that snobbery had a whiff of old-money anti-Semitism to it, as the film studios of the 1920s were built by Jewish immigrants— Jack Warner, David O. Selznick (via his father, Lewis), Louis B. Mayer, Samuel Goldwyn, Carl Laemmle. Hollywood created a vision of the American dream that was flashier and breezier than the WASP aristocracy could tolerate.

But in Nichols's case, intellectual snobbery produced the greater fault line. New York was the incubator of artistic endeavor, the laboratory of progressive thought, and the arbiter of cultural value. While Hollywood pandered to America's slavering id, New York flattered its ego. In 1966, as *Who's Afraid of Virginia Woolf?* was in postproduction, Leonard Bernstein had just won a Grammy for his Symphony no. 3 (*Kaddish*). Truman Capote's newly published bestseller, *In Cold Blood*, was blurring literary boundaries between fiction and nonfiction. Nichols continued to socialize with Susan Sontag, the reigning public intellectual of the era; Stephen Sondheim, lyricist for *West Side Story* and *Gypsy*; and best friend Richard Avedon, the most famous photographer in the world. It's not irrelevant that Nichols lived among the towering figures of his era as a matter of course in his daily life. He was part of a circle that shaped the culture at large—the influencers of his day—and it elevated the quality of life all around him, from the books he read to the music he listened to, the art he saw, the conversations he had, and the food he ate. No wonder he was reaching for Olympian-style achievement with his first film.

Nichols was the quintessential New Yorker, straddling the heights of civilization in a high-wire act that would leave anyone with a sense of vertigo. "He was a great artist, but he was also great at civilized living," Tom Stoppard, the playwright, said about Nichols after working with him on the 1983 Broadway production of *The Real Thing*. "He just thought we are all part of this marvelous civilization at its best, and he was sensitive to the fact that civilization at its worst was happening simultaneously just out of sight."

From the New York perspective, the battles Nichols fought at Warner Brothers—whether swatting away Warner's multiple directives to shoot the film in color or whittling Lehman's screenplay back to the purity of the original Albee script—seemed wholly justified. He was fending off the barbarians at the gate. Nichols's final production battle over the composer was the last straw for Jack Warner, but since Nichols's musical standards were being perpetually refined by his friends Bernstein, Previn, and Sondheim, who could blame him for wanting a score composed by someone other than a conventional Hollywood stalwart?

"The film starts with the moon and ends with the sun," Nichols said, eloquently describing not just its first and final shots but also its carefully mapped emotional transit from midnight to dawn. But he then divulged that the haunting opening image had an unlikely source. "The moon shot was from a vampire picture that Sam O'Steen found and spliced in . . . It was not shot for the film. We tried shooting the moon but the footage was awful." Nichols might as well have been speaking about the irony of his own ambitions: In other words, reaching for perfection sometimes requires cheating the details.

∼

In the months leading up to the summer 1966 release of *Who's Afraid of Virginia Woolf?*, several crucial screenings took place that could make or break the picture. One was the Production Code screening for the Motion Picture Association of America; one was for the National Catholic Office for Motion Pictures; and one was for Edward Albee. The moral purposes varied from one screening to the next: The Production Code screening was in service of public propriety; the Catholic Legion screening was in honor of religious sanctity. And while the Albee screening was a courtesy to the playwright, for Nichols, in particular, Albee's approval was paramount; it would be acknowledgment of the film's fidelity to the play, thereby ordaining its moral— that is, *artistic*—integrity. The studio flew Albee out to see the finished cut of the film in late February. He did not have high hopes for the production. Banished from the lot, Nichols agonized alone in New York, knowing Lehman would be present for the screening. Albee and Nichols were locked in a curious dance: each tethered to a reciprocal need for the play's integrity to remain intact, each hoping for an outcome of mutual respect. Whether those steps would be a tense tango or an easygoing watusi ("the dance made-a for romance," as the Orlons sang in 1962) remained to be seen.

When, initially, Albee had heard that Elizabeth Taylor and Richard Burton had been cast to play Martha and George—and not Bette Davis and James Mason, as he had hoped—he had gotten in touch with Davis. She was, of course, furious, telling Albee that Martha was a role she would have killed for. "It was to be my part," she said. If Uta Hagen had been cast in the film, Davis would have been disappointed but not heartbroken. "But to cast Miss Taylor," she moaned, "this beautiful, gorgeous young woman, is sickening for your play."

Yet, despite Albee's low expectations, after watching his play unfold on-screen, he acknowledged in his slightly begrudging manner that Nichols was a good director. "I found that he had a pretty good idea of what the play was about. There was at least one considerable intelligence at work. I tend to suspect that Mike Nichols deserves a great deal of the credit."

"I was very nervous because I cared a lot," Nichols said. "Albee called afterwards, and he said he was very happy. I *think* he was. He complained about the score, which was a good and a bad sign because at least he was complaining about something, so that maybe he wasn't being polite about the rest of it. Of course, if you're a writer like him you don't want *any* score. You want to hear the rhythm of the words."

At the beginning of production for *Virginia Woolf*, Jack Warner had sent Jeffrey Shurlock, the head of the Production Code, several iterations of the script to get a reading in anticipation of any obstacle with the censors. Shurlock's letter in response to the final script had not been encouraging. He had repeated his concerns about the profane language and the sexual references, concluding: "These items still seem to us to be unapprovable under Code requirements, but, as always, we will reserve our final opinion until we have a chance to see the finished picture."

Warner lived with trepidation about the questionable language throughout the production, and he was virtually apoplectic during the official "Decency Code" screening of *Who's Afraid of Virginia Woolf?* Following that screening at the Catholic Office for Motion Pictures at Warner Brothers in New York, Monsignor Thomas F. Little, who presided over the Office, and his chief associate, Father Patrick J. Sullivan, agonized over the movie's language. As promised, Jacqueline Kennedy attended the screening with Mike Nichols, and they were seated right behind the monsignor. When the film ended, Mrs. Kennedy turned to Nichols and, as rehearsed, said in direct earshot of the monsignor: "Jack would have *loved* this film," referring to her late husband. The monsignor overheard her, as planned, as did his associate. Eighty-one churchgoing volunteers—all college-educated film enthusiasts—attended that screening, too, and each one wrote a lengthy report for Monsignor Little and Father Sullivan to read in consideration of their final decision. "I must say I would not like to see the Lord's name become the easy recourse of a scriptwriter," one representative wrote in his report, "yet I feel very strongly that at this time an arbitrary blanket pronouncement regarding language by the Church would do nothing but assure its critics of a general lack of perception on the Church's part of the values of the film. There is something being said here which is quite valid and, in its own terms, very moral." Another wrote, "I can see little moral harm that will come from the use of vulgar language. Shock and disgust are not moral evils in themselves." Others disagreed: "I cast an emphatic vote for a condemned rating. This film has no redeeming social value." Still, the overwhelming majority of the eighty-one raters were in favor of approving the film. Warner Brothers expected a C rating ("condemned") or B ("morally objectionable in part for all").

While there is no question that the very glamorous Catholic first lady's opinion held sway, so did the surprising number of positive opinions from the volunteers. Warner and Lehman, in particular, were more than relieved when Monsignor Little announced a rating of A-4 ("morally unobjectionable for adults, with reservations"). "We put *Virginia Woolf* in what we call our 'think film category,' alongside

8 1/2 and *La Dolce Vita*," the monsignor explained. "I've never heard those words on a screen before, but I've heard them at Coney Island."

That was a monumental coup for Warner Brothers—not least because of the sly presence of Jacqueline Kennedy and her approving comment—but it still left the Production Code Administration screening. Although the Code's influence was waning with the changing mores of the 1960s, its oversight was still in place, and its rating could dramatically limit the distribution of the film. Following that screening in May, Shurlock told Warner that he had no choice but to withhold a Production Code seal of approval, thus vastly reducing the number of theaters that would be willing to show the film. Perhaps emboldened by the Catholic Office's decision, Warner had a private screening of *Virginia Woolf* in New York for Jack Valenti, who had just arrived from the Johnson administration as the new president of the Motion Picture Association of America, the Production Code's parent organization. VALENTI FACING FIRST FILM CRISIS was the *New York Times* headline for the film critic Vincent Canby's piece about the private screening. "Mr. Valenti is presented with one of the touchiest questions facing the film industry," he writes. "How can producers make admittedly adult films without alienating a mass audience that includes children?" Valenti was aware that all industry eyes were upon him. A decision to approve the film would deal a death blow to the Code, rendering it powerless. On June 11, just eleven days before the movie's scheduled premiere, Valenti overruled Shurlock and the Production Code Administration. The film's language, as Valenti predicted approvingly, would "hit the American public like an angry fist." *Virginia Woolf* could be shown across the country in the form Nichols had intended. By 1968 a new MPAA film rating system was put in place—G for general audience, M for mature audiences, R for restricted to adult accompaniment of anyone under sixteen, and X for no one under sixteen admitted. This may have been the first cultural boundary shattered by *Who's Afraid of Virginia Woolf?*, the film paving the way for more honest language in the public arena—even before the film's release.

This was the final victory Warner Brothers needed for national distribution of the film. On the eve of its premiere, *Life* magazine published a cover story called "Liz in a Shocker: Her Movie Shatters the Rules of Censorship." The reporter, Tommy Thompson, who had been on set in Northampton, wrote that *Who's Afraid of Virginia Woolf?* contains "eleven 'Goddamns;' seven 'bastards;' five 'sons of bitches;' and such assorted graphic phrases as 'screw you,' 'up yours,' 'hump the hostess,' and 'plowing pertinent wives.'" *Life* reported this list of profanities to underscore the Production Code obstacles the film had to hurdle to get to its national public release. The article began with this anecdote: "'If this obscenity is allowed,' raged one minister from his pulpit in 1939, 'then the very moral fiber of America is in grave jeopardy.'" That minister was referring to a single word in *Gone with the Wind*: "Frankly, my dear, I don't give a *damn*." Joseph I. Breen, the original "censor" in his role as president of the Motion Picture Producers and Distributors of America, had done everything in his power to get producer David O'Selznick to change the word to "darn."

"Disguising profanity with clean but suggestive phrases is really dirtier," Nichols told the *Life* magazine reporter. "It reminds me of an old Gary Cooper movie when somebody said, 'He's so poor he hasn't got a pot to put flowers in . . .' instead of 'a pot to piss in.' We feel the language in *Woolf* is essential to the fabric; it reveals who the people are and how they live."

Soon after the film was released, the *Paris Review* published an unusual piece in which Albee was interviewed by William Flanagan, his mentor and erstwhile romantic partner. In their conversation, Albee gave a thoughtful endorsement of the film. He allowed that, while he had been apprehensive about Nichols, the first-time director was "innocent to the medium and didn't know how to make the usual mistakes." Albee had been wary about the many ways Hollywood could have mutilated his script, but "I was startled and enormously taken with the picture," he told Flanagan. "More than that, I discovered that no screenplay had been written, that the play was there almost word for word. . . . So, really there wasn't a screenplay, and that delighted me."

As for the principals involved, Albee had typically strong opinions. "My second delight," he said, was "to appreciate that Mike Nichols understood not only the play, my intentions (pretty much, again with a couple of oversimplifications), but also seemed to understand the use of the camera and the film medium, all this in his first time around." And his third surprise—and equally, his delight—was with Elizabeth Taylor, who had been "quite capable of casting off the beautiful-young-woman image and doing something much more than she usually does in films." As for Lehman, Albee was clearly in the Nichols camp: "Lehman, who is credited with the screenplay, did write about twenty-five words. I thought they were absolutely terrible."

"I think I served Edward Albee and Elizabeth Taylor and Richard Burton well," Nichols said. "I did what I set out to do, which was to let *Virginia Woolf* take place on screen. I did not intrude myself terribly. I protected Albee's idea from misunderstanding, slurring, or twisting."

Lehman had sat with Albee during the screening. "He wept four times," Lehman told Thompson of *Life* magazine. Of course, those could have been the playwright's tears of pain at the "false notes" in the dialogue written by the man sitting next to him, but that seems unlikely. In that screening room, Albee was an artist watching his own precise understanding of things reflected back almost exactly as he intended. Years later, he admitted that he "damn near cried" on the Warner Brothers lot, telling Mel Gussow, his biographer, that part of his pleasure was relief. In the end, the highest endorsement Nichols could have hoped for came from Albee himself: "I found that it made an awfully good picture."

Chapter 13

Edward Albee and Mike Nichols
Dance the Watusi

PETRUCHIO: *Come, come, you wasp; i' faith, you are too angry.*

KATHERINA: *If I be waspish, best beware my sting.*

PETRUCHIO: *My remedy is, then, to pluck it out.*

KATHERINA: *Ay, if the fool could find it where it lies.*

PETRUCHIO: *Who knows not where a wasp does wear his sting? In his tail.*

KATHERINA: *In his tongue.*

PETRUCHIO: *Whose tongue?*

KATHERINA: *Yours, if you talk of tales; and so farewell.*

PETRUCHIO: *What! with my tongue in your tail? Nay, come again, Good Kate;*
I am a gentleman.

—SHAKESPEARE, *THE TAMING OF THE SHREW*, ACT II, SCENE I

In the spring of 1966, in the months before the world premiere of *Who's Afraid of Virginia Woolf?*, the Burtons were in Rome to star as Petruchio and Katherina in the film version of *The Taming of the Shrew*, directed by Franco Zeffirelli, in production at Cinecittà Studios. It seemed as if the couple were determined to play out every possible phase of their romantic relationship through the roles they chose, beginning with *Cleopatra*—where it all started—then *The V.I.P.s*, *The Sandpiper*, *Who's Afraid of Virginia Woolf?*, and now this. When *The Taming of the Shrew* came out the following year, *Look* magazine quipped, "What other young couple would go to such lengths to make home movies for their fans?"

That April, Edward Albee spent a weekend in Rome as Zeffirelli's guest. He was so taken with the heady swirl of international glamour that he wrote a one-page story called "My Weekend in Rome, a theme," an absurdist caricature of his visit, and sent it to his former lover and mentor William Flanagan. He described a house filled with interesting people, including Rudolf Nureyev, the dancer, another guest that weekend, and then portrayed the dinner he had with the Burtons:

> The nice Italian man [Zeffirelli] took my playmate and me to dinner with two nice people. A man and a woman [Richard Burton and Elizabeth Taylor]. We sat in a little room so nobody could see us. Why? The man had a beard. The lady didn't. She had a white dress, and she had on a lot of pearls and emeralds. She was very pretty. She came in with a big furry coat on. She took it off and said, I don't want to sit on my chinchill. What is a chinchill? [*sic*]
>
> We ate lots and drank a yellow wine, except the lady, who drank a yellow sparkling something. She had purple eyes. She was pretty . . . The nice lady and the man with the beard talked to me a lot. They asked me how I liked a movie they moved around in [*Who's Afraid of Virginia Woolf?*] I said I liked it fine. They liked that. When we left the room, the nice pretty lady kissed me and asked me if she could move around in a play I made someday. I said that would be fun. . . . oh, yes, the pretty lady smelled pretty, too. She said she liked to get presents.

∿

As the drumroll for the release of *Who's Afraid of Virginia Woolf?* was getting louder, its principals were getting on with their lives. While the Burtons were filming in Rome, Albee's new play, *A Delicate Balance*, was gearing up to open on Broadway in the fall. Mike Nichols was in pre-production for his next film, *The Graduate*. And Ernest Lehman was still in high-level negotiations for his four-picture deal with several studios, which would lead to his eventual producer-screenwriter role for *Hello, Dolly* in 1969 and as first-time director of *Portnoy's Complaint* in 1972. The press coverage of *Virginia Woolf* had begun long before the film went into production, insinuating the enigmatic title into the collective conscience as if it were a riddle, the name itself functioning as a kind of meme, generating a swell of curiosity about the film. The stars attached to the production provided further seasoning to the riddle, and the gravitas of the playwright, along with the gamble of a first-time director, generated innumerable *Rashomon*-like angles for the press to go at the production without repeating what had already been reported. By the time *Virginia Woolf* was released in movie theaters, Albee was a household name, his place in the canon of American theater already well secured. Of course, "Dick and Liz" were a singular "meme" unto themselves, underscored by the tabloid scandal that continued to reverberate in references to the torrid origins of their marriage whenever the couple was mentioned in print. Nichols's name was not yet as widely known to the American public, but those who determined media coverage in New York were more than willing to provide a collective megaphone for his apotheosis from Broadway to Hollywood.

Beginning with the play's success on Broadway, the *New York Times* reported on the incremental stages of *Virginia Woolf*'s progress to the big screen in more than a dozen articles that appeared with each new development leading up to the film's release, from the initial sale of the rights to Warner Brothers in March 1964 all the way up to the last-minute controversies surrounding censorship and the Hays Code. During production, there had been a cover story on Nichols in the *Saturday Evening Post*; a cover story on the Burtons in the *Ladies' Home*

Journal; a feature on Lehman in *Cosmopolitan*; endless small items in *Variety* and the *Hollywood Reporter*; and, during the Northampton shoot, a three-part feature in the *Boston Globe*. Several months before the film was released, *Look* magazine published a feature on the movie called "The Night of the Brawl" that began: "Here they are, again, fans," describing Taylor as "the anti-heroine of all the young homemakers" and Burton as "the matinee idol of the brainy set." And, two weeks before the world premiere in Los Angeles, *Life* magazine ran an eight-page feature on the movie with Taylor on the cover; on the eve of the film's premiere, *McCall's* magazine also ran a multipage feature; and *Playboy's* "Interview" of the month of June was with Nichols. On "earned media" alone, the film had achieved a level of cultural saturation beyond Warner Brothers' wildest imaginings.

Who's Afraid of Virginia Woolf? had its premiere at the Pantages Theatre in Los Angeles on June 21, 1966, followed by a wide national release. Among the glittering array in the audience were Hollywood friends Julie Andrews, Anne Bancroft, Candice Bergen, Rock Hudson, and André Previn; movie-star royalty such as Fred Astaire, Joan Crawford, Gregory Peck, Ginger Rogers, Mickey Rooney, Rosalind Russell, and James Stewart; industry stalwarts including the Redgraves—Lynn, Michael, and Vanessa—and the Newmans, Paul and Joanne (Woodward); and members of the press from all over the country. There was not an empty seat in the house.

"Mike and I sat in the back row," Sam O'Steen said. "Mike was a basket case. So, the picture started, and he said, 'That's a light print. Jesus!'"—complaining that the overall black and white film tones weren't rich enough. "And I said, 'Come on, Mike, settle down.'" Nichols squirmed next to O'Steen, counting the imperfections, inventing flaws, "moaning and groaning throughout the screening." From O'Steen's perspective, the audience's enthusiastic laughter and intermittent gasps were a clear indication that they loved the movie. But as soon as it was over, Mike grabbed O'Steen's arm. "Let's get out of here. I don't want to see anybody." O'Steen remembered fleeing the theater and driving off with Mike. Later, they got word that everyone was looking for Nichols to congratulate him. He was the toast of the town, the auteur of the moment, but his moment of glory took place without him.

"I remember the opening night of *Virginia Woolf*," Nichols said. "When the second reel came on, it was about twelve to sixteen points darker than the first. I thought I was going to have a heart attack. I went running to the projectionist and felt crazy. I couldn't stop bitching about it in my head." Mike remembered, too, the next day, when he read the review in the *Los Angeles Times*. "History was written in fire last night," the reviewer asserted—the best endorsement anybody could have hoped for. "All I could think was 'Yeah, but that *reel*,'" Nichols said. It was his defense mechanism. Obsessing over an incidental—and maybe nonexistent—flaw was his way of protecting himself from the terror of uncertainty, of not knowing how other people would react. If the film flopped, he could always blame it on that second reel.

As a first-time director, Nichols believed (rightly or wrongly) that his entire future in Hollywood depended on *Virginia Woolf*. But the premiere was also a nail-biting affair for everyone else involved in the production. Certainly, it was Lehman's calling card for the four-picture deal he was shopping around, and its success would only elevate his status and increase his value. And no one had more invested in the film's financial success than Jack Warner. He had relented against his better instincts more often on this picture than ever before, his nerves consistently frayed by the demands of "the creatives." He had no idea what his $7.5 million gamble would yield. For the Burtons, too, superstar status was on the line. When *Who's Afraid of Virginia Woolf?* had premiered on Broadway in 1962, the Kennedys had reigned supreme as America's most glamorous couple; the play had called into question all such myths of marital perfection (presciently, as it turned out). Now, four years later, everyone knew that the media had passed the Kennedy throne to Dick and Liz—and here, again, was *Who's Afraid of Virginia Woolf?*, a referendum on their star power: Its success or failure would determine whether the Burtons stayed on top. They were anxious in absentia—Elizabeth and Richard stayed in Rome, missing the premiere and the opportunity to face the judgment of their peers.

"Edward Albee's *Who's Afraid of Virginia Woolf?*, the best American play of the last decade and a violently candid one, has been brought to the screen without pussyfooting," wrote Stanley Kauffmann in the *New York Times* after the film's premiere. He had just become the drama critic for the *Times* after years as a film critic for the *New Republic*. "This in itself makes it a notable event in our film history. . . . Mike Nichols, after a brilliant and too-brief career as a satirist, proved to be a brilliant theatrical director of comedy. This is his debut as a film director, and it is a successful Houdini feat."

Two weeks after the film's release, Bosley Crowther, the official film critic of the *New York Times*, weighed in with the opinion of record: "After all the initial commotion over *Who's Afraid of Virginia Woolf?*—all the wailing of the censors, the shouting of the reviewers, and the mumbling and grumbling of those patrons who have come away stunned and confused—there remains one simple statement to be made about this film: it is a magnificent triumph of determined audacity."

Other publications were even more effusive than the Gray Lady. This from the *Hollywood Reporter* the day after the film opened: "The screen has never held a more shattering and indelible drama than *Who's Afraid of Virginia Woolf?* Edward Albee's stage play was a masterpiece. The makers of this film have created from it a motion picture masterpiece. It will be nominated for every category in next year's Academy Awards, and it deserves to win them all. It will tote up an equally impressive score at the box office. *Who's Afraid of Virginia Woolf?* is an instant film classic, and Warner Bros. deserves the highest credit for making it a movie without compromise."

Variety hailed it as "a keen adaptation and handsome production by Ernest Lehman, outstanding direction by Mike Nichols in his feature debut," and claimed that the "four topflight performances score an artistic bullseye."

Not all the reviews were glowing. "The movie isn't all that good, but it's reasonably entertaining and effective within certain limitations, some evitable and some inevitable," wrote Andrew Sarris, the film critic for the *Village Voice*, once the bible for progressive thinking and existential ruminating in downtown Manhattan. "Why Jack Warner should be applauded for bringing a Broadway hit to the screen is a bit beyond me." Sarris considered the play "brilliant when it comes to Living and a bad play about Life. . . . It's too bad really because *Virginia Woolf* is at its best when it doesn't mean anything, but simply Is."

The *Village Voice* was often guilty of registering a patent, too-cool-for-school dismissal of mainstream culture—in this case, the mass-media machinery of Hollywood. But Susan Sontag—a bona fide public intellectual, a breed that had its moment in the 1960s and '70s—had no such qualms. "To me the direction of the actors in *Virginia Woolf* is brilliant," she told *Newsweek* later that year. Sontag meant this sincerely—she was not prone to say what she did not believe—but, equally, she was in full "logrolling" mode, that is, plugging her good friend Mike. "Elizabeth Taylor gave the best performance of her life. She's a real actress. If someone has the capacity, [Nichols] can get it out of them. . . . He's one of the few people in this country who could direct Brecht properly."

Resistance to what was billed as a controversial film turned out to be sporadic. Because of the obscenities, officials in Nova Scotia banned *Virginia Woolf* from all the theaters in the province; in Tennessee, the Nashville police chief also deemed the film obscene, shutting it down at the prominent Crescent Theater and arresting the theater manager. But there was also support in the unlikeliest places: Sister Mary Cecile, a nun from Detroit, told the National Catholic Theater Conference in New York, attended by 1,500 members, that *Who's Afraid of Virginia Woolf?* was "the best film in years" and that the dialogue was "part of the film's crusty layer."

A day after the film opened at the Criterion Theatre in Manhattan, Vincent Canby, the *Times'* other drama critic, interviewed moviegoers as they left. By then, after one day, almost two thousand people had seen the film in New York. Of the patrons he interviewed, "none of them found the language shocking," he reported. One fifteen-year-old, in the company of his mother, said, "I've heard worse."

~

Any number of historical events might explain why *Who's Afraid of Virginia Woolf?* struck such a deep cultural chord when it came out in 1966. It was a transitional moment in a transformative decade. After the Cuban missile crisis of 1962, the threat of the atomic bomb was a lingering menace in the souls of average Americans. The crisis was followed by the assassination of President Kennedy the next year, which destroyed the national mood of optimism and hope, tearing a sorrowful hole through the fabric of the country: It felt as if there had been a death in every family. Throughout the 1960s, the civil rights movement leveled an urgent corrective to the status quo, unsettling the currents of middle-class American life. Surely, in 1966, many middle-aged adults who had grown up during the Depression and come of age during World War II were no longer swayed by the myths about love, romance, and sex they had grown up with. That version of "living happily ever after" was not coalescing with the reality of marriage and parenthood they were experiencing in their daily lives. More to the point, in the wake of so much cultural disruption, they were sick of pretending that the cartoon versions of marriage put forward by Hollywood—from *Pillow Talk* to *The Parent Trap*—and in television programming from the Ricardos to the Cleavers to the Nelsons passed for a believable reflection of actual human experience. People were looking for answers about the meaning of things without quite knowing the questions.

One 1960s cultural phenomenon in particular suggests the timeliness of the film. "While in 1932 there were only three marriage counseling centers in the entire U.S., by 1968 there were 1,800 licensed marriage counselors in California alone," reports the medical historian Wendy Kline. This statistic suggests that in the mid-1960s, people were acknowledging that marriage required attention—maintenance, even. *Who's Afraid of Virginia Woolf?* provided, among other things, cold comfort to audiences who could watch George and Martha's marriage-in-distress on the big screen and recognize areas of turbulence in their own relationships. The brutally honest portrayal of marriage in *Virginia Woolf* was a welcome, if bracing, surprise, and a strangely palatable relief: George and Martha's extreme behavior provides a cushion of distance for any couple in the audience to view the marital discord on-screen in the abstract yet still be able to measure their own marriages against it. At the same time, there is enough verity in *Who's Afraid of Virginia Woolf?* to glean that it is not just about one marriage; it's about marriage.

∼

Marriages tend to straddle a common paradoxical line. In public, couples by and large conform to a standard social etiquette, where bickering, say, is to be avoided. At home, though, behind closed doors, the private, truer reality of marital coalescence is lived out at the deeper, more intimate, and murkier foundation of emotional attachment. There, spouses are freer to let down their guard; behavior is less self-conscious, often defaulting or regressing to patterns established in early childhood with one's parents. The couple's tender and momentary gestures of love and regard for each other can reassure and gratify, until their absence or withdrawal lays bare a vulnerability, like opening a trap door into a netherworld of ever-accruing inadvertent slights, unintended rejections, and simmering resentments, magnified by betrayals—whether incidental (a forgotten birthday or anniversary) or monumental (sexual, financial, or legal deception). The result might be flickering hatred, retaliatory behavior, or intermittent loneliness. Couples are likely to incorporate these pesky emotional nicks and wounds into the natural flow of their days, often swallowing the impulse to get even, opting for silence as the simpler course, because the infraction just might seem too petty to make an issue out of. But those moments add up, and the injustices collect, and raising them without seeming insane in the moment requires distance, control, circumspection, and stamina. Then, too, the balance of power in marriage is always shifting from one spouse to the other according to circumstance. Equally, disappointment in one spouse or another is a fluctuating inevitability. Such are the trials that come with the territory of deep attachment and that test every marriage in varying proportion and over the course of time.

Mike Nichols was often asked to explain what *Who's Afraid of Virginia Woolf?* is about, and he always responded with the same neutral, if literal, description. "It is about a couple who comes home late after a party. She has invited another couple over for a nightcap. They drink and they argue and then the guests go home." One of the razor-sharp edges straddled in George and Martha's late-night domestic odyssey is the formal dichotomy of *pretext*—the social situation in Nichols's summary of what the play is about—versus the *subtext*, the underlying feelings and psychological motivation that drive the behavior of the two couples, fueling the in-vino-veritas conversations that drag on into the wee hours of the night until dawn. In *Who's Afraid of Virginia Woolf?*, the pretext—two faculty couples having a very late, extended nightcap—and the subtext, the host couple getting to the marrow of their own love by making mincemeat of their guests, merge and become indistinguishable.

While unique as characters, George and Martha are representative of any married couple in that they are always aware of the private subtext playing out below the public face of their relationship. These subtextual dynamics are drawn out in extremis, X-rayed. In the first few scenes of *Who's Afraid of Virginia Woolf?* Martha endures two slights in her entreaties for affection, the first when she asks George for a wet, sloppy kiss, which George rejects, and the second, when she sidles up to him for a simple "snuggle" before the guests arrive. Both are seemingly incidental requests, yet the rejections cut deep and unleash an accumulated anger proportional to the depth—and history—of the wound. Her fury is a tempest of revenge that thrashes George throughout the rest of the evening. Why does George reject her? From what we know so far, they have just arrived home from a party at two A.M. and she tells him that she has invited another couple over for a nightcap. He is understandably annoyed by it, tired, put out. He accuses her of always springing things on him. No wonder he doesn't feel affectionate at that hour.

All of this is recognizable and believable and could be true of any couple. As we get to know more about them, we piece together aspects of their behavior that become more specific to who they are. George, a college professor, is cerebral. Martha, an intelligent and educated (prefeminist) housewife, is visceral. Martha is passionate and wild, a "party girl" at heart. George is reflective, reserved, and intellectual. Martha wants more stimulation in her life, more meaning. She, like the Bette Davis character she described, is *discontent*. George, withdrawn and seemingly unambitious, is a disappointment to her, but the question lingers: Was he drained of his lifelong ambition by Martha's overbearing demands, or did he withhold the achievement she expected of him just to spite her? Regardless, he, too, is trapped in a tangle of resentments, and his clearest impulse seems to be to fend Martha off.

We learn quickly enough that they are raging alcoholics who have let their inner demons out for the night, perhaps a regular occurrence, and we watch their indecent, undignified, and increasingly vicious behavior reveal secrets particular to their marriage—and indicative of the dynamics of all marriage. Martha tears George apart, humiliating him in front of the guests. Then she betrays George outright by bedding the handsome younger man, "the historical inevitability." She is getting even with George for rejecting her affection, but, equally, she is testing the depth of George's love for her. It gets to George, and he does break down; in his jealousy, he plots his own revenge. Very human, very believable.

~

Nichols had psychological insights about the meaning of *Virginia Woolf*, as well. "The cruelty here is that it's the weakling ultimately laying the trap," he observes. In Nichols's interpretation—bearing the imprint of mid-century prejudices about gender roles—George holds a stealth kind of power and prevails as the ultimate victor: "George is subjugated by Martha, we think; he is the patsy of all her jokes. The guests laugh at him, encouraged by Martha, yet he's laying the trap all the time." Nichols admires Albee for the plot construction, the way George is strategic in mining Nick for information about him and Honey; George will then use their own confessions as weapons against them. All of this occurs as Martha badgers him, repeatedly, humiliates him all night long, breaking several golden rules of marriage—mutual respect being one of them. She sneers at his career failures in front of the guests. When he breaks a bottle of gin, for example, she screams: "You can't afford to lose good liquor, not on your salary, not on an associate professor's salary." Her infractions over the evening are outrageous, unrelenting, the ultimate one being blatant infidelity. By the end of the piece, George asserts the only power he has left—withdrawing his love. This is Martha's ultimate fear, his ultimate revenge—and he does that by killing off their son, "the little bugger," murdering the secret fantasy that symbolizes the core of their attachment. "I think [*Virginia Woolf*] is pleasurable because of the revenge," Nichols asserts. "The revenge of the guy who never made it. Nobody ever kissed George's ass. They're kissing Martha's ass and he has to live with that." As enlightened as Nichols could be, the chauvinism of his generation comes through in his view of George as the ultimate victor of the evening—and in the marriage. "[George] turns the tables and realizes that he is the strong one and Martha's the weak one," Nichols claims. Yet Albee himself would not have agreed with this conclusion. There is no victor in *Who's Afraid of Virginia Woolf?* No one wins as the sun comes up. They are both afraid of "Virginia Woolf"—that is, the examined life. In the dawn's early light, both George and Martha are compelled to engage in the struggle to come to terms with each other and to come to terms with themselves. We are left with their trepidation but willingness to move forward together, equally, up the stairs, into bed, and on to tomorrow.

The plot seems to run rampant with one psychologically sadistic feat after another—one for George, then one for Martha, then one for George—volleying not back and forth so much as spiraling into a disgraceful emotional squalor that leaves them both splayed and spent, all the way down to the very marrow of their vulnerability. Appearances are deceptive, though. "At first, Nick and Honey appear to be close, and George and Martha appear to be enemies," Nichols says, explaining the dichotomy of the neutral public face of marriage versus the more authentic private reality. "Of course, it's the other way around and our slow discovery of that is an important skein in the plot. . . . Nick and Honey are constructs—they don't love each other; they don't know who they are. They are a pure façade." In the end, George and Martha come back together, ready to move forward with a few illusions peeled away, one hand in the other, one step at a time, further into the uncharted emotional depths at the core of their marriage—a courageous act, after all.

~

Who's Afraid of Virginia Woolf? was both a product of the 1960s and a catalytic influence that came to define that decade. Not long after *Virginia Woolf* came out, "wife-swapping" or "key parties" swept through upper-middle-class suburbs as a sophisticated entertainment, and marriage counseling would become more of a necessity. As marriages were falling apart, the college-aged children of the American mainstream were rejecting their parents' way of life, not drinking alcohol so much as getting stoned and listening to a new breed of music. Bob Dylan's "Positively 4th Street" and "Like a Rolling Stone" topped the charts soon after rehearsal began for *Virginia Woolf* at Warner Brothers. The Beatles' innocent rock and roll was fast becoming more experimental, spiritual, psychedelic, and absurdist; the Rolling Stones' song "Mother's Little Helper" was a dark but catchy tune about parental instability, and their hit "Let's Spend the Night Together" contained one of the most overt references yet to sex in a rock and roll song. When the Stones appeared on *The Ed Sullivan Show* in January 1967, they were forced to change the words to "Let's spend *some time* together."

There are hints of this generational shift in the film itself, in an unlikely place: Alex North's score. North utilized the folk ballad style that was emerging in contemporary music, and on campuses across the country, from Woody Guthrie and Pete Seeger to Bob Dylan, Joan Baez, and Peter, Paul and Mary. As the film opens, the melodic theme begins with the strumming of a guitar. The music is a late-night serenade, plucked string by string as George and Martha walk the length of the campus from the party to their house. The informal quality of the music conjures a balmy, almost melancholic intimacy that makes the film immediately accessible. While Albee blanched at what he considered the film's treacly music, it is very possible that the musical score made the movie just that much more palatable to the mainstream public. Lehman deserves credit for two unpredictable choices that served the chemistry of the film and added to its box office success: casting Taylor to play Martha, and hiring North to compose the music, which brought a hearth-like warmth to the stormy domestic drama.

In the mid-1960s, the "kids" were rejecting the hypocrisies of their parents' generation. To younger viewers, George and Martha represented what was wrong with their parents, and they applauded the film's honesty as a useful indictment of what was fraudulent about the conventional middle class. *Who's Afraid of Virginia Woolf?* brought into public view the "closed-door argument in the other room." Finally! The honest dialogue and direct language had countercultural appeal for the younger generation.

In early 1967, *Mad* magazine, the beloved comic bible for disaffected teenagers who would grow up to create shows like *Saturday Night Live*, published a six-page graphic caricature of the movie called "Who in Heck Is Virginia Woolf?" that could easily define the "stoned humor" of that generation—that is, subverting the pretext by exposing the subtext. In the opening panel, George and Martha, drawn to comic perfection by Mort Drucker, stand in the domestic storm of their living room. "Well here we are . . . me, the DIRTY ROTTEN DAUGHTER of the University President . . . and you, a DIRTY ROTTEN HISTORY TEACHER!" Martha says. "It's 2:00 o'clock in the morning and we've just returned from a faculty party to our DIRTY ROTTEN HOME." George stands next to her and responds: "Right! And now, we're going to play DIRTY ROTTEN

GAMES for the rest of the night. Because through these games, the author plans to dramatically strip away our facades and reveal the fulsome phantasmagoria of base rot that permeates our souls." No one is a more perceptive psychologist than one's own kids, and in this snide and snarky feature, *Mad* put its finger on the way teenagers in the 1960s saw their parents, whether it was true or not.

The sexual revolution was nascent when *Who's Afraid of Virginia Woolf?* was released. But soon, "sex, drugs and rock and roll" would become the native call of the youth generation. Not that *Virginia Woolf* was a singular catalyst, but its timing was consistent with wider cultural forces that reflected the film as a harbinger and icon of its moment. Of course, it would be Nichols's next film, *The Graduate*, the following year, that spoke more directly to the alienation that propelled the youthquake of the 1960s; countless teenagers recognized themselves in the disenfranchised Benjamin Braddock. While *Virginia Woolf* was loud and bawdy in its indictment of mid-twentieth-century marital hypocrisy, it provided a kind of mirror for an adult audience, the Baby Boomers' parents. *The Graduate* renders marital hypocrisy anew, now from the perspective of Benjamin on the brink of his own coming of age. Mrs. Robinson and Martha share the same discontented marital terrain. They are women of the same age who are unhappy in their marriages, unhappy in their lives. They represent the "problem that has no name," depicted at the dawn of second-wave feminism, although they—and many in their audience at the time—didn't yet realize that they were not alone with that condition.

∽

"Elizabeth Taylor and Richard Burton probably do more acting per frame of film in *Who's Afraid of Virginia Woolf?* than you have ever seen in your life. You can't call it overacting because it's not just that Taylor and Burton are performing as George and Martha, it's that George and Martha are performing as George and Martha," observed the *New York Times* film critic A. O. Scott in 2010. "Now, if your friends behaved this way when you came over to their house for a drink, you would run for the door, or maybe call the cops. But, when movie stars do it, they win Oscars."

On April 10, 1967, the 39th Academy Awards Ceremony took place at the Santa Monica Civic Auditorium, but Bob Hope almost didn't have a televised show to host that night. The American Federation of Television and Radio Artists had been on strike, and it was settled just two hours before the telecast was supposed to begin. "Welcome to the on again, off again, in again, out again, 39th Academy Awards," Hope said in his opening monologue. "This is the big night. What tension. What drama. What suspense. And that was just deciding whether the show was going on or not." California governor Ronald Reagan was in the audience, and Hope acknowledged him in a corny—if prescient— joke: "Pretty soon we're going to need another category: Best Performance by a Governor."

Who's Afraid of Virginia Woolf? received thirteen Oscar nominations. The nominees for Best Actress alongside Taylor were Vanessa Redgrave in *Morgan*; Anouk Aimee in *A Man and a Woman*; Lynn Redgrave in *Georgy Girl*; and Ida Kaminska, for *The Shop on Main Street*. Burton was nominated for Best Actor, and his stiffest competition, by far, was Paul Scofield in *A Man for All Seasons*. Taylor had already won an Oscar for her role in *BUtterfield 8*, but this was Burton's fifth Academy Award nomination, and he really wanted a win. Elizabeth held out hope that they might be the first couple to walk away with husband-and-wife Oscars, perhaps carrying their on-screen lives, once again, into their real-world marriage.

But at the ceremony itself, they were nowhere to be found. That spring the Burtons were residing in Saint-Jean-Cap-Ferrat, just outside Nice, where Richard was shooting *The Comedians*. Elizabeth had wanted to attend the Academy Awards ceremony in Los Angeles; in fact, Jack Warner expected her to be there as a kind of command performance. He sent her a telegram, practically begging: "Do not burn the bridges you have built." But Richard couldn't bear the idea of losing yet again, particularly with the likelihood that Elizabeth could win. In a clever, if manipulative, gambit, he told her that he "dreamed her plane had crashed returning to California, and that it was he who found her body." That was enough to dissuade Taylor from the idea of attending. She issued an official excuse to the press, claiming an obligation to stay in Nice because of Burton's production schedule on *The Comedians*.

Lee Marvin presented the award for Best Actress, and when he announced Taylor as the winner, there was thunderous applause—not only as a show of affection from the industry but also as a clear statement that she had earned this ultimate accolade of her profession. Anne Bancroft (who was then in production as Mrs. Robinson in *The Graduate*) accepted the Oscar for Taylor: "Miss Taylor regrets very much that she can't be here tonight," Bancroft said. "I'm sure she must be very, very proud—not half as nervous as me, I'm sure. She thanks you very, very much. Thank you."

Then, when Scofield won for Best Actor, it dealt Burton a double wound. Not only did he have his wife's Best Actress Oscar to contend with, but, equally, he felt a private rebuke. Scofield was known as "the Shakespearean actor who had not abandoned the stage for movies." Scofield's Sir Thomas More in *A Man for All Seasons* was a sainted, historical figure—a marked contrast to Burton's George, a diminutive and bitter history professor. While Scofield "had ably and nobly recreated his stage role for the film. . . . Burton had created George wholly from his own psyche, a more emotionally challenging feat," write Sam Kashner and Nancy Schoenberger. "Alas, Burton lost to a saint." Richard would write in his journal: "We heard that E had won the Oscar and I hadn't! Bloody cheek. But P Scofield won, so that's all right." Indeed, he was proud of Elizabeth's much-deserved win, and he was gentlemanly about his loss, even sending a congratulatory telegram to Scofield, who, in turn, sent him a conciliatory note. Still, Burton was hurt by it.

The Best Director Award went to Fred Zinnemann for *A Man for All Seasons* (which Zinnemann had opted to direct over *Who's Afraid of Virginia Woolf?*), and while, for Nichols, it chafed, he acknowledged that he knew how Burton felt about losing to someone he respected. Nichols considered Zinnemann an eminence, so the blow was less painful. Nichols did make an appearance onstage to accept the Oscar for Best Supporting Actress on behalf of Sandy Dennis, who was in New York shooting the film *Sweet November*. Nichols smiled giddily and spoke succinctly. "Sandy thanks you very much," he said. "I thank Sandy. It's nice to be up here." It was a gracious thing to say—elegant, genuine, and humble, in striking contrast to Nichols's 1959 Emmy Awards turn at the podium, where he had smiled unctuously and ingratiatingly as he delivered an unprecedented repudiation of the television industry, making a mockery of the award ceremony itself.

While Best Picture went to *A Man for All Seasons*, *Who's Afraid of Virginia Woolf?* walked away with five Oscars that night. Aside from Taylor and Dennis, Haskell Wexler won for Cinematography, proving Jack Warner's skepticism unfounded, and delivering a happy reproach to Nichols, who had berated Wexler relentlessly throughout the production. Richard Sylbert also won for Best Art Direction, and Irene Sharaff for Best Costume Design.

But for Warner, the success of *Who's Afraid of Virginia Woolf?* was measured not only by its Oscars haul; the 1966 box office gross of $14.5 million made it the third-highest-grossing film that year. Warner Brothers' gamble had paid off. The studio doubled its money.

One month after the Academy Awards ceremony in 1967, Albee's new play, *A Delicate Balance*, won the Pulitzer Prize, "the award that had been denied Albee for *Who's Afraid of Virginia Woolf?* in 1963," wrote Mel Gussow in his biography. When Albee heard the news, he considered refusing the prize, telling a reporter for the *World Journal Tribune* that "the Pulitzer committee had rejected my nomination for *Virginia Woolf* without either seeing or reading the play." He decided to accept the Pulitzer for *A Delicate Balance*, explaining his reasoning: "If I refused it out of hand, I would not be as free to criticize later prizes given. I don't wish to embarrass other recipients of the prize by appearing to suggest that they follow my lead. The Pulitzer Prize is still an honor."

But that didn't stop Albee from using his Pulitzer acceptance speech to settle old scores. "I would suggest that the Pulitzer Prize is in danger of losing its position of honor and could foreseeably cease to be an honor at all," he lectured. "Certainly something should be done to counter the feeling in the arts that the prize is not always given to the best work in any given year. Certainly, something should be done to counter the feeling that the trustees will, from time to time, pass over a controversial work in favor of one more conventional. . . . Or, failing that option, choose to make no award at all." He used his prize money to set up a fund in the name of John Gassner, the Pulitzer Prize juror who, along with John Mason Brown, had nominated *Virginia Woolf* to the committee in 1963 and had vocally resigned from the Pulitzer jury when the prize was withheld. Gassner, a professor at Yale, had recently died, and the fund honoring him was intended to go to the Yale School of Drama, to aid young playwrights or to help train young drama critics.

Albee's deferred Pulitzer Prize—passed over for *Who's Afraid of Virginia Woolf?*, victorious for *A Delicate Balance*—would also create another notable symmetry between his career and Nichols's. In 1968, one year after losing out at the Academy Awards to Zinnemann for Best Director, Nichols would take home his first Oscar—for *The Graduate*.

~

Despite Albee's initial relief about the fidelity of Nichols's *Who's Afraid of Virginia Woolf?* to the play, over the years he was to change his mind about the film and about the actors. By 1996, he had seen the movie eight times, and he said, "In spite of everything, it's not bad. The only trouble with it is that it's completely humorless." Although he always thought that Taylor was far too young for the role, it was, he said, "the best thing she's ever done."

After a long career as a film director, Nichols expressed his own reservations about *Who's Afraid of Virginia Woolf?*, the movie that had launched his film career. Asked by Gussow, Albee's biographer, if he would change anything in the film, Nichols said, "I would change everything. But it has a lot of life to it. It's a great script. It's a great play. It hasn't died in that way that some things from the stage died in being transferred." He said that he still thought of *Virginia Woolf* as a play and marveled that he was able to make a movie where people just sat around the living room and talked. He acknowledged the honesty of the dialogue. "It didn't seem like a play, and I think that's more Edward's accomplishment than mine. I think the things they're saying are forever shocking, not shocking because of the anger or the violence, but shocking because they're so alive. They're alive and recognizable and funny. The dialogue is so arresting. It was outside and beyond all conventions."

Marriage in Relief: An Epilogue

Women have served all these centuries as looking-glasses possessing the magic and delicious power of reflecting the figure of man at twice its natural size.

—VIRGINIA WOOLF, *A ROOM OF ONE'S OWN*

In the history of movies about marriage, *Who's Afraid of Virginia Woolf?* draws a clear dividing line. Those that preceded *Virginia Woolf* addressed the central relationship at varying distances, with other themes often predominating; in those films that followed, marriage could be approached more directly as the driving narrative force. There is not a precise genre of marriage films—although there are enough films about the subject to establish one. For the most part, movies about marriage tend to focus on the traditional model—monogamous heterosexual couples—with the boundaries of convention being tested to propel the plot. As the idea of marriage in contemporary Western societies evolved over the years, the narrative possibilities expanded to include mixed-race couples, same-sex couples, and other configurations that were previously taboo in mainstream cinema.

Even as our culture has expanded the scope of what a marriage can look like, the complex of emotions at the core of marital attachment has remained remarkably constant throughout my lifetime. And, for me, *Who's Afraid of Virginia Woolf?* comes closer than any movie I know to examining that emotional core. In these final pages, let us consider *Virginia Woolf*'s lineage amid the corpus of marriage movies before and since.

~

At the beginning of the twentieth century, *Women in Love*, by D. H. Lawrence, was one of the first novels to challenge the inevitability of marriage, raising questions about the institution itself and offering alternative ways of living—a departure from the literary novels preceding it that explored marriage within the conventions of society, such as *Middlemarch*, by George Eliot, *Madame Bovary*, by Gustave Flaubert, or *The Portrait of a Lady*, by Henry James. Lawrence didn't consider the questions he pondered about marriage to be a radical gambit, yet *Women in Love* prompted an ugly, drawn-out obscenity trial in London when Lawrence's British publisher put out a tentative limited-edition version in 1920. "I do not claim to be a literary critic, but I know dirt when I smell it, and here is dirt in heaps—festering, putrid heaps which smell to high Heaven," wrote one W. Charles Pilley at the time in the conservative journal *John Bull*. The novel was first published commercially in 1921—in the United States.

Women in Love revolves around Ursula and Gudrun Brangwen, sisters of marriageable age, and follows their courtships with Rupert Birkin and Gerald Critch, two best friends. The women try to figure out how to make their relationships work across class hierarchies, societal conventions, and individual predispositions, often questioning whether marriage is even a worthy pursuit. The novel opens with an idle conversation between the two sisters:

> "Ursula," said Gudrun, "don't you really *want* to get married?"
> Ursula laid her embroidery in her lap and looked up. Her face was calm and considerate.

"I don't know," she replied. "It depends on how you mean."

Gudrun was slightly taken aback. She watched her sister for some moments. "Well," she said ironically, "it usually means one thing! But don't you think anyhow, you'd be"—she darkened slightly—"in a better position than you are now?"

A shadow came over Ursula's face. "I might," she said. "But I'm not sure."

Again, Gudrun paused, slightly irritated. She wanted to be quite definite. "You don't think one needs the experience of having been married?" she asked.

"Do you think it need *be* an experience?" replied Ursula.

"Bound to be, in some way or other," said Gudrun, coolly. "Possibly undesirable but bound to be an experience of some sort."

"Not really," said Ursula. "More likely to be the end of experience."

That was a shocking conversation in 1920. But when *Women in Love*, the movie, was released in the United States in 1970—fifty years after the controversial publication of the book—the Brangwen sisters, who questioned marriage as the only destiny for a woman, struck a chord with the burgeoning feminist movement. The only real controversy created by the film was a homoerotic scene in which Rupert and Gerald strip off their clothing, fireside, and embark on a wrestling match in the nude—visible genitalia and all—which reverberated in that post-Stonewall moment when the gay rights movement was nascent. While some critics considered the movie to be "purple cinema"—like purple prose, because of the flamboyant style of its director, Ken Russell, as well as the erotic quality of Lawrence's writing—audiences were receptive to the film's interrogation of marriage, which would have been less likely before the new realism in cinema, ushered in by *Who's Afraid of Virginia Woolf?* several years earlier.

Lawrence and Albee share few artistic affinities, but each came out of the bohemian literary cohort of their day—Lawrence was part of London's Bloomsbury circle in the 1920s and Albee cavorted with the New York poets in Greenwich Village in the 1950s. Both were unintentional provocateurs: *Women in Love* was among the first novels to challenge the inevitability of marriage so directly, and almost half a century later, *Who's Afraid of Virginia Woolf?* was ahead of the curve in examining marriage itself—the marrow of it—and breaking through to the cultural mainstream. "There is nothing in the film that is not in the novel," Larry Kramer, the producer and screenwriter of *Women in Love*, told William F. Buckley on *Firing Line*, responding to his question about the extent and purpose of the sex scenes in the film. "A great deal of the dialogue itself is Lawrence's own." The same can be said of *Virginia Woolf*, the movie, in relation to the play. Neither film departed from the author's or the playwright's original intentions; both addressed the concept of marriage from the perspective of the individuals involved, without holding the institution itself up as an ideal. The excesses of *Women in Love* raised eyebrows in some quarters; there is an infamous scene in which Rupert demonstrates to a table of elegant luncheon guests the proper way to eat a fig, as if he were performing cunnilingus. Nevertheless, Glenda Jackson won an Academy Award for Best Actress for her performance as Gudrun; the film also brought Oscar nominations to Russell for Best Director and Kramer for Best Adapted Screenplay—much like the configuration of accolades accorded by the Academy to *Who's Afraid of Virginia Woolf?* four years earlier.

While Lawrence anticipated the shortcomings of marriage for women in the modern era, *Who's Afraid of Virginia Woolf?* was pivotal in addressing the "discontent" of married women so directly. When Mike Nichols later said, referring to women like Martha, that "there's no such thing as a tough woman alone in a room," he was countering predominating attitudes at the time that wrote off a strong-willed woman as a "bitch." In other words, Nichols urged his contemporaries to see the fuller picture. Martha stands up for herself, demands her rights—at times defiantly—and expects equality. That she suffers lone-liness when George withholds his affection is merely human. She's discontented because George no longer seems worthy of her respect, no longer worth the effort and the energy. "If you existed, I'd divorce you," she tells him. But that is because he has not only failed her expec-tations of him; he has also failed, primarily, to simply make her feel loved. George, like so many men of his generation, falls short of the promise of the mid-century male hero—some embodiment of financial success, professional standing, and personal responsibility—exemplified by Martha's father (the college president). George is a man who—as Virginia Woolf herself implied about the exaggerated stature of men reflected in women's eyes—"no longer seems twice as tall" in Martha's estimation. And yet, a woman like Martha could still smart when that man in the room (to paraphrase Nichols) caused her to feel lonely and unloved.

Before *Virginia Woolf*, movies about marriage hewed to the conven-tions of their time. *The Women*, for example, released in 1939, is a time capsule of the strict cultural mores of wealthy white Americans in the 1930s, among whom marriage was expected to be a rock-solid institu-tion, its boundaries clearly circumscribed and delineated. Directed by George Cukor and based on the Broadway play by Clare Boothe Luce, *The Women* offers a sharp satire of high society and an indictment of the power imbalance between men and women, focusing on Mary Haines (played by Norma Shearer), a wife and mother thoroughly contented with her child, her stately home, and her (apparently) fairy-tale marriage. The drama begins when some treacherous friends set a trap for Mary in which she learns about her husband's affair. She is crushed. "It's an old story," her mother says, assuring her that she is not the first wife to suffer a husband's infidelity. "He isn't bored with you; he's bored with himself," the older woman astutely observes.

The Women is about the breakup of a seemingly perfect marriage from a (prefeminist) woman's perspective. One brilliant stroke is that men are often discussed but not a single man appears in the movie. We never see the interactions between Mary and her husband, Stephen, that result in their divorce; their arguments take place behind closed doors—in keeping with the era, the words muffled and indecipherable to the movie audience. The strictures of decorum that circumscribed representations of marriage in the 1930s are epitomized by *The Women* and stand in striking contrast to the agonizing emotional honesty of the brutal on-screen arguments between the likes of George and Martha. In the 1930s, infidelity was presented as a sin that necessitated divorce, but by the 1960s, the world had changed.

In 1949, *Adam's Rib*, another romantic comedy directed by Cukor, stars Spencer Tracy and Katharine Hepburn as Adam and Amanda Bonner, husband-and-wife lawyers. Their marriage gets played out through a legal battle between Adam, the district attorney, and Amanda, who is in private practice—a lively proxy for their underlying marital dynamics. The conflict begins with an argument between them at breakfast over an article in the morning paper: *A woman who suspected her husband of having an affair followed him to an assignation with his paramour, pulled a gun on the couple, and shot him outright. He was hurt, albeit not fatally.* Adam asserts that the woman is guilty of a heinous crime; Amanda counters that the woman was justified, driven by her husband's deceit. In the DA's office, the case lands in Adam's docket and he becomes the prosecuting attorney; Amanda, intent to prove her point, offers to represent the woman as her defense attorney. As *Adam's Rib* sails along on a current of snappy patter, a battle of the sexes plays out at arm's length through fast-talking comedy, without the confrontational emotional and psychological probity of *Who's Afraid of Virginia Woolf?* It would be fifteen years before the American public was ready for George and Martha, without the pretext or the distraction of the courtroom sport.

In 1990, the producer-director team Ismail Merchant and James Ivory would make *Mr. and Mrs. Bridge*, a film based on the novels *Mrs. Bridge* (1959) and *Mr. Bridge* (1969), by Evan S. Connell. The film is a slow-drip examination of a marriage in the 1940s, when the common vocabulary for emotional expression was more limited, and open discussion of feelings less encouraged. Set in Kansas City, *Mr. and Mrs. Bridge* puts under the microscope the manners and mores of upper-middle-class life in the Midwest and, specifically, among the conservative country-club set—in effect, where Connell, the author, was born and raised. Merchant-Ivory were known for their meticulous period detail, and the 1940s world they create for Walter and India Bridge, played by the married couple Paul Newman and Joanne Woodward, is of forensic, museum-quality accuracy, from the Bridges' stalwart, three-story white clapboard house to the cars they drive, the clothes they wear, the tables they set, the glasses they drink out of, down to the white lace doilies on the mahogany furniture in the living room.

The Bridges are approaching fifty, but they seem older by today's standards. In fact, their conversations are monosyllabic and virtually monotonal—traditional, ritual-defined, regional. The modern enthusiasms of their teenaged children cause Walter and India to scratch their heads. Their marriage is solid but lacking. One poignant moment takes place in a bank vault, where Walter is showing India their financial papers should anything happen to him. She picks up a cherished locket from the safe-deposit box and grows pensive. "Do you remember that evening on my parents' front porch before we were married?" she asks, looking up at Walter. "It was in the summertime," she continues. "Remember the azaleas by the porch?" He draws a blank. She reminds him that he read poetry to her. Then, turning to make sure that no one is around to hear her, she asks him, with a strained expression on her face: "Walter, do you love me?" He looks at her quizzically. "Well, *do* you?" she persists. He twitches slightly. "If I didn't," he musters, "then I wouldn't be here." This is an unsatisfactory answer, and she strains not to cry. "Couldn't you *tell* me once in a while?" she says. "Would that hurt you so very much?" He is at a loss, not really knowing what to say. "India, I am not very good at this sort of business," he says, as if to wash his hands of her question. "You used to be," she says, indignance edging into her disappointment. He is silent, perhaps chastened, but he will have the final word, as men were customarily expected to at the time. "Well, for better or worse, I turned out to be an attorney and not a poet," he explains. Surrounded by the rock-solid physical evidence of their material security—the inner sanctum of a bank vault—Walter implies that he believes his ability to provide for India is proof enough of his love.

The Man in the Gray Flannel Suit, the novel by Sloan Wilson published in 1955, was a bestseller, and the film, directed by Nunnally Johnson, was released the following year. Marriage is addressed here through the lens of middle-class male ambition in the era of lockstep societal conformity. Tom Rath, played by Gregory Peck, is a suit-and-tie professional who commutes to work in midtown Manhattan from suburban Connecticut, where he lives with his wife, Betsy (Jennifer Jones), and their three young children. Betsy, like Martha, is *discontent*. She finds the ordinary circumstances of their life boring and depressing. She expected more of Tom, who, like George in *Virginia Woolf*, has lost his drive, his courage, and his individuality. When Tom is given a new career opportunity, Betsy encourages him to pursue it, and then, in his new job, she pushes him to speak truth to power, unlike the "yes" men all around him. In the end, Tom wins his boss's respect for his honesty, and he is rewarded for it. (Behind every great man, the saying used to go, is a woman.) While the novel is a morality tale about the soul-draining effects of conformity, the movie holds the marriage itself in steady focus as a driving force for Tom's success and the couple's happiness—in keeping with the upwardly mobile aspirations of the mid-century American middle class. Tom and Betsy's arguments touch on issues fundamental to couples who are trying to understand each other, even as the dialogue is tailored to a plot that is not, in and of itself, driven by their marriage.

Richard Yates's novel *Revolutionary Road* was set in the same mid-1950s suburban milieu as *The Man in the Gray Flannel Suit*, and there are overlapping themes. The film version, however, directed by Sam

Mendes, was not made until 2008, and like *Mr. and Mrs. Bridge*, it accurately reconstructs the period in which the novel takes place. Frank and April Wheeler (Leonardo DiCaprio and Kate Winslet), in their mid-thirties, with two small children, feel trapped by their conventional lives. April, too, is *discontent*. Despite her efforts to break free of the workaday suburbs and move the family to Paris, the plan is thwarted when April learns that she's pregnant. On top of that, Frank gets a big promotion at work, which makes him trepidatious about leaving the security—and the new prestige—of his job. Paris becomes an unreachable goal. Mendes was able to foreground Frank and April's marital arguments with emotional potency, underscoring the crisp, recognizable language of the book with pointed psychological resonance about the marriage. "In my mind, [*Revolutionary Road*] is trying to be a sister film to *Who's Afraid of Virginia Woolf?*, *Scenes from a Marriage*, and those sorts of movies," Mendes said.

The 2016 film *Fences* provides another historicized glimpse of a midcentury American marriage. Directed by Denzel Washington, based on the Pulitzer Prize–winning play by August Wilson, it is among the best-received mainstream films to center the portrayal of a Black couple. This period piece takes place in segregated 1950s Pittsburgh. Troy Maxson, played by Washington, is a sanitation worked married to Rose, played by Viola Davis. Money is tight, and the movie, set mostly inside their house or in their "fenced-in" backyard, captures the tensions that mount in a marriage burdened by financial constraint, compounded with the pressure of accommodating to an oppressive social structure. Troy can be charming, a raconteur—yet equally righteous, stubborn, and explosive. Over the years, their conflicts deepen, amid Troy's self-destructive tendencies and Rose's shifting loyalties between him and their son, Corey, played by Jovan Adepo. When Troy reveals the affair he is having with a woman named Alberta, then confesses that she is pregnant with his child, Rose shuts down emotionally. She tries to maintain the status quo, going about her daily routines with dignity and earnest resolve, keeping their domestic tableau in order, proceeding without having the option of leaving. In one ugly scene, enduring yet another of Troy's dispiriting messes, she poses a question that must have seemed eternal to so many wives of that generation. "What about my life?" she asks her husband. Why did she have to sacrifice everything for him?

The Lion in Winter, a 1968 film directed by Anthony Harvey, based on the play by William Goldman, offers an entirely different example of a historical couple enacting timeless marital dynamics, and, indeed, it has often been compared to *Who's Afraid of Virginia Woolf?* When the original print of *Lion* was restored in 2016, Kenneth Turan, the film critic of the *Los Angeles Times*, wrote that "the element of the picture that has aged not even a little bit, is the spectacular lead performances by Katharine Hepburn and an on-fire Peter O'Toole, two master battlers going at each other hammer and tongs like a 12th century version of *Who's Afraid of Virginia Woolf?*"

Based on the marriage between King Henry II of England (O'Toole) and Eleanor of Aquitaine (Hepburn), *The Lion in Winter* is an elevated historical drama featuring sophisticated dialogue. The king keeps Eleanor imprisoned in France—a marital entrapment of historical magnitude—and the film opens with her spectacular arrival at his castle for Christmas with a full royal armada. "How dear of you to let me out of jail," Eleanor says to the king with sunny disdain. "It's only for the holidays," says Henry, bowing to kiss her hand. Their fierce and seething, if utterly polite, squabbles throughout the film revolve around a King Lear–like decision about which of their three conniving sons should inherit the throne. As historical epics go, it stands out for its biting wit, building intricate plots and schemes around the same fundamental marital dynamics as in *Who's Afraid of Virginia Woolf?*, albeit overlaid with medieval detail. "Give me a little peace," Henry beseeches Eleanor after one argument. "A little? Why so modest?" Eleanor says blithely, always strategizing his death. "How about eternal peace? Now, there's a thought."

Eleanor of Aquitaine, like Martha, is *discontent*. She is disappointed not only in her husband but also in her three sons. "I don't much like our children," she tells Henry. She, too, feels trapped, her literal (and historically factual) imprisonment standing as an apt metaphor for the feelings of boredom, hopelessness, and rage that the Marthas of American society in the mid-twentieth century experienced as "the problem that has no name." *The Lion in Winter* clads in epic splendor the battle between husbands and wives that George and Martha enact without the regalia of the royal court, in the intimate, tattered, drunken comfort of their living room.

~

Who's Afraid of Virginia Woolf? was released as the stigma of psycho-therapy was eroding and the practice was growing in popularity. Several movies came out in the early 1970s that examined marriage as if from a psychotherapist's-eye view. One was *Diary of a Mad Housewife*, directed by Frank Perry and released in 1970. Tina Balser, played by Carrie Snodgress, is an attractive and urbane Manhattan housewife married to a narcissistic, autocratic, social-climbing lawyer (Richard Benjamin). Despite their posh lifestyle—a classic six on Central Park West—he belittles her in social situations and treats her like a servant at home. Tina begins a sexually satisfying affair, but her lover is also verbally abusive; in group therapy, her psychiatrist dismisses her marital complaints as neurotic—*her* fault and not her husband's. Even when her husband confesses to having an affair, she accepts it, without confessing that she, too, has a lover. Over the course of the film, Tina unravels, driven slowly insane by the gaslighting mechanisms of a male-dominated society. *Diary* puts *Virginia Woolf* in striking relief; Martha, despite her unharnessed bad behavior, is a nascent feminist who stands up for herself, refusing to be cowed by her husband. Tina, by contrast, is so bound up in status and heteronormative convention that she cannot see her way out of her victimization, and remains imprisoned by her marriage and by society, trapped in her discontent.

In 1973, a breakthrough documentary series called *An American Family* was broadcast on PBS. Craig Gilbert, the producer, with Alan and Susan Raymond on the cameras, recorded three hundred hours of live footage of Bill and Pat Loud, an affluent couple with five children in Santa Barbara, California, who agreed to be the subjects of this cinematic experiment. Gilbert had interviewed two dozen families before choosing the Louds. The producer claimed that the idea for the series came out of his own life. "My marriage, my parents, television and really something about the country," he told the *Washington Post* in 1973.

The filmmakers followed the Louds around in their daily lives for seven months. At first, the Louds seemed like the very image of the American dream. The series captured the tedium of family life, as well as their marriage playing out before the camera in real time. Viewers saw touching moments interspersed with the mundane tensions any couple might have—but also unanticipated circumstances: Pat's angry outburst when she learns of Bill's extramarital affair; the ensuing arguments that lead to their separation; and the emotional turmoil of their divorce. Other unexpected dramas large and small unfolded over the twelve-episode series—for instance, their oldest son, Lance, who was almost twenty, revealed his homosexuality on national television, a surprise to his parents as much as to the entire viewing public. "The Louds are neither average nor typical," Gilbert said in introducing the first episode of the series. "No family is. They are not 'the' American family. They are simply 'an' American family."

Some critics agreed, considering *An American Family* to be a corrective to idealized fictional representations on television, pointing out that the Louds had no connection to *Ozzie and Harriet* or *The Brady Bunch*. "In this light," the film historian Jeffrey Ruoff writes, "*An American Family* may be more effective as a critique of family life on fictional television than as a statement about contemporary American society." While reviewers ascribed a "soap opera" fascination to the series, "others intuited that the Louds stood for more than themselves, as in [the journalist] Shana Alexander's comment that the documentary depicted 'a genuine American tragedy.'" *An American Family* was later considered the prototypical "reality show" years before the genre emerged. During the show's run, the family appeared on *The Dick Cavett Show*. Pat Loud disparaged her decision to allow the filming of her family, complaining that the series "makes us look like a bunch of freaks and monsters. . . . We've lost dignity, been humiliated, and our honor is in question." Luckily, the cameras are not always rolling in the course of our own daily lives; challenges to our dignity occur at every turn, and our unfiltered emotional reactions do not necessarily reflect our best selves.

Scenes from a Marriage, directed by Ingmar Bergman and released in the United States in 1974, was a breakthrough film (edited down from a six-part miniseries) that took several cues from *Who's Afraid of Virginia Woolf?* Having directed the European premiere of *Virginia Woolf* a decade prior, Bergman had a deep understanding of Albee's play. In *Scenes from a Marriage*, Bergman took the essential question of *Virginia Woolf*—who's afraid to live without illusions—and expounded on it.

Scenes from a Marriage opens with Johan and Marianne, a Swedish couple, being interviewed for a magazine feature as exemplars of the "ideal marriage." He is confident and self-aggrandizing; she is prim, subservient. Only when asked about employment does she allow that, contrary to her image as a devoted wife and mother, she is also a lawyer, and works for a large law firm. Marianne has been untouched by psychotherapy and has no awareness of the women's movement: Despite her career, she is bound to the then-common gender role of doormat wife in a typical bourgeois marriage.

Marianne's awakening occurs throughout the film. Several years transpire, and Johan and Marianne—once the very model of the perfect couple—are now separated. On the eve of their divorce, Johan comes over for dinner, and, after several drinks, Marianne reads a few of her evolving revelations about herself from her diary: "I go on faking relationships with others, with men, always putting on an act in a desperate attempt to please. I've never considered what I want, but only, 'What does he want me to want?' It's not unselfishness, as I used to believe. It's cowardice. Worse, it stems from being ignorant of who I am." She turns to Johan, who has fallen asleep. He has not heard a word she said. Her growing self-awareness is cast against his unexamined chauvinism, egocentricity, and diminishing career. In striking contrast to the film's opening scene, Marianne is now empowered by her new self-discovery. In the end, she sheds the restraints of her discontent, in contrast to Johan, whose initial cock-of-the-walk arrogance has withered. As the movie ends, he complains of being passed over for a prestigious position at work, and admits to feeling like a failure, a relic at the age of forty-five, a deadweight in his field, impotent.

The presentation of Johan and Marianne as an ideal couple at the beginning of the film—like the Louds in *An American Family*—turns out to be a facade. And the role reversal at the end is a poignant rebuttal to the clear delineation of gender roles in society—and in movies—up until that point. Bergman is successful in systematically anatomizing and undoing the couple's illusions in *Scenes from a Marriage*. In *Who's Afraid of Virginia Woolf?*, by contrast, George and Martha's illusions are exploded in a less linear, more assertively emotional, and by far more direct dissection of who they are to each other. "In content, [*Scenes from a Marriage*] is a child of the stage, most obviously Strindberg's *Dance of Death*, Ibsen's *A Doll's House* and Albee's *Who's Afraid of Virginia Woolf?*" wrote T. E. Kalem, *Time* magazine's drama critic, in 1974.

~

A Woman Under the Influence, directed by John Cassavetes and released in 1974, was a tour de force, not only because of its intimate cinema verité camerawork, but also because of its haunting portrait of marital dysfunction. Nick and Mabel Longhetti, played by Peter Falk and Gena Rowlands, are a working-class couple in Los Angeles. The film opens with Mabel handing their three young kids off to her mother so she and Nick can have a "date night." But Nick—a city utility worker—is part of a crew called to respond to a water main break, and, once again, she is left alone, discouraged, despondent, enraged. To cheer herself up, she goes out, picks up a man at a local bar, gets drunk, and brings him home—a revenge fuck to get even with Nick. In the morning, Nick arrives home with his crew of dirty, sweaty co-workers, and Mabel is forced to welcome them like a dutiful housewife and make the bunch of them a hearty breakfast of spaghetti. We discover that Mabel is mentally dissociated—or is it repressed accumulated rage that makes her unable to speak normally? Her comments of endearment to some of the men make them all uncomfortable—no one more so than Nick, her husband, who reprimands her in a verbally abusive way.

The film unfolds with a series of ugly scenes in which Nick—inarticulate, reactive, and brutish—abuses Mabel verbally and physically, and she becomes increasingly detached from reality. Nick and his mother put her into a treatment center for six months, but when she's released, her condition has not improved. Two questions linger: Was she driven mad because of Nick's oppressive behavior, or was she chemically imbalanced all along? And why is Nick's behavior—equally unhinged, as well as volatile and antisocial—acceptable, when he is just as crazy as Mabel? In the end, despite the shaming, the humiliations, and the disappointments, the love between them is clear, and they find their way back to each other, if only in a single tender moment at the end.

The 1979 film *Too Far to Go* was based on John Updike's twenty-four short stories about Joan and Richard Maple, written over the course of twenty years. Together, the stories chart the evolution of the Maples' marriage and divorce. They are a winning New England couple (played by Blythe Danner and Michael Moriarty), classy and credentialed in an Ivy League sort of way. They have four kids and a dog or two, a big, comfortable house, and spend summer weekends at a small beachside cottage on the Cape. As the film opens, they have just agreed to be divorced. It's all so amicable, in keeping with their just-so-civilized mode of behavior—despite their repressed rage, resentment, and bitterness over the years.

The story unfolds in flashbacks to moments in their marriage. In one sequence, they are on vacation in Puerto Rico without the kids. They are stuck in a room with two single beds side by side, and are now lying down in the late afternoon, each in their own bed, discussing the tiffs they have had throughout the day. Joan turns to Richard and invites him into her bed. "I would like to," he says, looking over at her. "But it's too far to go." She glares at him in a flash of anger, then turns her head in sorrow. "Jerk" is all she can muster at his piercing slight. While she is visibly wounded by Richard's sly rebuff, her New England reserve prevents her from screaming at him. Still, it is that singular moment in which she decides the marriage is over. This scene parallels George's rejections of Martha's bids for intimacy in *Who's Afraid of Virginia Woolf?* The difference is that Joan simmers in decorous silence through this and other betrayals before they agree to end the marriage. Martha, by contrast, never holds back, and, as far as we know, she and George are still together after all these years.

~

No one outside a marriage can experience the bond that keeps any two people together. Certainly, couples recognize in other people's marriages the dynamics that ring true about their own. Couples socialize together, observe one another—compete with, rely on, flirt around, gossip about, and use others in service of their own marriages. They learn quickly from experience how to identify the subtextual signals of marital discord in others from the most casual social interactions—one half of a couple's disparaging, offhanded remark about the other at a dinner party, say, or the spouse who is *too* friendly to someone else's partner at an afternoon barbecue. Couples are the structural foundation of most societies on earth. Every marriage tells a story. Examples can be set. Lessons can be learned. Warnings can be heeded. But, ultimately, finally, profoundly, each marriage is its own reason for being, with its own chemistry and constellation of circumstances that make it specific to that couple while also representative, by the nature of marriage, of all couples.

By the 1980s, the realities of marriage itself—as opposed to the dramas of courtship and romance—had become a more common subject for cinematic scrutiny. In *Shoot the Moon* (1982), for example, Alan Parker handles the discord between George and Faith Dunlap (Albert Finney and Diane Keaton) as an honest, intelligent, and believable depiction of a good marriage gone sour. George is a writer whose international success has diminished his home life in his eyes, rendering his lovely wife, their vibrant children, and their enviable Marin County existence as something of a noose around his neck. The film opens with George in a tuxedo crying alone in the den, the voices of Faith and the kids in the background as she gets dressed for an evening event—a literary awards dinner at which George is being honored. As they leave the house, George tells Faith she looks good, and asks if that's the same dress she wore to the ceremony the year before. "Oh," she says, embarrassed. "Does it still have the stain from the wine you spilled on me?" He frowns, disparaging her for "always remembering the wrong things." On arrival at the event, the cameras flash, and George is asked how he should be identified. "George Dunlap and *friend*?" the photographer asks. "I'm not his friend," Faith interjects. "I'm his *wife*." George's affair with the "friend" is an open secret, which, over the course of the film, will lead to the sad dissolution of what appears to have had all the ingredients of a solid marriage. "*Shoot the Moon* is not the historical record of this marriage, but the *emotional* history," Roger Ebert wrote when the film came out. "[The film] contains a raw emotional power of the sort we rarely see in domestic dramas."

In the late 1980s, *sex, lies, and videotape*, Steven Soderbergh's low-budget film debut, was an unexpected success. Original, astute, and visually stylish, the story unfolds around John and Ann (Peter Gallagher and Andie MacDowell), a young, affluent couple in Baton Rouge, Louisiana. Chaos ensues when John's college friend Graham (James Spader) returns to Baton Rouge for unexplained reasons. While John and Ann's marriage plays a significant role in the film, the gravitational weight lies with Graham and his mysterious pervy-artist-inquisitor demeanor. Intentionally or not, he exposes with psychological poignancy the hypocrisies of Ann and John's picture-perfect marriage—which was never on solid ground to begin with—resulting in the union's inevitable demise. In 2006, Soderbergh interviewed Mike Nichols while watching *Who's Afraid of Virginia Woolf?* together. While *Virginia Woolf* was a decided influence on Soderbergh, he pointed out that *Carnal Knowledge*, the fourth film Nichols directed—and another four-character chamber piece—was an even more specific reference for *sex, lies, and videotape.*

"Perhaps no filmmaker has covered the tonal bases of marital strife quite as comprehensively as Woody Allen," wrote Guy Lodge, the film critic for the *Guardian*, in 2017, and "never more scarringly than in *Husbands and Wives.*" Woody Allen's twenty-first film, released in 1992, stars Mia Farrow, with whom he had been romantically involved for twelve years. The bitter lawsuits and custody battles that were to become a real-life scandal soon after this film was released, and which would scar Allen's legacy permanently, hover somewhere beyond the frame. But however conflicted we may feel about Allen as an artist (and as a person), *Husbands and Wives* is a masterpiece of social observation, psychological acuity, and filmmaking experimentation. "*Husbands and Wives* de-romanticizes modern love, revealing it as a human condition ultimately motivated by logic rather than impulse: the heart may flutter or bleed, but it's a resilient, flexible muscle that can adapt to the most exigent of circumstances," wrote Steve Davis, the longtime film critic of the *Austin Chronicle*, when the movie came out. "It's Allen's *Scenes from a Marriage.*"

Husbands and Wives opens with Jack and Sally (Sydney Pollack and Judy Davis), who have been married for more than twenty years, arriving for dinner at Gabe and Judy's apartment (Woody Allen and Mia Farrow). The couples are old friends, and Sally makes a surprising announcement: "Jack and I are separating." This sends Gabe and Judy into turmoil, and Judy erupts in anger. "How could you do this?" she says, accusingly, meaning: *How could you threaten our marriage—or all marriage—by separating after all these years?* Sally will later tell Judy at lunch that her anger that night was "because *you* wanted to do what we did," and she advises Judy that she can't stay with Gabe simply out of fear. A series of touch-and-go ancillary flings ensue: Jack moves in with his young, blonde aerobics instructor ("It's like your IQ is suddenly in remission," Gabe tells Jack, who responds by saying it's a relief not to face Sally's endless "Radcliffe judgments" all the time); Sally gets involved with a co-worker of Judy's (Liam Neeson); and Gabe, who teaches writing at Columbia, has a protracted, if inappropriate, flirtation with a twenty-year-old student (Juliette Lewis). Throughout, Gabe and Judy have honest conversations about their love for each other, their ambivalence about each other, and their on-again-off-again phantom idea about the child that she wants to have, and that he doesn't—an echo of George and Martha's "little bugger."

Allen, ever the auteur, adds a layer of canny storytelling with cut-in sequences in which each character intermittently speaks into the camera—as if in a therapy session or documentary-style interview—providing a retrospective description of the film's action while it's happening, giving the viewer clues about where the story is going before we get there (foreshadowing the "confessional" segments that are now a staple of the reality TV formula). Jack and Sally will end up back together. "Here's to a good marriage," Jack says, toasting the four of them at dinner several months later. "Finally, the *best* two people could hope for." Soon after that, Gabe and Judy separate, agreeing that it is for the best. In *Husbands and Wives,* Jack and Sally—like George and Martha in *Virginia Woolf*—are introduced as the couple with the problems; Gabe and Judy—like Nick and Honey—seem happily married. "It's the essential contradiction in *Who's Afraid of Virginia Woolf?*" Nichols said. "Nick and Honey, the young couple, appear to be close. And George and Martha appear to be enemies, but, of course, it's the other way around."

In the 2000s several movies addressed marriage itself from various narrative distances: *Mr. and Mrs. Smith* (2005), for example, anatomizes the Smiths' relationship by proxy—as a shoot-'em-up comedy thriller about rival contract killers who are married to each other (Brad Pitt and Angelina Jolie). Just as in *Adam's Rib,* where the Bonners' marriage plays out as a courtroom drama, the underlying dynamics of the Smiths' relationship get played out in high-production violence as an extreme—if darkly comedic—metaphorical equivalent to the domestic arguments, the revenge fantasies, or the secret desires of any married couple. A similar transformation is at work in 2022's *Everything Everywhere All at Once*, where the long-suffering union of Evelyn (Michelle Yeoh) and Waymond (Ke Huy Quan) is refracted as a multiversal action flick. This Best Picture Academy Award winner gestures toward how a couple can unlock hidden potentialities in each other—and how the effort required to sustain a marriage over decades of struggles can be, for lack of a better word, superheroic.

Released in 2010, *The Kids Are All Right*, directed by Lisa Cholodenko, is as nuanced an examination of a same-sex marriage as any film had yet depicted. Nicole and Jules (Annette Bening and Julianne Moore) are raising two now-teenaged children each of them had given birth to, both conceived from the same sperm donor. The film is an honest and insightful portrayal of the realities and complexities of married life as the balance of power shifts back and forth over the simplest things, from the distribution of labor over domestic chores to whose wishes come first based on the income they bring in. Deeper emotional conflicts are at play, as well, with accusations hurtling from one spouse to the other about parenting skills, and an exposed affair (across gender lines) threatening the foundation of the marriage itself. The movie does not foreground the couple's difference from the norm but, rather, reflects an underlying sameness of marriages, gay and straight alike.

Chris & Don: A Love Story (2007), directed by Tina Mascara and Guido Santi, is a clear-eyed, touching documentary about the thirty-year relationship between Christopher Isherwood, the renowned British author, and Don Bachardy, the artist, who were thirty years apart in age. The film includes passages read from Isherwood's diaries and footage of Bachardy making drawings of Isherwood as he was dying from prostate cancer in 1986. At the time of its release, Stephen Holden, writing in the *New York Times*, called it "one of the ultimate true stories of a proto-gay-marriage succeeding in a forbidding climate."

In 2015, *45 Years*, a British film by Andrew Haigh, was released in the United States. It introduces us to Kate and Geoff Mercer (Charlotte Rampling and Tom Courtenay) around the occasion of their forty-fifth wedding anniversary. Geoff receives some unexpected news of a seemingly innocuous nature about a girlfriend who died before he and Kate were married. Over the course of the film, Kate learns that Geoff had been in love with the girlfriend when she died, and becomes increasingly disturbed about this previously unknown information. During their grand, celebratory anniversary party, Geoff makes a toast, taking Kate's hand to lift together in his, but, in a strikingly symbolic moment, she yanks her hand away, realizing that their entire forty-five-year marriage was based on a lie.

Marriage Story (2019), by Noah Baumbach, is the most direct descendant of *Who's Afraid of Virginia Woolf?* and *Scenes from a Marriage* in the twenty-first century so far: a modern, moving, and original tableau about marriage that is recognizable and accessible, with true-to-life resonance. Charlie and Nicole Barber (Adam Driver and Scarlett Johansson) are a New York couple married ten years. Charlie runs a theater company; Nicole is an actress; they have an eight-year-old son, Henry. They are undergoing a painful divorce. The film opens with a series of vignettes showing each of them going about their days as the other lists in tender voice-over the qualities they like about each other. The film then cuts to the office of the couple's "separation mediator" as they listen to him explain that things will get inevitably more contentious during a divorce. "I like to begin with a note of positivity for the people I work with to remember why they got married in the first place," he says, asking them to read the lists we just heard out loud to each other. Nicole has no patience for this exercise and gets angry when she is prodded to read her list. "I'm going to go if you guys are just going to sit around and suck each other's dicks," she says, and leaves the room.

Nicole, originally from Los Angeles, has been offered a starring role in a TV series and returns there with Henry. Charlie keeps talking of her eventual return to New York, but Nicole, whose career is taking off, wants to stay in L.A. Soon, she files for divorce. A cross-country battle escalates over Charlie's attempt to win her back, then over custody of Henry. In one significant monologue, Nicole explains to her powerful divorce lawyer (Laura Dern) her own, modern-day version of "the problem that has no name." Initially, in their marriage, she says, they communicated so well: "It was better than the sex, the talking, although the sex was also like the talking, you know, everything is like everything in a relationship." By most measures, Charlie is a good guy—thoughtful, responsible, sensitive; at the same time, he proceeded for so long with an innate belief that his needs took priority over Nicole's. She describes how, at the beginning, she had been the "marquee" attraction in the theater company, but over the years, Charlie, as the director, became more prominent. "It would have been fine, but I got smaller," she says, in a kind of free-associative reverie about what went wrong. After Henry was born, she realized that everything in the apartment was Charlie's. "I didn't even know what my taste was because I'd never been asked to use it. I didn't even pick our apartment, I just moved into his." When she got the offer for the TV series, for which she would make a lot of money, he made fun of it. "But this is who I am, and this is what I'm worth, and maybe it's stupid but at least it's *mine*. If he had just taken me into a big hug and said, 'Baby, I'm so excited for your adventure, of course I want you to have a piece of earth that's yours,' well, then, we might not be getting divorced. . . . but that's when I realized he truly didn't *see* me. Also, I think he slept with the stage manager, Marianne."

∼

Why are there so many movies about romance and so few, by comparison, about marriage? Obviously, romance is dreamier, sexier, full of hope and possibility. The love story is what myth is built on—in literature, opera, theater, poetry, film, and popular culture. We could trace a line from Cupid and Psyche, Orfeo and Eurydice, to Tristan and Isolde, Romeo and Juliet, Anna Karenina and Count Vronsky; from Dick and Liz, to Brad and Angelina, to Beyoncé and Jay-Z. Stories about romantic love are, to some extent, erotic fantasies in the guise of social ritual, the circumstances of the characters providing ample distractions, with plot twists delaying gratification as the story builds toward consummation—that is, marriage by any other name—or its obstruction. Romance is the halcyon childhood of marriage before the realities set in.

Why do people cry at weddings? When I was younger, I thought it was because of the poetic nature of the betrothed avowing themselves to each other at the altar in front of family and friends, in a moment of pure grace, their love—and love above all—being ordained for all to see. With age and over time, I wonder if the tears aren't a bit more wistful: less, perhaps, about the couple at the altar than in welling sadness and nostalgic lament about an increasingly abstract, once-imagined ideal of love, clarified in maturity as something of a beautiful childhood fantasy. The happily-ever-after part of romantic love becomes a fairy tale the older we get, but with the wisdom of experience, hope is sustained in watching some couples turn that illusory promise into genuine love.

Look around at all the couples you know, or those you observe walking on the street, passing by in their cars, or dining out in restaurants. How do any two people end up together, and what are the odds of them staying the course of a lifetime? Perhaps they were lucky enough to have been drawn together initially in the alchemy of love—being in love—the aura, the euphoria, the aching physical attraction, the awe of seeing one's own set of ideals personified in the beloved, the suspension of disbelief in seeing one's dreams come true in another single individual who, miraculously, seems tailor-made for you. And then, the intoxicating levitation that comes with being recognized equally by that dream-come-true, being seen and wanted in the same way. Other-worldly, magical, like a drug: You never want it to end. Perhaps simply blinded by love, the two of you marry. Realities set in. Circumstances take over. Twenty years go by. Good and bad things happen. The level of attachment deepens and solidifies long after the magic dissipates. You are bound by feelings now so familiar from habit, so native in proximity, essentially familial and intertwined with needs that echo from the core of attachment to your parents. You look at your spouse and wonder what happened to the personification of that ideal. Again, if you're lucky, you might summon a kernel of the initial infatuation and, perhaps for a fleeting moment, remember why you fell in love with them in the first place. "Who's afraid of Virginia Woolf?" George asks Martha in the wee hours of dawn. "I am, George," Martha says. "I am." After all is said and done, they have seen the raw truth about each other, and, in their messy wisdom, they are willing to move forward together, a little more honestly than before—scared, but willing, but scared.

My regard for *Who's Afraid of Virginia Woolf?* veers toward the romantic, as I am convinced that genuine love is the foundation on which George and Martha play out their unrelenting display of rancorous one-upsmanship, turning on each other hurtfully and destructively with mutual venom and bile. The existentialist in me accepts that their bad behavior, while extreme, is based on emotions that are universal. George and Martha are closer to the truth of marriage—if, perhaps, its uglier dimensions—than the typical anodyne characterizations of married life in mainstream movies. *Who's Afraid of Virginia Woolf?* is an incisive investigation of the psychological under-pinnings of any marriage—love, need, tenderness, attraction, disappointment, rejection, resentment, misunderstanding, revenge, hatred, (the imbalance of) power—that define (it seems to me) the emotional core of spousal attachment.

On one draft of the screenplay for *Who's Afraid of Virginia Woolf?*, Ernest Lehman scrawled this observation: "When two people hate each other as much as George and Martha appeared to, and stay together year after year, it can only be because side by side with that hatred, is deep love almost ashamed to come out from the hiding place into which it has been slowly forced."

There are good and bad marriages. Some marriages get derailed for the wrong reasons, others for the best. Elizabeth Taylor and Richard Burton, for example, married each other *twice* and divorced *twice* before they called it quits, and Mike Nichols married and divorced three different women before he married Diane Sawyer—who turned out to be, famously, the best thing that ever happened to him. Lehman married his wife, Jacqueline, when he was twenty-seven, and they stayed the course until her death fifty-two years later. Marriage is not an easy condition to maintain. It starts out as a fairy tale and ends up a labyrinth of emotional, psychological, circumstantial, and ethical challenges. It takes work. And it takes love. But is it worth it? Well, if you ask George and Martha—representative of so many couples, for better or worse, in sickness and in health—they would probably say it depends on the day.

ACKNOWLEDGMENTS

My first thank you goes to Adam Eaglin, my literary agent, for the conversations that led to the genesis of this book and also for his steady guidance along the way. Next, an editor is a writer's best secret weapon, and I am more than grateful to Ben Hyman, my editor, for the pleasure of his wisdom, taste, masterly invisible hand, and our easy compatibility. I want to acknowledge, too, the entire Bloomsbury team for their exacting standards and collegial house manner.

My gratitude extends to those individuals who were helpful in untold ways—offering relevant information, providing resources, lending personal support or institutional assistance, in alphabetical order: Bill Goldstein; Rebecca Boucher; Eric Colleary and Steve L. Wilson, curators, respectively, of theater and of film at the Harry Ransom Center, Austin; Annabel Davis-Goff; Eric Himmel; Nailah Holmes at the Billy Rose Theatre Division, New York Public Library for the Performing Arts; Jakob Holder of the Edward Albee Foundation; Andy Howick of mptv Images; Edward Kosner; Tom Kirdahy; Bill Jacobson; Gerard Malanga; Lee Manchester; Greg Pierce, curator of film, the Warhol Museum, Pittsburgh; Jeff Roth at the *New York Times*; Rajendra Roy and Josh Siegel, curators in the Film Department at the Museum of Modern Art; Bree Russell, curator, Warner Bros. Archives; and Valentina Rice.

A delighted thank you to the friends with whom I watched and discussed *Who's Afraid of Virginia Woolf?* over drinks and dinner on several evenings: Tamara Jenkins and Jim Taylor; Hernan Diaz and Anne Ross; Alison Maclean; Lisa Schwarzbaum; Frank Tartaglione; and Alan Coulter and Kim Knowlton.

Finally, thank you, Richard Press, my husband, my reader, my sounding board, my reservoir of inspiration, who can be, intermittently, Martha to my George, and George to my Martha, with whom I have traveled the vicissitudes and back. And beyond the realm of our marriage, a singular thank you for designing the cover of this book.

NOTES

PROLOGUE

xii *If Bette Davis had deliberately set out*: *New World Encyclopedia*, s.v. "Bette Davis," https://www.newworldencyclopedia.org/entry/Bette _Davis.

xiii *Albee joked with great trepidation*: William Flanagan, "Edward Albee, The Art of Theater No. 4," *Paris Review*, no. 39 (Fall 1966).

xvi *Mike Nichols gave* Playboy *an interview*: "*Playboy* Interview: Mike Nichols," *Playboy*, June 1966, 63.

CHAPTER ONE: THE COLLEGE OF COMPLEXES

1 *If you removed the homosexuals*: Fran Lebowitz, "The Impact of AIDS on the Artistic Community," *New York Times*, September 13, 1987.

1 *Albee's eyes fell on one quip*: Mel Gussow, *Edward Albee: A Singular Journey* (New York: Applause Theatre Books, 2001), 87.

2 *I was told that [the Village]*: Edward Albee, "Audio Biography," Academy of Achievement, June 2, 2005, achievement.org/achiever/edward-albee /#interview.

2 *For most of the people in [my] class*: Anatole Broyard, *Kafka Was the Rage: A Greenwich Village Memoir* (New York: Crown, 1993), 56.

3 *I had an awful lot of jobs*: "Albee," Talk of the Town, *New Yorker*, March 25, 1961, 31.

3 *There were a lot of saloons*: Albee, "Audio Biography."

3 *He had this wonderful, Jesuit-trained mind*: Gussow, *Edward Albee*, 78.

3   *It was part of the learning experience*: Ibid., 81.

4   *There was no sense of monogamy*: Robert Heide, phone interview by author, October 21, 2022.

4   *He was very much an orphan*: Gussow, *Edward Albee*, 87.

4   *"Duet for Three Voices"*: Richard Howard, *Quantities* (Middletown, CT: Wesleyan University Press, 1962), 55.

4   *Flanagan and Albee shared a weakness for alcohol*: Christopher Bram, *Eminent Outlaws: The Gay Writers Who Changed America* (New York: Twelve Books, 2012), 76.

5   *A feeling of danger*: Gussow, *Edward Albee*, 80.

5   *I have no idea who my natural parents were*: "Albee," 30.

6   *I used to make old-fashioneds*: Gussow, *Edward Albee*, 43.

6   *I was given all the things*: Ibid., 36.

6   *If I did not behave*: Ibid., 39.

6   *It was not just her casual racism*: Mel Gussow, unpublished interview with Noel Ferrand, 1993, Mel Gussow Collection, Harry Ransom Center, University of Texas at Austin. Hereafter cited as Gussow Collection.

7   *The absence of affection at home*: Mel Gussow, unpublished interview with Albee, November 10, 1994, Gussow Collection.

7   *Valley Forge Concentration Camp*: "Albee," 30.

7   *Ed is an adopted child*: Gussow, *Edward Albee*, 53.

8   *How dare you come home at five in the morning*: Ibid., 79.

8   *I'd learned to hate their politics*: Ibid., 70.

9   *A homosexual who*: John Skow, "Edward Albee's Vortex of Violence," *Saturday Evening Post*, January 18, 1964.

9   *Diminishing human agency*: Hannah Arendt, *The Human Condition*, 2nd ed. (Chicago: University of Chicago Press, 1998), jacket copy.

10   *There was no preparation*: Gussow, *Edward Albee*, 93.

10   *You must remember I'd been watching*: William Flanagan, "Edward Albee, The Art of Theater No. 4," *Paris Review*, no. 39 (Fall 1966).

11   *The best fucking one-act*: David Crespy, *Richard Barr: The Playwright's Producer* (Carbondale: Southern Illinois University Press, 2013), 80.

13   *Give authority to the playwright*: Ibid., 79.

13   *Albee could be rather stiff*: Ibid., 81.

13   *There is a whole crop of American writers*: Ibid., 83.

13   *Edward was able to parlay*: Robert Heide, "Carousing in the Village with Terrence and Edward," *WestView News*, May 3, 2020.

14   *The Albees at home were amusing*: Gussow, *Edward Albee*, 141.

14   *A couple who once adopted a son*: Skow, "Edward Albee's Vortex of Violence."

14   The American Dream *is the substitution of artificial values*: Edward Kosner, "Social Critics, Like Prophets, Are Often Honored from Afar," *New York Post*, Friday, March 31, 1961.

16   *I do think you would be amused*: Albee to Barr, 1960, Richard Barr–Clinton Wilder papers, Billy Rose Theatre Division, New York Public Library for the Performing Arts.

16   *I like that little play you showed me*: Crespy, *Richard Barr*, 100.

17   *The first time I laid eyes on Terrence McNally*: Albee interview, in *Terrence McNally: Every Act of Life*, directed by Jeff Kaufman (The Orchard, 2018).

17   *The parties of Morris's that I attended*: Bill Berksen, "Morris Golde," in *Since When* (Minneapolis: Cogg House, 2018).

18   *Edward was the first boyfriend I ever had*: McNally interview, in Kaufman, *Terrence McNally*.

18   *Bill's collapse, as Bill will have it*: Gussow, *Edward Albee*, 155.

19   *I must tell you that we artists*: Thomas Mann, *Death in Venice* (New York: Ecco, 2009), 136.

19   *I will discover one day that I am thinking*: Gussow, *Edward Albee*, 151.

21   *Willard and Marie were the last of the great bohemians*: Marc Siegel, "Bitch," in *The Films of Andy Warhol*, vol. 2 (New Haven, CT: Whitney Museum of American Art / Yale University Press, 2021), 311.

21   *They wrote and filmed and drank*: Lee Manchester, "Who's the Source for Virginia Woolf?," *Wagner Magazine: The Link for Alumni and Friends*, Winter 2013–14, https://wagner.edu/wagnermagazine/whos-the-source-for-virginia-woolf/.

21   *He used to come every time to eat*: Ibid.

22   *Watching their arguments was a little like*: Scott MacDonald, *A Critical Cinema 5: Interviews with Independent Filmmakers* (Berkeley: University of California Press, 2006), 39–40.

22 *I'm bored when people read aloud to me*: Gussow, *Edward Albee*, 154.

22 *The dilemma of George/Martha will not leave me*: Ibid., 155.

CHAPTER TWO: MARQUEE DREAMS

24 *Their plays . . . disrupted the comfortable certainties*: Martin Esslin, introduction to *Absurd Drama* (New York: Penguin Books, New Impression Edition, 1965).

24 *The Theatre of the Absurd . . . tends toward a radical devaluation of language*: Martin Esslin, *The Theatre of the Absurd* (New York: Knopf Doubleday, 2004), 26.

24 *Writing a two act play that seems unlikely*: "Theater: The Un-Angry," *Time*, February 3, 1961.

25 *about a two-in-the-morning drunken party*: Talk of the Town, *New Yorker*, March 25, 1961, 32.

25 *barbed, poised, and elegantly guarded*: William Flanagan, "Edward Albee, The Art of Theater No. 4," *Paris Review*, no. 39 (Fall 1966).

25 *When I sit down to work*: Talk of the Town, 32.

25 *Angry? No, I'm not angry*: Edward Kosner, "Social Critics, Like Prophets, Are Often Honored from Afar," *New York Post*, Friday, March 31, 1961.

25 *When I was told*: Edward Albee, "Which Theater Is the Absurd One?," *New York Times*, February 25, 1962.

26 *Edward was very supportive*: *Terrence McNally: Every Act of Life*, directed by Jeff Kaufman (The Orchard, 2018).

26 *[Bill] was very, very important in my education*: Mel Gussow, unpublished interview with Albee, London, November 10, 1994, Gussow Collection.

26 *McNally . . . would win the Stanley Award*: "McNally Wins Writer's Prize," *New York Daily News*, n.d., ca. July 21, 1962.

27 *Intrigued as I had been*: Alan Schneider, *Entrances: An American Director's Journey* (New York: Viking Penguin, 1986), 221.

27 *Edward was both taciturn and shy*: Ibid., 271.

27 *I found* Dream *a charming and well crafted "cartoon"*: Ibid., 289.

28 *I remember vividly the hand-to-hand passage*: Ibid., 309.

28   *Martha is hurt and wants to lash out*: Ibid., 310.

29   *No one liked the play*: David Crespy, *Richard Barr: The Playwright's Producer* (Carbondale: Southern Illinois University Press, 2013), 112.

29   *He hoped to take at least one "fuck" uptown*: Ibid., 113.

29   *Indeed, I did name the two lead characters George and Martha*: Flanagan, "Edward Albee," 13.

30   *He agreed to rent the theater to them*: Schneider, *Entrances*, 312.

30   *I never got to play George*: Ibid., 313.

30   *I have just read the best American play*: Mel Gussow, *Edward Albee: A Singular Journey* (New York: Applause Theatre Books, 2001), 166.

31   *If we had opened with that play*: Ibid., 167.

31   *Schneider gave Pinter the Albee script to read*: Schneider, *Entrances*, 315.

32   *She was a great actress*: Ibid., 313.

32   *There is no maid, no chaise longue*: Helen Markel Herrmann, "Saint Joan from Wisconsin," *New York Times*, September 30, 1951.

32   *I had the reputation for being unbelievably choosy*: Crespy, *Richard Barr*, 116.

32   *After class I ran home*: Uta Hagen and Herbert Berghof papers, Billy Rose Theatre Division, New York Public Library for the Performing Arts.

33   *If I hesitated, it was about Alan*: Susan Spector, "Telling the Story of Albee's Who's Afraid of Virginia Woolf?," *Theatre Survey* 31, no. 2 (November 1990): 177–99.

33   *I was more insecure than I am now*: Alan Levy, "The A* B** B*** of Alan Schneider," *New York Times Magazine*, October 20, 1963, 40.

33   *We had a long talk, and he was wooing me*: Uta Hagen and Herbert Berghof papers.

33   *I spent five hours talking her into accepting the part*: Schneider, *Entrances*, 313.

34   *I thought it would be interesting to cast Uta*: Recorded interview with Edward Albee, n.d.

34   *A script the size of the London telephone directory*: Spector, *Theatre Survey*.

35   *He didn't feel "butch enough, jock enough"*: Gussow, *Edward Albee*, 170.

35   *The funding had come together*: Ibid., 167.

35 *It was Wilder who realized*: Ibid.

36 *I am writing you in reference*: Albee/Leonard Woolf correspondence, Leonard Woolf Papers, The Keep, University of Sussex, U.K.

36 *I have no objection*: Ibid.

36 *There are two equal roles in this play*: William Flanagan, "Edward Albee, The Art of Theater No. 4," *Paris Review*, no. 39 (Fall 1966).

37 *Barr and Wilder [the producers] made some stupid announcements*: Uta Hagen and Herbert Berghof papers.

37 *Edward reading George badly*: Ibid.

37 *Just before everyone could commit suicide*: Schneider, *Entrances*, 318.

37 *She was wearing these sort of pulpit glasses*: Spector, *Theatre Survey*.

38 *Uta worked from inside*: Schneider, *Entrances*, 321.

38 *To me, that was not only precedent-setting*: Crespy, *Richard Barr*, 117

39 *He begged for help*: Schneider, *Entrances*, 325.

39 *I loved working with Arthur Hill*: Mel Gussow, unpublished interview with Uta Hagen, October 1, 1999, Gussow Collection.

39 *the best thing Schneider did is that he didn't interfere*: Spector, *Theatre Survey*.

39 Edit *me, Alan. Don't* direct *me*: Levy, "The A* B** B*** of Alan Schneider," 40.

40 *She was working the way an actress*: Spector, *Theatre Survey*.

40 *The child is "a 'beanbag'"*: Schneider, *Entrances*, 324.

41 *Melinda, whose New York debut this was*: Ibid., 322.

41 *We had changed out Honey*: Ibid., 320

42 *Albee let me stage each scene*: Ibid., 322.

42 *Albee considered it "marvelous"*: Mel Gussow, unpublished interview with Albee, n.d., Gussow Collection.

42 *He was very insecure with women*: Mel Gussow, unpublished interview with Albee, December 21, 1995, Gussow Collection.

42 *As a director he was tough:* Mel Gussow, "Alan Schneider, Pioneering Director, is Dead," *New York Times*, May 4, 1984

43 *Astonished, excited and ineffably moved*: Crespy, *Richard Barr*, 119.

CHAPTER THREE: WILD APPLAUSE

44　*If you take the cha cha out of Duchamp*: Ray Johnson, *Back to Ray Johnson: What a Dump*, exhibition at David Zwirner Gallery, New York, April 8–May 22, 2021, https://www.davidzwirner.com/exhibitions/2021/ray-johnson-what-a-dump/press-release.

44　Who's Afraid of Virginia Woolf? *opened on Broadway*: "Who's Afraid of Virginia Woolf?," *Playbill*, https://playbill.com/production/whos-afraid-of-virginia-woolf-billy-rose-theatre-vault-0000002773.

44　*"Jesus H. Christ," she barks*: Edward Albee, *Who's Afraid of Virginia Woolf?* (New York: Pocket Books, 1962), 3.

47　*The producers had sent opening night invitations*: David Crespy, *Richard Barr: The Playwright's Producer* (Carbondale: Southern Illinois University Press, 2013), 120.

47　*When the play ended at 11:40*: Mel Gussow, *Edward Albee: A Singular Journey* (New York: Applause Theatre Books, 2001), 178.

47　*Tonight belongs to the actors*: Crespy, *Richard Barr*, 120.

48　*We had a party afterwards at our apartment*: Terrence McNally, Mercedes Ruehl, and Jakob Holder, interview by Michael Riedel, Edward Albee Tribute, Theater Talk, August Wilson Theatre, December 6, 2016, https://www.youtube.com/watch?v=1Isyq4jPOA0.

48　*With the first reviews*: Alan Schneider, *Entrances: An American Director's Journey* (New York: Viking Penguin, 1986), 328.

48　*A sick play about sick people*: Robert Colemen, "Theater Review," *New York Daily Mirror*, October 15, 1962.

48　*Is 3 ½ hours long*: John Chapman, "A Play Lies Under the Muck in *Who's Afraid of Virginia Woolf?*," *New York Daily News*, October 15, 1962.

48　*It is a horror play written by a humorist*: Walter Kerr, "Theater Review," *New York Herald Tribune*, October 15, 1962.

49　*Thanks to Edward Albee's furious skill*: Howard Taubman, "The Theater: Albee's Who's Afraid," *New York Times*, October 15, 1962.

49　*One of those works that extend the frontiers of the stage*: John Lahr, *Tennessee Williams: Mad Pilgrimage of the Flesh* (New York: Norton, 2015), 441.

49   *Gore Vidal's sister, Nina Steers, sent Wilder a note*: Richard Barr–Clinton Wilder papers, Billy Rose Theatre Division, New York Public Library for the Performing Arts.

49   *I remember being enthralled and overwhelmed*: Eric Grode, "George and Martha, 50 Years Together," *New York Times*, September 27, 2012.

49   *There was an air of excitement*: Colleen Dewhurst, *Colleen Dewhurst: Her Autobiography* (New York: Scribner, 1997), 243.

50   *I was teaching at M.I.T. at the time*: Grode, "George and Martha, 50 Years Together."

50   *The flash of the moment of truth*: Gussow, *Edward Albee*, 204–5.

50   *Broadway did make a difference*: Ibid., 183.

51   *Do you think Elizabeth Taylor will marry Richard Burton?*: Sam Kashner and Nancy Schoenberger, *Furious Love: Elizabeth Taylor, Richard Burton, and the Marriage of the Century* (New York: Harper Perennial, 2011), 35.

52   *The problem lay buried, unspoken, for many years*: Betty Friedan, *The Feminine Mystique* (New York: W. W. Norton, fiftieth anniversary edition, 2013), 1.

52   *"Head and master" laws gave husbands*: Stephanie Coontz, "Mystifying 'The Feminine Mystique': Four Myths About Betty Friedan and Feminism," Council on Contemporary Families, University of Texas at Austin, https://sites.utexas.edu/contemporaryfamilies/2013/02/18/four -myths-about-betty-friedan/.

52   *For many women, and not a few men*: Louis Menand, "Books as Bombs: Why the Women's Movement Needed 'The Feminine Mystique,'" *New Yorker*, January 24, 2011.

53   *The hopeless emptiness of everything in this country*: Richard Yates, *Revolutionary Road* (New York: Vintage, 2000), 200.

54   *I meant the title to suggest that the revolutionary road of 1776*: Interview with Richard Yates, *Ploughshares*, Issue 3, Winter 1972.

54   Revolutionary Road *comes out of a tradition of marital literature*: Sam Mendes, interview by Charlie Rose, *Charlie Rose*, January 1, 2009, https:// charlierose.com/videos/12468?autoplay=true.

54   *O'Neill . . . wrote characters that cannot survive without their illusions*: John Simon, "Making the Scene," *Washington Post*, August 1, 1999. (The exact

quote in this review of Gussow's biography of Albee is "O'Neill says you have to have false illusions. Virginia Woolf says get rid of them.")

55   *He said that the play comes to life outside the theater*: Nancy Kelly, interview by Studs Terkel, 1964, Studs Terkel Radio Archive, https://studsterkel .wfmt.com/programs/discussing-whos-afraid-virginia-woolf-edward -albee-and-interviewing-nancy-kelly-and.

55   *This is excellent TV*: Stephen J. Bottoms, *Albee: Who's Afraid of Virginia Woolf?* (Cambridge: Cambridge University Press, 2000), 19.

55   *For Dirty Minded Females Only*: Crespy, *Barr*, 121.

56   *The Literate Are Seldom Rich*: Ibid.

56   *People who wouldn't come to see*: Schneider, *Entrances*, 328–29.

56   *Hateful is the proper word*: Philip Hope-Wallace, "Who's Afraid of Virginia Woolf?," *Guardian*, July 21, 1963.

57   *What a hangover on the day of reckoning*: Ingmar Bergman website, https:// www.ingmarbergman.se/en/production/whos-afraid-virginia-woolf.

57   *A shaking, spiritual striptease-act*: Ibid.

57   *If they are very good actors, they will find it*: Bottoms, *Albee*, 131.

58   *With his unblinking view of life*: "A Snub of Edward Albee," Pulitzer Prize website, https://www.pulitzer.org/article/snub-edward-albee.

59   *It made you uncomfortable*: Grode, "George and Martha, 50 Years Together."

59   *There was an inevitability about psychoanalysis*: Anatole Broyard, *Kafka Was the Rage: A Greenwich Village Memoir* (New York: Crown, 1993), 52.

60   *Marrying for love*: Stephanie Coontz, "Marriage Evolves," *Newsday*, June 30, 2011.

61   *It happened slowly, imperceptibly*: Christopher Bram, *Eminent Outlaws: The Gay Writers Who Changed America* (New York: Twelve Books, 2012), 80.

61   *The American theater, our theater, is so hungry*: Richard Schechner, "Who's Afraid of Edward Albee?," *Tulane Drama Review* 7, no. 3 (Spring 1963): 7–10.

61   *Hayes berates the New York theater*: Joseph Hayes, "Theater Misrepresents Life in America," *New York Times*, August 11, 1963.

62   *Albee begins by describing the idyllic summer*: Edward Albee, "Who's Afraid of the Truth," *New York Times*, August 18, 1963.

64 *A homosexual daydream*: Philip Roth, "The Play That Dare Not Speak Its Name," *New York Review of Books*, February 25, 1965.

64 *The "infantile sexuality" of "homosexual theater"*: Donald M. Kaplan, "Homosexuality and American Theater: A Psychoanalytic Comment," *Tulane Drama Review* 9, no. 3 (Spring 1965): 25–55.

64 *The fact is that without the homosexual American*: Bram, *Eminent Outlaws*, 81.

64 *The principal charge against homosexual dramatists*: Stanley Kauffmann, "Homosexual Drama and Its Disguises," *New York Times*, January 23, 1966.

65 *The great artists so often cited as evidence*: "The Homosexual in America," unsigned essay, *Time*, October 31, 1969.

66 *I was part of the gay community critical*: Terrence McNally, Mercedes Ruehl, and Jakob Holder, interview by Michael Riedel, Edward Albee Tribute, Theater Talk, August Wilson Theatre, December 6, 2016.

66 *I read it and I was so disturbed*: Gary Ross, "Never Just a Writer," *Los Angeles Times*, March 25, 2001.

67 *Ernie let's face it*: Ibid.

CHAPTER FOUR: HOLLYWOOD BOUND

69 *Probably no one in Hollywood*: Peter Bart, "Woolf at Hollywood's Door," *New York Times*, July 12, 1964.

70 *What I hope to do*: Ibid.

70 *He scrawled a list of Marthas*: Ernest Lehman Collection, Harry Ransom Center, University of Texas at Austin. Hereafter cited as Lehman Collection.

71 *I started getting very excited*: Mel Gussow, *Edward Albee: A Singular Journey* (New York: Applause Theatre Books, 2001), 233.

71 *The opulence of Cleopatra's palace*: Sam Kashner and Nancy Schoenberger, *Furious Love: Elizabeth Taylor, Richard Burton, and the Marriage of the Century* (New York: Harper Perennial, 2011), 59.

71 *Why did I think Elizabeth would be right?*: Gussow, *Edward Albee*, 233.

72   *They had cut out the heart, the essence*: Jerry Vernilye and Mark Ricci, *The Films of Elizabeth Taylor* (New York: Citadel, 1976), 28.

73   *Fisher, whom Taylor's friends secretly referred to*: Truman Capote, *Portraits and Observations: Essays by Truman Capote* (New York: Random House, 2007), 314.

73   *Elizabeth and Burton are not just* playing *Antony and Cleopatra*: Kashner and Schoenberger, *Furious Love*, 27.

73   *At first the romance struck some people as too campy*: C. David Heymann, *Liz* (New York: Birch Lane, 1995), 250.

73   *I lust after your smell*: Kashner and Schoenberger, *Furious Love*, 26.

74   *I was the happy recipient*: Ibid., 48.

74   *It was the real thing, and everybody knew it*: Heymann, *Liz*, 250.

74   *Who do you love*: Kashner and Schoenberger, *Furious Love*, 26.

75   *Burton did most of the talking*: Ibid., 27.

76   *Like tributes paid to royalty by their subjects*: Ibid., 44.

77   *They would show the world*: Ibid., 87.

78   *You've only to read the first lines*: Ibid., 138.

78   *I think you're too young*: Roy Newquist, "Behind the Scenes of a Shocking Movie," *McCall's*, June 1966, 89.

78   *Lehman had made his list of Georges*: Lehman Collection.

79   *Who was truly touched by the finger of God*: Hume Cronyn, *A Terrible Liar* (New York: William Morrow, 1991), 330.

79   *Imagine the lines around the block*: Newquist, "Behind the Scenes of a Shocking Movie," 89.

79   *Lehman scribbled notes on hotel stationery*: Lehman Collection.

81   *Nichols and May at the Blue Angel*: Gene Knight, "The Knight Watch: Comedy Team Scores at The Blue Angel," *New York Journal American*, October 24, 1957.

81   *Arthur, this is your mother*: Mike Nichols and Elaine May, undated video clip, YouTube, https://www.youtube.com/watch?v=lKLitNv_kU.

82   *Because their act was so intelligent*: "Nichols and May: Take Two," *American Masters*, 1996.

82   *Nichols and May opened their show on Broadway*: *Playbill*, https://playbill.com/production/an-evening-with-mike-nichols-and-elaine-may-john-golden-theatre-vault-0000008447.

82 *Opening night was a gala*: Sam Kashner, "Who's Afraid of Nichols and May," *Vanity Fair*, December 20, 2012.

83 *I felt a real connection to him*: Gussow, *Edward Albee*, 235.

84 *I'll be on the* Cleopatra *set most days*: *Becoming Mike Nichols*, directed by Doug McGrath (HBO, 2016).

84 *With Suzy and Mike*: Michael Guerrin, unpublished interview with Richard Avedon for *Le Monde*, 1993, provided to the author.

85 *We talked about books, about feelings*: John Lahr, "Making It Real," *New Yorker*, February 13, 2000.

86 *I saw it on the second night*: Susan King, "Mike Nichols: It's a Wonderful Life," *Los Angeles Times*, June 9, 2010.

86 *I'm on her side. I'm on his side*: Gussow, *Edward Albee*, 235.

87 *There are two equal roles in this play*: William Flanagan, "Edward Albee, The Art of Theater No. 4," *Paris Review*, no. 39 (Fall 1966).

87 *Funny. Humor. Funny*: Mel Gussow, unpublished interview with Albee, December 21, 1995, Gussow Collection.

88 *It was his core text*: Mark Harris, *Mike Nichols: A Life* (New York: Penguin, 2021), 32.

88 *Lehman's screenplay had been completed*: Lehman Collection.

89 *They actually love each other very much*: "Steven Soderbergh & Mike Nichols Who's Afraid of Virginia Woolf? Audio Commentary," YouTube, https://www.youtube.com/watch?v=4l4zhoHMeoY.

89 *Hallelujah. We've got Mike*: Lehman Collection.

CHAPTER FIVE: IF YOU GIVE ME CHOCOLATE, I'LL GIVE YOU FLOWERS

90 *Abstruse! In the sense of recondite*: "Steven Soderbergh & Mike Nichols Who's Afraid of Virginia Woolf? Audio Commentary," YouTube, https://www.youtube.com/watch?v=4l4zhoHMeoY.

91 *My play is not a farce*: Roy Newquist, "Behind the Scenes of a Shocking Movie," *McCall's*, June 1966, 88.

91 *Young god he needed to be*: "Soderbergh & Nichols."

91 *I did a reading at the Cherry Lane theatre*: Rose Eichenbaum, *The Actor Within: Intimate Conversations with Great Actors* (Middletown, CT: Wesleyan University Press, 2011), 99.

91   *Piazza, who, it turned out, was having a very clandestine affair*: Ibid.

92   *She would be called out by critics*: Lee A. Daniel, "Sandy Dennis, Film and Stage Veteran, Dies," *New York Times*, March 4, 1992.

93   *Wexler shot a series of luscious*: Sandy Dennis screen test, YouTube, https://www.youtube.com/watch?v=pNRGkAqjF34.

93   *It's a matter of tapping your unconscious*: "Soderbergh & Nichols."

93   *He was incredibly smart and fun to be with*: Mark Harris, *Mike Nichols: A Life* (New York: Penguin, 2021), 150.

95   *On the front lawn*: Ernest Lehman journal, June 5, 1965, Lehman Collection.

96   *I think I just heard somebody at the piano*: Lehman journal, May 28, 1965.

96   *Every morning*: Norman Podhoretz, *Making It* (New York: Random House, 1967).

97   *Don't worry about the technical stuff*: Harris, *Mike Nichols*, 156.

99   *Oh, you found me*: Lehman journal, June 4, 1965.

100 *Ernie—the enclosed clipping speaks for itself*: Lehman journal, June 7, 1965.

101 *I'm learning things I had not known*: Lehman journal, May 18, 1965.

101 *I'm absolutely overwhelmed with anxiety*: Lehman journal, May 19, 1965.

103 *Albee's pen was just in flames*: "Soderbergh & Nichols."

103 *I was a prick some of the time*: Ibid.

104 *Lehman was very talented*: Ibid.

105 *During the course of these two hours*: Ibid.

105 *I was feeling a little stiff backed*: Lehman journal, May 20, 1965.

107 *Nothing on* Who's Afraid of Virginia Woolf? *means anything to me*: Lehman journal, June 3, 1965.

CHAPTER SIX: FLIES IN THE OINTMENT

108 *I don't know why you want to make a movie like this one*: Ernest Lehman journal, May 17–18, 1965, Lehman Collection.

110 *The start date is June 28*: Lehman journal, June 1, 1965.

110 *Taylor's one-million-dollar contract included*: Lehman Collection.

111 *When I was twelve*: Mike Nichols, interview by Charlie Rose, *Charlie Rose*, August 7, 1992, https://charlierose.com/videos/16142.

112 *It's the director's job to tell the story*: Ibid.

112 *It depressed Mike because he realized*: Lehman journal, June 25, 1965.

113 *Hacks only imitate*: Lehman journal, June 22, 1965.

113 *It was my fault for having Elizabeth Taylor and Richard Burton*: Lehman journal, May 18, 1965.

114 *The film is a piece of shit*: Mark Harris, *Mike Nichols: A Life* (New York: Penguin, 2021), 173.

114 *Warner said to me and Lehman*: Mark Harris, *Pictures at a Revolution* (New York: Penguin, 2008), 101.

114 *Here's the thing about black and white*: Ibid.

114 *All right, black and white*: Harris, *Pictures at a Revolution*, 101.

115 *I was a real snot*: Ben Gazzale, unpublished interview with Nichols, 2010, American Film Institute.

116 *The only trouble with all this*: Lehman journal, June 11, 1965.

117 *How did I look*: Lehman journal, June 13, 1965.

117 *She is so famous*: Lehman journal, June 14, 1965.

117 *A few little wisps of bad feeling*: Lehman journal, June 15, 1965.

119 *I'm glad you were willing*: Lehman journal, June 16, 1965.

119 *My parents used to fight*: "Soderbergh & Nichols."

120 *You gotta have these bookshelves*: Harris, *Mike Nichols*, 176.

120 *For the opening scene on the set*: "Soderbergh & Nichols."

120 *It was an eerie experience*: Lehman journal, June 28, 1965.

121 *Did you send flowers and champagne*: Lehman journal, June 25, 1965.

122 *Elizabeth seemed to go at me*: Lehman journal, May 28, 1965.

123 *It is nothing less than sumptuous*: Ibid.

124 *I could have written half of a screenplay*: Lehman journal, June 30, 1965.

125 *It was an unexpected convergence*: Jane Fonda, *My Life So Far* (New York: Random House, 2005), 163.

125 *In the middle of the party*: Harris, *Pictures at a Revolution*, 107.

126 *There is no such thing*: Mel Gussow, unpublished interview with Nichols, August 30, 1965, Gussow Collection.

126 *Like asking a chocolate milkshake*: Lehman journal, July 6, 1965.

CHAPTER SEVEN: THE MOST FAMOUS COUPLE IN THE WORLD

127 *A good marriage*: Mel Gussow, unpublished interview with Albee, November 3, 1995, Gussow Collection.

127 *"Exhilarating" is how Ernest Lehman described the first day*: Lehman journal, July 6, 1965, Lehman Collection.

129 *The close relationship between Nichols and the Burtons*: C. Robert Jennings, "All for the Love of Mike," *Saturday Evening Post*, October 9, 1965, cover story.

129 *I realize we sound like an atom bomb project*: Ibid.

130 *I had never seen people treated like that*: Mark Harris, *Mike Nichols: A Life* (New York: Penguin, 2021), 177.

130 *Her legs are too short for the torso*: Capote, *Portraits and Observations: Essays by Truman Capote* (New York: Random House, 2007), 35–36.

131 *She had never once been asked to rehearse*: Harris, *Mike Nichols*, 177.

131 *At noon, someone poured Bloody Marys*: Lehman journal, July 6, 1965.

133 *The only trouble was that she looked ravishingly beautiful*: Lehman journal, July 8, 1965.

133 *The only time she flashed me a look*: Lehman journal, July 8, 1965.

133 *My job is not to say*: Mel Gussow, unpublished interview, Gussow Collection.

133 *More productions that year than any individual Shakespeare play*: Mel Gussow, *Edward Albee: A Singular Journey* (New York: Applause Theatre Books, 2001), 66.

134 *Mike cited another interpretation from an acquaintance*: Mel Gussow, unpublished interview with Mike Nichols, August 29, 1965, Gussow Collection.

135 *I don't want to upset Mike*: Lehman journal, July 7, 1965.

135 *We note that it still contains a good deal of the profanity*: Geoffrey Shurlock to Jack Warner, October 9, 1965, Lehman Collection.

135 *In 1951, he cautioned George Stevens*: Tommy Thompson, "Raw Dialogue Challenges All Censors," *Life*, June 10, 1966, 92.

136 *Mike was reluctant to shoot any protection shots*: Lehman journal, July 7, 1965.

136 *He was certain that Burton could play himself*: Ibid.

137 *They had a real student-teacher relationship*: Harris, *Mike Nichols*, 177.

137   *It was very cathartic*: Sam Kashner and Nancy Schoenberger, *Furious Love: Elizabeth Taylor, Richard Burton, and the Marriage of the Century* (New York: Harper Perennial, 2011), 145.

137   *Reverting to their favorite pastimes*: Ibid., 107.

138   *A new tantrum was brewing in anticipation*: Lehman journal, July 9, 1965.

138   *Elizabeth Taylor's lush, glossy beauty*: Kashner and Schoenberger, *Furious Love*, 117.

139   *Not exactly a happy picture*: Lehman journal, July 12, 1965.

140   *That old house contained a few faculty offices*: Gloria Steinem, email to author, April 5, 2022.

140   *Mike would play all four roles*: Lehman journal, July 7, 1965.

140   *He had an intuitive grasp*: Louis Menand, "Who Was Mike Nichols When He Wasn't Playing Mike Nichols?" *New Yorker*, February 1, 2021.

141   *I can't believe a man with a face*: Lehman journal, July 9, 1965.

142   *Listen, Ernie, you must be sure to tell them*: Lehman journal, July 13, 1965.

142   *On practically every point Mike fought him effectively*: Lehman journal, July 14, 1965.

144   *Isn't there some way you can make Harry Stradling like me*: Lehman journal, July 16, 1965.

145   *She's the greatest looking middle-aged lady*: Lehman journal, July 15, 1965.

147   *If that's the kind of picture you want to make*: Lehman journal, July 21, 1965.

148   *I'm so sorry. I have to fire you*: Harris, *Mike Nichols*, 173.

149   *I could simply order the picture in color*: Lehman journal, July 16, 1965.

CHAPTER EIGHT: THE ART OF FILMMAKING

151   *My father basically had two ways*: John Preston, "Bernardo Bertolucci on Being Burned by Hollywood," *Telegraph*, April 19, 2013, https://www.telegraph.co.uk/culture/film/9984513/Bernardo-Bertolucci-on-being-burned-by-Hollywood.html.

151   *He always lived like a prince*: Ash Carter and Sam Kashner, *Life Isn't Everything: Mike Nichols, as Remembered by 150 of His Closest Friends* (New York: Picador, 2020), 239.

151   *Anything he did, he did well*: Annabel Davis-Goff, phone interview by author, February 15, 2023.

152 *Just enough to sound like someone who can play*: C. Robert Jennings, *Saturday Evening Post*, October 9, 1965.

152 *Taught him how to be a rich person*: Ash Carter and Sam Kashner, "Mike Nichols's Life and Career: The Definitive Oral History," *Vanity Fair*, September 2015, https://www.vanityfair.com/hollywood/2015/09/re membering-director-mike-nichols.

152 *Just ask them about themselves*: Carter and Kashner, *Life Isn't Everything*, 72.

153 *I had some apprehension about Mike*: Mel Gussow, unpublished interview with Ernest Lehman, August 30, 1965, Gussow Collection.

153 *My job is not to fix what Albee wrote*: Mel Gussow, unpublished interview with Mike Nichols, August 30, 1965, Gussow Collection.

153 *Every line in the film is my play*: Mel Gussow, *Edward Albee: A Singular Journey* (New York: Applause Theatre Books, 2001), 243.

153 *He met his first wife*: Mark Harris, *Mike Nichols: A Life* (New York: Penguin, 2021), 61.

154 *Was a snob, but a funny, brilliant snob*: Ibid., 86.

154 *I was jealous*: Ibid., 80.

154 *Mike would bring people as presents for us to play with*: Ibid., 127.

155 *When she pulled a knife on me*: Ibid., 145.

155 *I'm on her side. I'm on his side*: "Steven Soderbergh & Mike Nichols Who's Afraid of Virginia Woolf? Audio Commentary," YouTube, https://www .youtube.com/watch?v=4l4zhoHMeoY.

157 *I want it bright, bright, bright*: Herb A. Lightman, "The Dramatic Photography of *Who's Afraid of Virginia Woolf?*," *American Cinematographer*, April 28, 2020, https://theasc.com/articles/the-dramatic-photography -of-virginia-woolf.

158 *We all found each other through rehearsals*: "Soderbergh & Nichols."

158 *Nichols had designed everything in the refrigerator*: Gussow, *Edward Albee*, 239.

159 *Taylor wanted to create her own Martha*: Ibid., 238.

159 *Richard is about the sound*: "Soderbergh & Nichols."

160 *I can't act until you say "action"*: Lehman journal, July 26, 1965, Ernest Lehman Collection, Harry Ransom Center, University of Texas at Austin.

161 *All in all, the first day was a very slow day*: Ibid.

161 *We were all awed by Elizabeth's knowledge*: "Soderbergh & Nichols."

165 *There is a slight air of dissatisfaction*: Lehman journal, July 27, 1965.

166 *Everybody seemed to be going about things the wrong way*: Thomas Thompson, "Liz in a Shocker," *Life*, June 10, 1966.

166 *I find that very few people on the picture*: Lehman journal, July 29, 1965.

167 *I think he wants to leave the picture*: Ibid.

168 *I'm sick and tired of you getting angry*: Ibid.

170 *I hate publicity*: Cynthia Lindsay, "Who's Afraid of Filming Virginia Woolf?," *Cosmopolitan* magazine, October 1965.

170 *The parking spaces outside Stage 8*: C. Robert Jennings, *Saturday Evening Post*, October 9, 1965.

171 *Mike's a very disturbing man*: Ibid.

CHAPTER NINE: THOSE DAMNED GUESTS

173 *Don't talk to me about hatred*: Merve Emre, "Jonathan Franzen Thinks People Can Change," *New York* magazine, October 11–24, 2021, 66.

174 *We were at it so long*: "Steven Soderbergh & Mike Nichols Who's Afraid of Virginia Woolf? Audio Commentary," YouTube, https://www.youtube.com/watch?v=4l4zhoHMeoY.

176 *Some performers greatly aid the cameraman*: Peter Bart, "The Woolf's Young Turk," *New York Times*, September 18, 1966.

177 *If there's a phony premise*: Gussow, unpublished interview with Nichols for *Newsweek* article, 1965, Gussow Collection.

177 *We understood the power of this material*: Rose Eichenbaum, *The Actor Within: Intimate Conversations with Great Actors* (Middletown, CT: Wesleyan University Press, 2011), 99.

178 *Sandy [Dennis] does a lot with her voice*: "Soderbergh & Nichols."

178 *There is never a false moment with Sandy*: George Segal, interview by Foster Hirsch, 2018, https://vimeo.com/286713672 [password Segal].

178 *Honey has to be annoying*: "Soderbergh & Nichols."

179 *She counted on all that in some semi-conscious way*: Ibid.

179 *Oh, Martha, she's frightening to play*: Kevin Kelly, "On the Set with the Burtons," Part II, *Boston Globe*, September 20, 1965.

179 *Elizabeth had a mouth on her:* Ash Carter and Sam Kashner, *Life Isn't Everything: Mike Nichols, as Remembered by 150 of His Closest Friends* (New York: Picador, 2020), 102.

179 *When they were called back to the set after lunch:* Ibid., 101.

180 *At the end of the day:* Ibid.

180 *I saw a kind of arrogance I didn't want:* Ann Guerin, "Happy to Be a King," *Life*, November 19, 1965.

CHAPTER TEN: THE PRODUCER'S OTHER CHEEK

185 *Extinction is the rule:* Carl Sagan, *The Varieties of Scientific Experience: A Personal View of the Search for God* (New York: Penguin, 2006), 66.

186 *It was one of the nicest times that we have had:* Ernest Lehman journal, July 29, 1965, Lehman Collection.

187 *You can spend $1,500, Ernie:* Lehman journal, August 4, 1965.

187 *Now Ernie found himself in a trap:* Lehman journal, August 19, 1965.

189 *Even though I had only six hours of sleep:* Lehman journal, August 16, 1965.

189 *The other "major emergency":* Lehman journal, August 5, 1965.

190 *What a shitty thing to do:* Detailed handwritten notes of the phone conversation, Lehman Collection.

191 *I was being George and Elizabeth certainly was being Martha:* Lehman journal, August 5, 1965.

191 *Elizabeth had occasionally found it difficult:* Sam Kashner and Nancy Schoenberger, *Furious Love: Elizabeth Taylor, Richard Burton, and the Marriage of the Century* (New York: Harper Perennial, 2011), 62.

191 *On the surface everything is wonderful:* Lehman journal, August 20, 1965.

192 *He was a guy who would go into a White Castle:* Ash Carter and Sam Kashner, *Life Isn't Everything: Mike Nichols, as Remembered by 150 of His Closest Friends* (New York: Picador, 2020), 19.

193 *It was the cheek that I had used so many times:* Lehman journal, August 16, 1965.

193 *I could stay on this plane forever:* Lehman journal, August 21, 1965.

194 *Mr. Mendenhall is a very witty and vibrant man:* Lehman journal, August 22, 1965.

195 *It's easier to obtain an audience with President Johnson*: Jim Morse, "Dick and Liz Come to Mass," *Boston Herald*, August 29, 1965.

196 *Martha walks stumpy*: Gussow, unpublished notes for *Newsweek* article, 1965, Gussow Collection.

197 *Mike and I thought it unwise*: Roy Newquist, "Behind the Scenes of a Shocking Movie," *McCall's*, June 1966, 138.

198 *We had an agreement with the college*: Ibid.

198 *My mind is made up, Mike*: Lehman journal, August 23, 1965.

199 *To many it seemed like asking Debbie Reynolds*: Kevin Kelly, "On the Set with the Burtons," Part II, *Boston Globe*, September 20, 1965.

200 *If you don't do something about this immediately*: Lehman journal, August 27, 1965.

201 *There was no way not to love Elizabeth*: "Steven Soderbergh & Mike Nichols Who's Afraid of Virginia Woolf? Audio Commentary," YouTube, https://www.youtube.com/watch?v=4l4zhoHMeoY.

201 *There were almost no pictures of Ernie*: Lehman journal, September 16, 1965.

202 *Home on vacation, he and his friends from Choate*: Mel Gussow, *Edward Albee: A Singular Journey* (New York: Applause Theatre Books, 2001), 56.

202 *Beneath the towering elm*: Howard Thompson, "Making of 'Virginia Woolf' Film Enlivens Smith College Campus," *New York Times*, August 28, 1965.

203 *It's the great speech in the play*: "Soderbergh & Nichols."

203 *Every camera shot should convey an emotion*: Howard Thompson, "Unafraid of Virginia Woolf," *New York Times*, September 5, 1965.

203 *Richard was not so great at remembering long things*: "Soderbergh & Nichols."

204 *It looked like high noon*: Ibid.

204 *It looked to the drivers on Route 10*: Kevin Kelly, "The Burtons Appear," Part I, *Boston Globe*, September 19, 1965.

205 *When people say that it spoils the claustrophobia*: "Soderbergh & Nichols."

205 *I am moody, vicious, and dangerous tonight*: Lehman journal, September 17, 1965.

205 *Sometimes, when he couldn't perform*: Kashner and Schoenberger, *Furious Love*, 146.

206 *Hey, you two guys got passes*: Kelly, "On the Set with the Burtons."

207 *I had two cameras almost side by side*: "Soderbergh & Nichols."

208 *It was a symptom of how green I was*: Ibid.

CHAPTER ELEVEN: GETTING TO THE MARROW

209 *Menken and Maas were notorious bickerers*: Marc Siegel, "Bitch," *The Films of Andy Warhol*, vol. 2 (New Haven, CT: Whitney Museum of American Art / Yale University Press, 2021), 311.

210 *You don't seem to be able to finish your sentences*: *Bitch*, directed by Andy Warhol (1965), Andy Warhol Museum, Pittsburgh.

210 *Willard and Marie introduced me to the poetry of Ezra Pound*: Gerard Malanga, unpublished memoir, shared with author.

211 *Looked just like Broderick Crawford in drag*: Lee Manchester, "Who's the Source for Virginia Woolf?," *Wagner Magazine: The Link for Alumni and Friends*, Winter 2013–14, https://wagner.edu/wagnermagazine/whos-the-source-for-virginia-woolf/.

212 *They had what you'd call a symbiotic relationship*: Ibid.

213 *There will be a lot said tonight about excellence*: 1959 Emmy Awards, YouTube, https://www.youtube.com/watch?v=0Bk6VcZpboc.

214 *They're all so great and the play absolutely soars*: Lehman journal, September 27, 1965, Lehman Collection.

214 *I wouldn't say she is particularly gifted*: James Agee, "Films," *Nation*, December 23, 1944.

215 *When Elizabeth as Martha cries "I'm not a monster!"*: Lehman journal, September 27, 1965.

216 *Haskell Wexler fiddles around*: Lehman journal, September 29, 1965.

216 *I don't think anybody realizes how difficult it is*: Ibid.

217 *Somebody brings in a small* Matisse: Ash Carter and Sam Kashner, *Life Isn't Everything: Mike Nichols, as Remembered by 150 of His Closest Friends* (New York: Picador, 2020), 239.

217 *I started traveling coach in airplanes*: Ibid., 194.

218 *It is to the advantage of studios and directors*: Herb A. Lightman, "The Dramatic Photography of *Who's Afraid of Virginia Woolf?*," *American Cinematographer*, April 28, 2020, https://theasc.com/articles/the-dramatic -photography-of-virginia-woolf.

218 *The surprising thing about Mike Nichols*: Ibid.

220 *Those who suffer from the disorder*: Elizabeth Svoboda, "All the Signs of Pregnancy Except One: The Baby," *New York Times*, December 5, 2006.

220 *Bertha Pappenheim, a well-to-do Austrian woman*: Melinda Guttmann, *The Enigma of Anna O* (Chicago: Moyer Bell, 2001) 8.

221 *Nichols worried about how it might affect the shoot*: Lehman journal, September 28, 1965.

221 *Sandy is eating too heavily*: Lehman journal, October 13, 1965.

221 *Dennis had gotten married*: Milestones, *Time*, October 22, 1965.

223 *Elizabeth had a baby shower for Sandy*: Lehman journal, December 6, 1965.

223 *Terrible news in the paper today*: Lehman journal, December 20, 1965.

223 *If I'd been a mother*: David Hutchings, "Sandy Dennis," *People*, March 13, 1989.

224 *You really have guts buying a car like that*: Lehman journal, October 22, 1965.

225 *He was considering* Hello, Dolly *with the idea of casting Elizabeth Taylor*: Lehman journal, November 8, 1965.

225 *Well, you're overweight enough and you're Jewish*: Sam Kashner and Nancy Schoenberger, *Furious Love: Elizabeth Taylor, Richard Burton, and the Marriage of the Century* (New York: Harper Perennial, 2011), 173.

225 *A 1966 white Oldsmobile Toronado*: Lehman journal, November 10, 1965.

226 *It was the kind of acting*: Lehman journal, October 15, 1965.

227 *The Burtons are great to work with*: Lightman, "Dramatic Photography of *Who's Afraid of Virginia Woolf?*"

228 *Elizabeth didn't mind looking puffy and haggard*: C. David Heymann, *Liz* (New York: Birch Lane, 1995), 280.

228 *That thrilling thing that I've only seen*: Mark Harris, *Pictures at a Revolution* (New York: Penguin, 2008), 275.

231 *At 9:00 o'clock tonight George stood with his hand in Martha's*: Lehman journal, December 13, 1965.

231 *Presents were being given all around*: Lehman journal, December 13, 1965.

231 *He could be incredibly cruel*: Annabel Davis-Goff, phone interview by author, February 15, 2023.

CHAPTER TWELVE: LABOR PAINS

232 *I never understood why they had to shoot*: Jakob Holder to author, email correspondence, August 25, 2023

233 *We've got a $7.5 million dirty movie on our hands*: Mark Harris, *Pictures at a Revolution* (New York: Penguin, 2008), 183.

233 *So, say George is speaking Latin and Martha is wailing*: Bobbie O'Steen, "Cut to the Chase," https://www.bobbieosteen.com/cut-to-the-chase/.

234 *It's unfair to expect me to write a score*: Lehman journal, January 5, 1966, Lehman Collection.

234 *I told him that if he tried to force me*: Ibid.

234 *In which Mike claimed that first*: Ibid.

236 *Ernie had signed Alex North as the composer*: O'Steen, "Cut to the Chase."

236 *He would invite his friend Jacqueline Kennedy*: Mark Harris, *Mike Nichols: A Life* (New York: Penguin, 2021), 191.

236 *Movie first, scene second, moment third*: O'Steen, "Cut to the Chase."

237 *Sam was listening to the currents*: Ibid.

237 *I mixed the picture*: Ibid.

238 *There's only one question the audience asks*: Mel Gussow, "Mike Nichols: Director as Star," *Newsweek*, November 14, 1966, cover story.

239 *He was a great artist*: Ash Carter and Sam Kashner, *Life Isn't Everything: Mike Nichols, as Remembered by 150 of His Closest Friends* (New York: Picador, 2020), 241.

240 *The film starts with the moon*: "Steven Soderbergh & Mike Nichols Who's Afraid of Virginia Woolf? Audio Commentary," YouTube, https://www.youtube.com/watch?v=4l4zhoHMeoY.

241 *It was to be my part*: Mel Gussow, *Edward Albee: A Singular Journey* (New York: Applause Theatre Books, 2001), 233.

241 *I found that he had a pretty good idea*: Ibid., 241.

241 *I was very nervous because I cared a lot*: "Soderbergh & Nichols."

241 *These items still seem to us to be unapprovable*: Geoffrey Shurlock to Jack Warner, October 9, 1965, Lehman Collection.

242 *I must say I would not like to see the Lord's name*: Tommy Thompson, "Raw Dialogue Challenges all the Censors," *Life*, June 10, 1966.

242 *I cast an emphatic vote for a condemned rating*: Ibid.

242 *We put* Virginia Woolf *in what we call our "think film category"*: Ibid.

243 *Mr. Valenti is presented with one of the touchiest questions*: Vincent Canby, "Valenti Facing First Film Crisis," *New York Times*, May 28, 1966.

243 *A new MPAA film rating system*: Leonard Leff and Jerold Simmons, *The Dame in the Kimono: Hollywood, Censorship, and the Production Code*, 2nd ed. (Lexington: University of Kentucky Press, 2001), 263, 265.

244 Who's Afraid of Virginia Woolf? *contains eleven "Goddamns;"*: Thompson, *Life*.

244 *Disguising profanity with clean but suggestive phrases*: Ibid.

244 *I was startled and enormously taken with the picture*: William Flanagan, "Edward Albee, The Art of Theater No. 4," *Paris Review*, no. 39 (Fall 1966).

245 *I think I served Edward Albee*: Gussow, "Mike Nichols."

245 *He wept four times*: Thompson, *Life*.

245 *He "damn near cried"*: Mel Gussow, interview with Albee, November 3, 1995, Gussow Collection.

245 *I found that it made*: Flanagan, "Edward Albee."

CHAPTER THIRTEEN: EDWARD ALBEE AND MIKE NICHOLS DANCE
THE WATUSI

247 *What other young couple would go to such lengths*: Sam Kashner and Nancy Schoenberger, *Furious Love: Elizabeth Taylor, Richard Burton, and the Marriage of the Century* (New York: Harper Perennial, 2011), 177.

247 *The nice Italian man [Zeffirelli] took my playmate*: Mel Gussow, *Edward Albee: A Singular Journey* (New York: Applause Theatre Books, 2001), 252.

249 *Here they are, again, fans*: "Elizabeth Taylor and Richard Burton: The Night of the Brawl," *Look*, February 8, 1966.

249 Who's Afraid of Virginia Woolf? *had its premiere*: "Who's Afraid of Virginia Woolf? 1966 Premiere," IMDb, list created by "nightopeningfan," December 31, 2019, https://www.imdb.com/list/ls093121382/.

249 *Mike and I sat in the back row*: Bobbie O'Steen, "Cut to the Chase," https://www.bobbieosteen.com/cut-to-the-chase/.

250 *I remember the opening night*: "Steven Soderbergh & Mike Nichols Who's Afraid of Virginia Woolf? Audio Commentary," YouTube, https://www.youtube.com/watch?v=4l4zhoHMeoY.

251 *Has been brought to the screen without pussyfooting*: Stanley Kauffmann, "Funless Games at George and Martha's: Albee's 'Virginia Woolf' Becomes a Film," *New York Times*, June 24, 1966.

251 *After all the initial commotion*: Bosley Crowther, "Who's Afraid of Audacity," *New York Times*, July 10, 1966.

251 *The screen has never held a more shattering*: James Power, "Who's Afraid of Virginia Woolf? Is a Motion Picture Masterpiece," *Hollywood Reporter*, June 22, 1966.

251 *A keen adaptation and handsome production*: "Who's Afraid of Virginia Woolf?," *Variety*, December 31, 1965, https://variety.com/1965/film/reviews/who-s-afraid-of-virginia-woolf-3-1200420919/.

252 *The movie isn't all that good*: Andrew Sarris, "Films," *Village Voice*, July 28, 1966.

252 *To me the direction of the actors in* Virginia Woolf: Mel Gussow, "Mike Nichols: Director as Star," *Newsweek*, November 14, 1966, cover story.

252 *Nova Scotia banned* Virginia Woolf *from all the theaters*: news item, *New York Times*, August 9, 1966.

252 Who's Afraid of Virginia Woolf? *was "the best film in years"*: Alden Whitman, "A Nun Applauds Virginia Woolf," *New York Times*, August 19, 1967.

253 *None of them found the language shocking*: Vincent Canby, "Public Not Afraid of Big Bad 'Woolf,'" *New York Times*, June 25, 1966.

253 *While in 1932 there were only three marriage counseling centers*: Wendy Kline, "The Surprising History of Marriage Counseling," *American Experience*, PBS, October 19, 2018, https://www.pbs.org/wgbh/americanexperience/features/eugenics-surprising-history-of-marriage-counseling/.

255 *It is about a couple who comes home late after a party*: Gussow, "Mike Nichols."

256 *The cruelty here is that it's the weakling*: "Soderbergh & Nichols."

258 *At first, Nick and Honey appear to be close*: Ibid.

259 *Well here we are . . . me, the Dirty Rotten Daughter*: Mort Drucker, "Who in Heck Is Virginia Woolf?," *Mad* magazine, no. 109, March 1967, 5–10.

260 *Elizabeth Taylor and Richard Burton probably do more acting*: A. O. Scott, "Who's Afraid of Virginia Woolf?," *New York Times*, June 11, 2010.

261 *Welcome to the on again, off again, in again*: Bob Hope, 39th Academy Awards, YouTube, https://www.youtube.com/watch?v=fjyi7oJVP_I&t =718s.

261 *Do not burn the bridges you have built*: Kashner and Schoenberger, *Furious Love*, 206.

262 *Dreamed her plane had crashed*: Ibid.

262 *The Shakespearean actor who had not abandoned the stage*: Ibid., 207.

262 *We heard that E had won the Oscar*: Ibid., 207.

263 *The 1966 box office gross of $14.5 million made it*: Joel Waldo Finler, *The Hollywood Story* (London: Wallflower, 2003), 358.

263 *Albee's new play*, A Delicate Balance, *won the Pulitzer Prize*: Peter Kihss, "Albee Wins Pulitzer Prize," *New York Times*, May 2, 1967.

263 *The award that had been denied Albee*: Mel Gussow, *Edward Albee: A Singular Journey* (New York: Applause Theatre Books, 2001), 268.

263 *If I refused it out of hand*: Judson Hand, "Albee Wins Pulitzer," *World Journal Tribune*, May 2, 1967.

264 *I would suggest that the Pulitzer Prize*: Dan Sullivan, "Albee Criticizes Pulitzer Board," *New York Times*, May 3, 1967.

264 *In spite of everything, it's not bad*: Gussow, *Edward Albee*, 243.

264 *I would change everything*: Ibid.

MARRIAGE IN RELIEF: AN EPILOGUE

266 *Women have served all these centuries*: Virginia Woolf, *A Room of One's Own* (Peterborough, ON: Broadview Press), 2001, 43.

267 *I do not claim to be a literary critic*: W. Charles Pilley, "Review of Women in Love," *John Bull* (London newspaper), September 17, 1921.

267 *Don't you really* want *to get married?*: D. H. Lawrence, *Women in Love* (New York: Oxford University Press, 1998), 5.

269 *There is nothing in the film that is not in the novel*: Larry Kramer appearance with William Buckley, "The New Realism in Movies," *Firing Line*, program 194, March 13, 1970, American Archive of Public Broadcasting, https://americanarchive.org/catalog/cpb-aacip-514-j38kd1rd6p.

277 *My marriage, my parents, television*: Matt Schudel, "Craig Gilbert, Creator of 'An American Family,' Called the First Reality TV Show, Dies at 94," *Washington Post*, April 18, 2020.

277 *The Louds are neither average nor typical*: Ibid.

277 An American Family *may be more effective as a critique of family*: Jeffrey Ruoff, *An American Family: A Televised Life* (Minneapolis: University of Minnesota Press, 2002), 112.

279 *In content,* [Scenes from a Marriage] *is a child of the stage*: T. E. Kalem, "Cinema: A Season in Hell," *Time*, September 30, 1974.

282 *[The film] contains a raw emotional power*: Roger Ebert, "Shoot the Moon," *Chicago Sun-Times*, January 1, 1982, https://www.rogerebert.com/reviews /shoot-the-moon-1982.

283 *While* Virginia Woolf *was a decided influence on Soderbergh*: Steven Soderbergh, email to author, October 26, 2023.

283 *Perhaps no filmmaker has covered the tonal bases*: Guy Lodge, "Bad Romance: A Thorny History of Marital Strife on Film, *Guardian*, May 5, 2017.

283 Husbands and Wives *de-romanticizes modern love*: Steve Davis, "Husbands and Wives," *Austin Chronicle*, September 18, 1992.

285 *One of the ultimate true stories of a proto-gay-marriage*: Stephen Holden, "A May-December Love for All Seasons," *New York Times*, June 13, 2008.

289 *When two people hate each other as much as George and Martha*: Lehman Collection.

BIBLIOGRAPHY

BOOKS

Bakewell, Sarah. *At the Existentialist Café.* New York: Other Press, 2016.

Biskind, Peter. *Easy Riders, Raging Bulls: How the Sex-Drugs-and-Rock 'n' Roll Generation Saved Hollywood.* New York: Simon & Schuster, 1999.

Bottoms, Stephen J. *Albee: Who's Afraid of Virginia Woolf?* Cambridge: Cambridge University Press, 2000.

Bram, Christopher. *Eminent Outlaws: The Gay Writers Who Changed America.* New York: Twelve Books, 2012.

Broyard, Anatole. *Kafka Was the Rage: A Greenwich Village Memoir.* New York: Crown, 1993.

Burton, Richard. *The Richard Burton Diaries.* Edited by Chris Williams. New Haven, CT: Yale University Press, 2012.

Capote, Truman. *Portraits and Observations: Essays by Truman Capote.* New York: Random House, 2007.

Carter, Ash, and Sam Kashner. *Life Isn't Everything: Mike Nichols, as Remembered by 150 of His Closest Friends.* New York: Picador, 2020.

Connell, Evan S. *Mr. Bridge.* Berkeley: Counterpoint, 2005.

———. *Mrs. Bridge.* Berkeley: Counterpoint, 2010.

Crespy, David. *Richard Barr: The Playwright's Producer.* Carbondale: Southern Illinois University Press, 2013.

Cronyn, Hume. *A Terrible Liar.* New York: William Morrow, 1991.

Dewhurst, Colleen. *Colleen Dewhurst: Her Autobiography.* New York: Scribner, 1997.

Esslin, Martin. *The Theatre of the Absurd.* New York: Knopf Doubleday, 2004.

Fonda, Jane. *My Life So Far.* New York: Random House, 2005.

Frankel, Glenn. *Shooting* Midnight Cowboy: *Art, Sex, Loneliness, Liberation, and the Making of a Dark Classic.* New York: Farrar, Straus and Giroux, 2021.

Friedan, Betty. *The Feminine Mystique.* New York: W. W. Norton, 2013.

Gitlin, Todd. *The Sixties: Years of Hope; Days of Rage.* New York: Bantam, 1987.

Gussow, Mel. *Edward Albee: A Singular Journey.* New York: Applause Theatre Books, 2001.

Harris, Mark. *Mike Nichols: A Life.* New York: Penguin, 2021.

———. *Pictures at a Revolution.* New York: Penguin, 2008.

Heymann, C. David. *Liz: The Intimate Biography of Elizabeth Taylor.* New York: Birch Lane, 1995.

Howard, Richard. *Quantities.* Middlebury, CT: Wesleyan University Press, 1962.

Kashner, Sam, and Nancy Schoenberger. *Furious Love: Elizabeth Taylor, Richard Burton, and the Marriage of the Century.* New York: Harper Perennial, 2011.

Lahr, John. *Tennessee Williams: Mad Pilgrimage of the Flesh.* New York: W. W. Norton, 2015.

Leff, Leonard, and Jerold Simmons. *The Dame in the Kimono: Hollywood, Censorship, and the Production Code.* Lexington: University of Kentucky Press, 2001.

Lehman, Ernest. "Fun and Games with George and Martha," unpublished production journal, 1965. Ernest Lehman Collection, Harry Ransom Center, University of Texas at Austin.

Maas, Willard. *Wagner Literary Magazine*, all four issues. New York: Wagner College, 2013.

Mann, Thomas. *Death in Venice*. New York: Ecco, 2009.

Paolucci, Anne. *From Tension to Tonic: The Plays of Edward Albee*. Whitestone, NY: Griffon House, 2005.

Podhoretz, Norman. *Making It*. New York: Random House, 1967.

Ruoff, Jeffrey. *An American Family: A Televised Life*. Minneapolis: University of Minnesota Press, 2001.

Schneider, Alan. *Entrances: An American Director's Journey*. New York: Viking Penguin, 1986.

Schulberg, Budd. *What Makes Sammy Run?* New York: Vintage, 1990.

Wanger, Walter, and Joe Hyams. *My Life with Cleopatra*. New York: Vintage, 1963.

Wasson, Sam. *Fifth Avenue, 5 A.M.: Audrey Hepburn, Breakfast at Tiffany's, and the Dawn of the Modern Woman*. New York: Harper Perennial, 2011.

Yates, Richard. *Revolutionary Road*. New York: Vintage, 2000.

Zeffirelli, Franco. *Zeffirelli: An Autobiography*. New York: Grove, 1986.

ARTICLES

Carter, Ash, and Sam Kashner. "Mike Nichols's Life and Career: The Definitive Oral History." *Vanity Fair*, September 11, 2015. https://www.vanityfair.com/hollywood/2015/09/remembering-director-mike-nichols.

"Elizabeth Taylor and Richard Burton: The Night of the Brawl." *Look*, February 8, 1966.

Flanagan, William. "Interview with Edward Albee." *Paris Review*, no. 39 (Fall 1966).

"Interview with Mike Nichols." *Playboy*, June 1966.

Jennings, C. Robert. "All for the Love of Mike." *Saturday Evening Post*, October 9, 1965.

Kelly, Kevin. Three-part piece about *Who's Afraid of Virginia Woolf?*, "The Burtons Appear," part 1; "Producer of 'Who's Afraid' Says He's Afraid of Publicity," part 2; " 'Luv, You Do Look a Fright,' Dick Tells Liz After Scene," part 3, *Boston Globe*, September 19, 20, 21, 1965.

Leff, Leonard J. "Play into Film: Warner Brothers' *Who's Afraid of Virginia Woolf?*" *Theatre Journal* 33, no. 4 (1981): 453–66. www.jstor.org/stable /3206770.

Lindsay, Cynthia. "Who's Afraid of Filming Virginia Woolf?" *Cosmopolitan*, October 1965.

Newquist, Roy. "Behind the Scenes of a Shocking Movie." *McCall's*, June 1966.

O'Steen, Sam. "Cut to the Chase." Interview by Bobbie O'Steen. https://www .bobbieosteen.com/cut-to-the-chase/.

Spector, Susan. "Telling the Story of Albee's *Who's Afraid of Virginia Woolf?*: Theatre History and Mythmaking." *Theatre Survey* 31, no. 2 (October 21, 2010).

Taubman, Howard. "The Theater: Albee's *Who's Afraid?*" *New York Times*, October 15, 1962.

Thompson, Thomas. "Liz in a Film Shocker." *Life*, June 10, 1966.

Tynan, Kenneth. "Interview with Richard Burton." *Playboy*, September 1963.

FILMS

45 Years (2015), directed by Andrew Haigh.

Adam's Rib (1949), directed by George Cukor.

An American Family (1973), created by Craig Gilbert.

Chris & Don: A Love Story (2007), directed by Tina Mascara and Guido Santi.

Diary of a Mad Housewife (1970), directed by Frank Perry.

Husbands and Wives (1992), directed by Woody Allen.

The Kids Are Alright (2010), directed by Lisa Cholodenko.

The Lion in Winter (1968), directed by Anthony Harvey.

The Man in the Gray Flannel Suit (1956), directed by Nunnally Johnson.

Marriage Story (2019), directed by Noah Baumbach.

Mr. & Mrs. Bridge (1990), directed by James Ivory.

Mr. & Mrs. Smith (2005), directed by Doug Liman.

Revolutionary Road (2008), directed by Sam Mendes.

Scenes from a Marriage (1973), directed by Ingmar Bergman.

sex, lies, and videotape (1989), directed by Steven Soderbergh.

Shoot the Moon (1982), directed by Alan Parker.

Too Far to Go (1979), directed by Fielder Cook.

A Woman Under the Influence (1974), directed by John Cassavetes.

The Women (1939), directed by George Cukor.

IMAGE CREDITS

Page One:

—Mrs. Frankie Albee and Edward: Courtesy of the *New York Times*

Page Two:

—Albee with William Flanagan: Courtesy of the Edward Albee Foundation

—Albee with Terrence McNally: Courtesy of the Edward Albee Foundation

—At the 1963 Tony Awards: Photo by Friedman-Abeles © The New York Public Library for the Performing Arts

Page Three:

—The first Broadway production: Photo by Friedman-Abeles © The New York Public Library for the Performing Arts

—A scene from the film: Photo by Mel Traxel/mptvimages.com

Page Four:

—Willard Maas and Marie Mencken: Beinecke Library, Yale University; by permission of Frank Polach

—Taylor and Burton: mptvimages.com

Page Five:

—Nichols setting up: Photo by Mel Traxel/mptvimages.com

—Martha delivers the line: Warner Brothers

—George looking in the fridge: © Bob Willoughby/mptvimages.com

Page Six:

    —Taylor and Burton in their roles: Warner Brothers

    —The thirty-two-year-old: © Bob Willoughby/mptvimages.com

    —George and Martha: Photo by Mel Traxel/mptvimages.com

Page Seven:

    —All photos © Bob Willoughby/mptvimages.com

Page Eight:

    —The guests arrive: © Bob Willoughby/mptvimages.com

    —Martha has changed: Warner Brothers

    —Honey senses: Courtesy *American Cinematographer* magazine, via Haskell Wexler

Pages Nine through Sixteen:

    —All photos © Bob Willoughby/mptvimages.com

INDEX

A NOTE ON THE AUTHOR

PHILIP GEFTER is the author of *What Becomes a Legend Most: The Biography of Richard Avedon*; *Wagstaff: Before and After Mapplethorpe*, which received the 2014 Marfield Prize for arts writing; and an essay collection, *Photography After Frank*. He is a regular contributor to the *New Yorker*'s Photo Booth, *Aperture*, and the *New York Times*, where he was an editor for over fifteen years. He also served as a producer on the award-winning documentary *Bill Cunningham New York*.